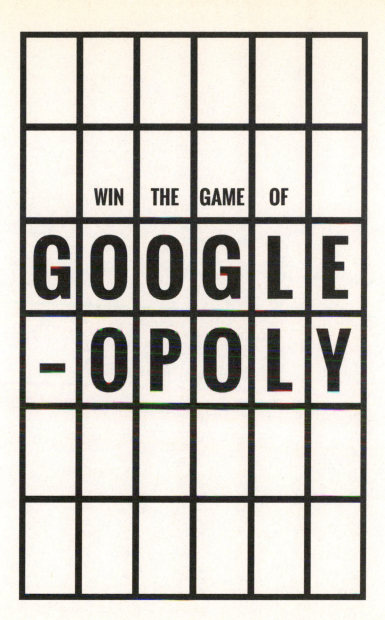

WIN THE GAME OF

GOOGLE
-OPOLY

SEAN V. BRADLEY, CSP

WIN THE GAME OF

GOOGLE -OPOLY

UNLOCKING THE
SECRET STRATEGY
OF **SEARCH**
ENGINES

WILEY

Every day I thank God for the gifts that he has blessed me with, and none are more special and incredible than my amazing and loving family. I dedicate this book to them; all of their love and support motivate me to do the absolute best in everything I do. Without them in my life, none of this is worthwhile.

- *My incredible wife Karina Bradley, who spent many hours late night brainstorming with me on this book!*
- *My daughters, Tianna Chanel Mick and Kalina Sarah Bradley.*
- *My sons, Sean V. Bradley II "The Sequel" and Xander K. Bradley.*
- *My Uncle Joey and Aunt Chickie, who are more like a mother and father to me.*
- *My mother, Anna Rodriguez; her hard life and suffering was not in vain. I am who I am in part because of her.*
- *My AWESOME "In-Laws" Robert Uriarte and Nilda Ortis. They have welcomed me into their lives as their own son.*

And a VERY special dedication to two very important people who are no longer with us:

- *In loving memory of my grandmother, Sarah Grimaldi; she was the most incredible person in my life and loved me so much.*
- *In loving memory of Karry Moore. He was a good friend and great business partner. It was from him I first learned about Video SEO, and he set me on my course to write this book.*

Contents

Acknowledgments

Writing this book has been a major accomplishment in my career and in my life. It is a milestone—one that I will always cherish. It is a little surreal to think of where I came from and then see where I am now in life. I am humbled and feel blessed for the opportunities that I have had. I have realized my goal of being a published author of a major publishing house—an accomplishment I could not have achieved without numerous amazing friends and experts of the highest level in digital marketing, SEO, video, social media, and so on, helping me by brainstorming, debating, synergizing, and providing good old inspiration!

I want to first thank JD Rucker, President of Dealer Authority. I live in New Jersey and JD lives in California. We spent many nights on GoToMeeting brainstorming ideas, theories, and details. You, my friend, are brilliant and awesome. Thank you so much for being a part of this book.

Thank you Tim Martell, President of Wikimotive. Tim, your intense passion for perfection and subject matter expertise inspired me to dig deep and exceed readers' expectations with this book. Your SEO philosophy and social media knowledge were much appreciated. Thank you so much for brainstorming with me and helping me with this book.

I even went international by connecting with Michael Cirillo, President of FlexDealer in BC, Canada. Thank you so much for your help and wisdom with this book. You were instrumental with your fundamental knowledge of Google's algorithms and advanced website design in relation to onsite SEO. And thank you for the hook-up with Rand Fishkin, Co-Founder of MOZ.

My man, Christian Jorn, CEO of Remora: Thank you so much, Christian, for all of your help and expertise on advanced SEO strategy as well as mobile SEO. You were truly awesome to brainstorm with, and I truly appreciate your help on this project. This is just the beginning!

Thank you so much, Eric Miltsch, for your help on this book. Your progressive understanding of where Google is now and where it's going in the future is amazing. You get Google!

Special thanks to my friend, AJ LeBlanc, Managing Partner of Car-Mercial. What can I say? We've come a long way! Thank you so much for inspiring me to write this book. The "Googleopoly" phrase came from you, and I turned a great thought into a great book! Also, thanks for allowing me to be a part of pioneering the entire video search engine optimization phenomenon in the automotive sales industry, years before anyone even understood what video SEO was. I learned so much from you and with you in regard to video and video SEO. But even more than that, thank you for being real. We both know that when there are millions of dollars, or, hell—sometimes even just pennies on the table, people start to act funny; you have always been 100 percent real with me. We have made millions and millions together, my friend, and we have millions more to make!

A big thank-you to Jim Ziegler, HSG, CSP, "The Alpha Dawg," President of Ziegler Super Systems. It is truly an honor to be mentored by a living legend in both the automotive sales industry and the National Speakers Association. I have learned plenty from you and know that my career has been accelerated by your guidance and friendship. It was you who suggested I join the NSA, and inspired me to achieve my CSP accreditation. And because of my affiliation with the NSA, I was given the opportunity to pitch my book to the prestigious John Wiley & Sons. Thank you, Jim, for being a great mentor.

Many thanks to Dr. Willie Jolley, CSP, CPAE, best-selling author of *A Setback Is a Setup for a Comeback*, Hall of Fame speaker, and another one of my awesome mentors. Thank you for seeing something special in me, for pushing me to write this book, and for always taking my calls, no matter how busy you are. I appreciate all of your guidance and advice, and all of your resources and recommendations.

Thank you Reverend Joe Cala (and my General Manager at Dealer Synergy). I was able to focus on writing this book because I was confident you could run my company. Thank you for being an amazing general manager and for being such a great friend. I have mad love for you and your family. I think it's so awesome that you married Karina and me and now we get to build this amazing company together with Karina and the rest of the team. Also, thank you for inspiring me to take the leap and write this book! You wrote two books to my one, and I am honored to say you are one of my greatest success stories. I am awed by what you do on a daily basis.

A shout-out to Anthony "AAA" Alagona—we did it, brother! We have come a *long* way from the Cha-Cha Lounge at the Limelight 21 years ago. I want to thank you for always having my back, from back then to today. You are appreciated. Congrats to you and Ambika!

I want to thank my Dealer Synergy team for being such an amazing group of talented, brilliant people! Thank you for all of the brainstorming on this book, the graphic design, assisting on research, and overall support. A special thank-you to Dana Goldberg for your insight, attention to detail, and creativity.

A shout-out to Phil and Ricardo Migliarese, owners of Balance Studios in Philadelphia. I am proud to say that they are my instructors (in Brazilian Jiu-Jitsu), as well as great friends. I have to say, Balance Studios is probably the most effective martial arts school in the country in terms of digital marketing, social media, video marketing, and search engine optimization. I have enjoyed my conversations and synergy sessions with Phil, and I am beyond grateful for the personal attention that Ricardo has given me with private lessons!

A special shout-out to my "Li'l Brother," Mark Gayed—I love you, brother, for always being supportive and believing in me. My best man at my wedding and my best friend, you are appreciated!

Thank you to Wiley for giving me the opportunity to share my knowledge and experience with the world. My team at Wiley, Shannon and Elizabeth, have been so awesome in guiding me through the process of becoming a first-time author. And wow! The Wiley marketing team is superb. I *love* the cover of this book. Thank you so much.

Thank you to my amazing family for being so supportive and understanding and allowing me the time to write this book. I loved reading chapters to my teenage daughters, Kalina and Tianna, and getting their opinions from the teenage perspective. Thank you to Li'l Sean for being such a great big brother for Xander. And thank you, Xander, for being such a loving little mini-me. Thank you to Karina Bradley, for being so supportive—for brainstorming with me, proofreading, and challenging me to constantly do more, be more, and achieve more. I am so blessed to have married my dream girl.

And most importantly, I thank God for blessing me with the gifts and the mind that I have and the tenacity and passion to do what I do. I know it is for Him. He has a purpose for me, as He does for everyone.

Introduction

Writing a book about a multibillion-dollar company—one of the most powerful companies on this planet and one that affects more than 1 billion people—can be an incredibly challenging task, but it has to be done. There are so many people, companies, brands, and so on that are in need of visibility, in need of people to buy their products and services, in need of building a brand and/or a fan base but do not know how. As a matter of fact, there are people who used to be successful—people who used to have huge fan bases and a huge clientele but now find themselves struggling, stressing, and losing revenue. They do not know how to stop the bleeding. They do not know how they can survive, never mind thrive! The world has changed, and if you do not change with it you will ultimately fail, or—if you are lucky—cling to the crumbs left behind by truly innovative and evolved companies and people. . . .

I am an avid learner, reader, and researcher. I try to absorb as much information as I possibly can, but when I was conducting research for this book, I was shocked to find that there were no other books in print about how to actually dominate Google's search engine for massive visibility. Sure, there were books out there that focused on SEO, or social media, video, reputation, digital marketing, and even on Google itself, but there was not one book written on how to leverage all the different aspects of Google with onsite and offsite resources that can and will get you indexed on page one of Google. I was determined to write a thorough book that could be used not to trick or beat Google, but to act as a true road map that would help people understand how Google works, what Google wants, and why—and then to show, step by step, a holistic approach to how you can create a customized plan for you, your business, or brand on how to give Google exactly what it wants and needs. In return, Google will give you exactly what you want . . . page one domination!

I have a very unusual background with an incredibly unique skill set. Traditionally, you would think that a business book author would have an MBA or doctorate degree. I don't. ☺

As a matter of fact, I dropped out of college my sophomore year, and I didn't even major in marketing, SEO, or anything like that. I was a Russian major at Rider University in New Jersey, in the Zeta Beta Tau fraternity and a cadet in the Army ROTC program. With all of that, I left, and life circumstances led me to car sales (I got fired from being a waiter). I worked in a car dealership for five years. I was a car salesman—actually, the best car salesman in the dealership: salesman of the month, salesman of the year. The average car salesman in the United States sells approximately 10 units per month and I was selling an average of 30 units per month and making over $120,000 at 24 years old. I guess like a lot of success stories, I was in the right place at the right time. I got into the automotive sales industry in 1999. This is literally the time that the Internet started to take off in our industry. People were going online to do research before they ever stepped foot into a car dealership. Because I looked so young (and so short), the management directed me to handle the Internet leads. And in no time I started to engage these Internet prospects and convert these Internet leads into Internet appointments into Internet sales! I was hooked; I quickly became addicted to the hunt and to the sale and, most honestly, the money! I was making so much money it was absurd. I went from being a college dropout making $30,000 as a waiter to making $120,000 almost instantaneously.

The next evolution in my career was to become an Internet sales manager/business development director. This meant that I was now in charge of building an entire department of Internet sales. I was no longer a one-man show. The dealership now wanted me to create and run a major profit center: the Internet Department, also known as the Business Development Center (BDC). The problem was that *no one* knew what to do. The Internet sprang up very quickly and very powerfully. So I went to the library, the bookstore, and the Internet, and researched everything I could on:

- The Internet
- Website design
- Search engine optimization
- Lead generation
- Third-party lead source providers
- Online classifieds
- Digital marketing

I even taught myself how to design websites in HTML, use editors like Microsoft Front Page and Adobe Dreamweaver, and code in Dynamic HTML and Java. I started to build my own websites, which I needed to drive traffic to. In the early 2000s I started to study search engine optimization (SEO) and tools like WebPosition Gold, Word-tracker, and other early SEO resources. I traveled all across the country, attending as many SEO workshops and seminars as I could find and got certified by the International Search Engine Optimization Academy in Advanced SEO. With all of this information, education, and the skills I was learning, I was building bigger and bigger success stories in the automotive sales industry, so much so that in 2004 I left the automotive sales industry at age 28 earning more than $160,000 per year at age 28 to start my first company: Dealer Synergy Inc.

For the past 11 years I have been the CEO of Dealer Synergy Inc. and personally trained over 11,000 automotive sales professionals as well as approximately 1,000 multimillion-dollar companies (car dealerships). Because of my consulting, training, and digital marketing strategies, I have helped my clients generate over $100 million in *additional* revenue.

In addition I have also had more than 1,000 articles published in more than 13 different national and international magazines that reach hundreds of thousands of readers on a monthly basis, and I have had a column in *AutoSuccess* magazine for the past seven years. I have been a keynote speaker or general assembly speaker for every major automotive sales industry event, workshop, or trade show, including:

- National Automobile Dealers Association convention
- American Truck Dealers Association convention
- Numerous State Dealers Association conventions
- J.D. Power & Associates Internet Roundtable
- Digital Dealer Conference & Exposition
- NCM & Associates Internet Sales Bootcamp (co-creator)
- Jim Ziegler's Dealer Battle Plan (co-creator)
- Internet Director Immersion Program (creator)
- The Internet Sales 20 Group (co-creator with Karina Bradley)
- Association of Automotive Internet Sales Professionals (charter member and general assembly speaker)

In addition to working with multimillion-dollar car dealerships, I have also had the honor of working with numerous publicly traded corporations like Autobytel Inc. (ABT) and Toyota. Autobytel has hired me to train their national sales team on Internet sales operations, and Toyota (the Boston region) recently had my www.internetsales20group.com national workshop's curriculum certified by Toyota corporate—meaning that any Toyota dealership from the Boston region that attended my three-day workshop on Internet sales, digital marketing, SEO, and more would receive Toyota certification credit. I have also been contracted by Carsdirect, a $1.1 billion corporation, to train their internal team on automotive Internet sales.

And if that wasn't enough, I pioneered the video search engine optimization phenomenon in the entire automotive sales industry back in 2006, about three years before anyone had video SEO on their radar. I had the amazing luck (destiny) of connecting with Karry Moore and AJ Leblanc of VSEO Inc. (now Car-Mercial). Karry and AJ are partners with John Ferber, the owner of USO Networks, the parent company of VSEO Inc. What is unimaginable is that John Ferber was the co-founder of Advertising.com, the world's largest digital marketing company. He sold the company in 2004 to AOL for $495 million. It is now worth $12 billion! So after John cashed in on Advertising.com, he started a new company, USO Networks, which specializes in video search engine optimization. They have proprietary software, patents, and so on, but they are not in the automotive industry. I connected with AJ and Karry and we hatched a plan to scale video SEO for the automotive industry, and for the first five years, I was the face of video SEO for the entire auto industry. Long story short, video SEO blew up big time, and I personally sold $10 million of video SEO for Car-Mercial. They grew beyond imagination to the point where they are about to be acquired for over $100 million!

So . . . I killed it in the automotive industry. My wife and I were making millions and millions of dollars, and we got bored; we wanted to venture off into other industries. My wife was a model back before she got into the corporate game and thought it would be awesome to get back into it. She was cast as an extra for a Barrington Levy Music video and was hooked on the music industry; she wanted to become a recording artist. Long story short again, we took an unknown female recording artist who had never been in a recording studio and in less than three years Karina Bradley had:

- Over 60 million online views
- Performed in front of millions of people
  - Approximately 1 million viewers on *CBS TalkPhilly*
  - Over 16 million listeners on Shade45 Sirius Satellite Radio
    - Six different live appearances on Sirius Satellite Radio on the *Miss Mimi* show and the *DJ Kay Slay* show
- Nine major music videos
- Become an official ASCAB recording artist
- Official BDS Spins on FM radio across the country
- Her music licensed by the *Tia and Tamera* show on the Style television network
- Performed live across the country
- Was the Philadelphia Fashion Week Red Carpet Hostess
- Had major label recording artists featured in her music, including:
  - Meek Mill
  - Papoose
  - Young Chris
  - DJ Diamond Kutz
  - Remy Ma (unreleased track)
- Produced by major music producers, such as:
  - Ruwanga "RU" Samath
  - Larry Tee
  - Certifyd Production Group
  - LA Dubb

Granted, my wife is model-beautiful and has a pop star voice. But that isn't enough; there are a lot of beautiful and talented women and men out there. We knew that talent was *not* going to be enough. She needed visibility; she needed a fan base. So, we created a massive digital marketing strategy for the Karina Bradley project, and it worked! We created a pop star!

We decided after three years of amazing and unbelievable experiences (that we will cherish for the rest of our lives) that we wanted another child. We also wanted to focus on our core businesses, which were already generating millions of dollars. So we decided to stop the KB project while Karina was at her peak. A lot of people didn't understand why. But it was a family decision: KB took it to an unthinkable level and could have easily gone on to the next stage of her career (we had label deals on the table), but it wasn't right for our family. So now, instead of splitting our attention between the automotive sales industry, training, consulting, digital marketing, and the music industry, we eliminated the music industry and immersed ourselves in our core competency with more intensity. We purchased a building in New Jersey for our production studio and to house our growing team of talented digital marketing specialists, graphic designers, social media content writers, online reputation managers, and, of course, our amazing video production team.

The past two-and-a-half years have been incredible and diverse. I have recently achieved my CSP accreditation from the National Speakers Association, which is the highest certification in the world for a professional speaker. It is like an accountant achieving his or her CPA.

I have had the honor of working with a wide group of clients. Above and beyond my core of automotive dealerships and recording artists, I have worked with professional athletes such as a Philadelphia Eagle who started his own fitness center (I helped consult on his digital marketing strategy). In addition to an NFL superstar I have worked very closely with Phil and Ricardo Migliarese, the co-owners of Balance Studios in Philadelphia, Pennsylvania. They have one of the most prestigious Brazilain Jiu-Jitsu and MMA schools in the United States, and numerous schools throughout the country and overseas. What is awesome about my relationship with the Migliarese brothers is that even though I have taught them so much in regards to digital marketing, SEO, video SEO, and so on, I have learned so much from them as well! Balance Studios is one of the most successful martial arts schools in Philadelphia and the tristate area. What is amazing to me is that Phil and Ricardo are not only world champion martial artists who train other champion martial artists, including numerous UFC fighters, but they also have by far the best digital marketing, SEO, video, social media, online reputation, digital PR, and branding compared to other martial arts schools in the country. They personify the Googleopoly strategy. My relationship with Balance Studio and its owners helped me understand the martial arts school business model and allowed me to work with other martial arts schools; one of my newest clients is Full Circle Martial Arts in Marlton, New Jersey. The owners are *incredible*: Steve, Deb, Matt, and their new partner, Paul Felder, "The Irish Dragon"—a CFFC champion and now an undefeated UFC fighter! We are working to crush the competition with a Googleopoly strategy.

I tell you all this *not* to impress you at all, *only* to impress upon you how serious the chapters in this book are. Like anything else in life, what you put into it is what you will get out of it. You can read this book and say wow, this is cool and not do anything with it, or you can truly internalize the lessons in this book, absorb all of the direction, tips, advice, secrets, and so on, and create a Googleopoly strategy for you or your business.

I charge $7,500–$10,000 to be a keynote speaker—that is usually one hour plus expenses (travel, lodging, etc.). This book, *Win the Game of Googleopoly*, is more than 76,000 words from 16 years of frontline experience and success, plus some wisdom from industry experts, pioneers, gurus, and leviathans in the Google/SEO space. I have all that information here in one consolidated format. One cohesive and holistic strategy for $25—I implore you to use this book as a reference guide for your evolution and success!

But wait . . . there's more! (I couldn't help it. It is the car salesman in me, LOL.)

I have put my whole Ninja Digital Marketing Team on creating the ultimate membership website: www.GoogleopolyBook.com.

GoogleopolyBook.com is *only* for people who purchase this book. Think of it like a DVD or Blu-ray Disc that has a ton of extra content above and beyond the movie itself. My feeling is that digital marketing, Google, algorithms, and technology change so quick that I felt the need to create a resource website for my readers that elaborates on the chapters in the book and contains:

- Video interviews with experts that contributed to the book
- Video tutorials on how to do the strategies that were listed in the book
- PowerPoint presentations
- Infographics
- Webinars
- List of social media sites
- List of Google algorithms and its updates in real time

And much, much more.

Enjoy this book and when you are done reading it, don't worry. There is a 24/7 interactive resource for additional information, education, training, guidance, resources, videos, and interviews at your fingertips!

CHAPTER 1

Either You Are Visible or You Are Invisible

As the old adage goes, if a tree falls in a forest and no one is around to hear it, does it make a sound? What about your marketing strategy? If you have the best product, service, widget, or invention and no one knows about it, does it truly exist? If the most talented person, the most innovative product, the greatest sales pitch to pass one's lips is created and no one is around to witness it, does it, he, or she exist?

The point is, you need an opportunity to do business, in order to do business. And regardless of your paradigm, whether you are a recording artist or owner of a small family–owned and operated bakery, your craft, talent, or passion is indeed a business and must be treated as such, if you expect it to evolve and earn money. Sure, I understand it is your passion, and it is easy to get caught up in the love of it, but at the end of the day, your passion is a business. Lady Gaga, Katy Perry, and Beyoncé are all brands, and despite all the fun it appears to be, they are in the business of sales: merchandise sales, record sales, concert sales. So yes, you need an audience. You can't sell something to an inanimate object. You need a real, live, breathing, responsive being to act as your audience, who essentially is going to purchase your product, idea, or talent.

In the performance and entertainment arena, you need an audience to develop a fan base from. You can't become famous if no one has ever heard of you. Even if you have the most incredible powerhouse singing voice known to man, if no one has ever experienced your game-changing talent, it is entirely irrelevant. The late Michael Jackson, formerly known as the King of Pop, exuded more talent in one pinky than some of us in our entire body. Yet, if Michael Jackson had a severe case of performance anxiety and put on historic concerts only in the privacy of his bathroom, with a shampoo bottle acting as his microphone, would he have left a legacy? Of course not! Because no one would have ever known of his talent. If no one has ever heard you or heard of you, you will never develop a fan base, get bookings or gigs, land a record contract, or become famous.

You could have the most amazing keynote speech, or be the most incredible speaker, trainer, or consultant, but if no one knows of your expertise, accomplishments, or capabilities, chances are you will not be recognized by the elite speaker bureaus and booked for speaking gigs worthy of your talent.

A career as a sales professional is no different. It can be rather frightening entering a career field that is solely or mostly based on commissions, such as a real estate agent or an automotive sales professional. Without the appropriate level of visibility, market awareness, and branding, you are going to have minimum success and starve (metaphorically speaking and sadly, in some cases, literally). On the other hand, a commission-based career can be extremely rewarding.

The field of sales is one of the most incredible careers one can embark upon. It allows you the ability to make as much money as you can earn, yet a large majority of those who enter the sales arena crash and burn, and are forced to leave their sales position for a traditional career or job with limited growth potential and no opportunity to earn massive revenue—and not because they lack the skill, ability, or talent, but because they lack an audience—someone to listen, someone to purchase whatever it is that they are selling. Why? Simply because they lack the knowledge to effectively prospect for new business, become visible, generate leads, and create new opportunities to do business.

To be clear, it doesn't matter what industry you are in. It doesn't matter if you are a sole proprietor, small business, corporation, doctor, lawyer, psychologist, dentist, chiropractor, singer, musician, speaker, sales professional, entrepreneur, or author/writer/blogger. Everyone needs visibility. Everyone needs an audience. Skill, desire, passion, likeability, intelligence, hard work, dedication, tenacity, desperation, need, and having a great product or service just aren't enough. The bottom line is that you are either visible or invisible. So unless you're David Copperfield or a ghost, being invisible isn't a desired result for any profession. So how can you become visible? Congratulations, my friend, for recognizing the importance of visibility (mind-set) and your commitment to reading this book (skillset). You have taken the first step toward visibility awesomeness!

With the sensory and content overloaded world we live in, it is difficult to become findable, never mind relevant, especially if you lack a strategy, resources, content, and a commitment to stay the course. This book is going to give you a methodical, proven approach to create a massive visibility strategy, while creating an unfair advantage over your competition, and consequently increasing your profits—a respectable goal for any business owner.

There is fierce competition out there, competition that comes in all shapes and sizes. And believe me, I've seen it. They are ready to inherit your customers the first opportunity they get. Chances are, when I say the word *competition*, a vivid picture of your direct competitor that offers similar or the exact products and services that you do comes to mind. You may even envision their horrid logo or obnoxious jingle, or hear the chant of their lame slogan, "ABC Competitor does it best, yup, no guess." But what about the competition of attention and stimulus? We live in the technology age, with tons of digital pieces starving for our attention—for example:

- Social media (the number one form of communication)
- Telephones (phone calls and texting)
- The Internet (surfing)
- Television, Netflix, Hulu, etc.
- Movies
- Sports
- Video games
- Radio
- Print (magazine, books)
- Nightlife (bars, clubs, casinos)
- And much, much more

You need to focus on how you, your company, and your product(s) are going to be found. How are you going to stand out against all of the noise from all of those different sources? You have to have a focused strategy, with a beginning, middle, and end in mind. I should probably mention here, early on, that I am a Franklin Covey Certified Trainer and Facilitator and continuous student of the *7 Habits of Highly Effective People*. I have adopted the seven habits into my personal and professional life and frequently apply these principles to all that I do. You will hear me mention these habits from time to time as they have become deeply rooted within me.

HOW DO I (YOU) GET FOUND?

First, you must begin with the end in mind. You know that you want to be found, but have you put enough thought into what it is exactly you want to be found for? What are your visibility goals? What is it specifically that you are trying to accomplish? What is your purpose? This is very important to acknowledge, for without a clear purpose, you have no guidance and without guidance, you cannot control where you are headed. Frankly, almost any road will get you there.

I suggest you take out a notepad or open a new Microsoft Word document and take some time to answer the following questions. These questions will get your mind set in the right direction and assist you in understanding how far on the path of visibility you currently are. Keep in mind, the only difference between where you are now and where you want to be is what you do. You already have a great product or service, or maybe you *are* the product—you just lack the roadmap to becoming visible. So, let's get those brain juices flowing and structure your end in mind.

What Is Your Product or Service?

Be specific, not generic, and make sure not to spread yourself too thin by trying to push too many services in one shot. By spreading yourself too thin, you risk diluting your relevancy and your potency, and furthermore, you risk taking away from your core competency. Chances are, you've probably heard the disparaging phrase "jack of all trades, master of none." While I am not implying that just because you are good at multiple things (notice I said "disparaging"), you cannot possibly master one or more of those things, I will say that it is my opinion that spreading your focus can have an adverse effect. Also avoid being too generic or vague. You need to find balance and a niche, and work on solidifying your existence within that niche. A rule of thumb I live by and a concept that will be introduced to you here shortly is "be careful of distractions disguised as opportunities."

I am going to provide a few examples that may or may not be the line of business you are involved in, but the basic principles may and can apply. In fact, many times you can grab nuggets from other industries and experience major success because you are doing something completely different from your competition. It provides your audience with a fresh perspective. A lot of times I see businesses that are trying to keep up with the big fish and mimic just about everything that they are doing. They are constantly in a state of exhaustion (physically and financially) because they are trying to keep up. It's important to be unique, a leader, a trend setter. Sometimes all it takes is a little risk to try something outside the box, and the payoff can be extremely rewarding.

If you are, for example, one of the following:

- **Car salesman.** Instead of thinking of yourself as just a car salesman, be specific. Do you sell new or pre-owned vehicles? If you sell new, then what franchises? Do you have the desire to represent a large dealership, small dealership, independent store, or large dealer group? Do you make an effort to work with law enforcement and military members? Or maybe you focus on or would like to become more active with being the go-to person for colleges. What is your personal primary market area (PMA)? If you sell pre-owned cars, what do you stock the most of, or what are the most requested pre-owned vehicles in your market (by brand and model)? Do you have certifications? Over 60 percent of Americans suffer from poor credit—do you specialize in credit needs?
- **Singer.** Instead of thinking of yourself as just a singer, be specific. What genre of music do you consider yourself? Pop, R&B, hip-hop, rock? It is no secret that there are many different types of singers and voices that range from power vocalist to gangsta rappers. There is obviously a big difference in style with a completely different audience base. The iconic Bruce Lee once stated, "I am all styles, I am no styles." This point of view may work well for a martial artist, but as a recording artist, you want to stay loyal to what your fans—or audience—are expecting from you and in turn willing to purchase. Too much diversity will only confuse them.
- **Speaker.** Instead of thinking of yourself as just a speaker, be specific. Are you a trainer? Are you a facilitator of a specific course? Are you a subject matter expert? Do you specialize in workshops, seminars, or webinars? Or maybe you deliver only keynote speeches? What is your niche? Are you a motivational speaker, technology speaker, or a sales

expert? Do you utilize a talent to deliver or solidify your message? As a Certified Speaking Professional with the National Speakers Association, I have had the privilege of sharing the same space with some of the world's top speaking professionals. Most recently, I was honored to be introduced to Erik Wahl, a fantastic graffiti artist and the author of *Unthink*. He utilizes the art of painting to deliver his speeches, awe his audience, and leave behind a real masterpiece. Another amazing speaker, Dan Thurmon, known as a dynamic keynote speaker, peak performance coach, and the author of *Off Balance on Purpose*, utilizes the art of comedy, coupled with juggling and acrobatics, to deliver his message. He guarantees a flipping good time, literally.

- **Restaurant owner.** Instead of thinking of yourself as just a person that owns a restaurant, be specific. What type of food do you specialize in? Is there a specific food you are famous or recognized for, or want to be? Do you have a secret recipe? What location are you based out of? Are you in the city or the suburbs? Do you have a single location or several locations? What are your demographics? What type of environment do you want to create—an upscale one or laid-back, cozy one? Either one will work, but it's important to the overall mission of the organization to have clarity. What type of clientele would you like to attract? Are you looking to attract a younger crowd, older crowd, families, or a mixture? Will you hold special events, like karaoke night or "kids eat free" night? How involved in the community are you or would you like to be? Do you have a theme? I recently threw an event in Dallas, Texas, and used Eddie Deen's Ranch as my event location. With its ranch-themed location resembling something out of a Clint Eastwood movie, with bull riding, square dancing, and BBQ-style cuisine, it does a great job of giving you that true Texas experience.

- **Martial arts school.** Instead of thinking of yourself as someone who just owns a martial arts school, be specific. What style of martial arts do you specialize in—Jiu-Jitsu, karate, judo? What is your specialty? Is it training law enforcement/military, kids' classes, or women's self-defense? What town or city is your school based in and how far can you draw students from? Answering these questions allows you to create a specific focus. I discuss this in later detail as we progress on our visibility journey.

- **Real estate agent.** Instead of thinking of yourself as just a standard real estate agent trying to sell properties, be specific. What kinds of properties are you trying to sell? Single homes, family homes, condos, apartments? Are you interested in acquiring homes too? Do you or have you considered flipping houses? Are you represented by a major real estate agency? Can you use its brand and credibility to perpetuate your individual credibility and brand? Is your only focus to sell properties, or have you considered selling home warranties as an additional source of income? What type of networking/referral systems have you built? Do you have relationships with home inspection agents or termite inspection agents? Do you focus on building relationships with real estate attorneys or homeowner insurance companies? What about landscapers, carpenters, and home builders? If not, then you are missing out on major opportunities. Think about it. You can build a strong referral business in all of these different areas. To get started, you can search for local companies in your area that fall within the categories of service mentioned earlier. Make a list of them and their addresses, and deliver a box of donuts and a box of joe along with a stack of business cards. Explain to them that you are looking to partner with some local businesses to create win-win solutions in which each refers business to the other. You reap what you sow. Partnering and nurturing relationships with other businesses will plant seeds that reap a great return.

What Is Your Value Package Proposition?

- What is different and better about you? What makes you unique?
- What awards have you won?
  - Have you been featured in any media—radio, TV, print, etc.?
  - "Best of . . . "
  - If you are a franchise, what awards has your franchise won? You can use that borrowed credibility.
  - What about reviews?
    - Google reviews
    - Yelp
    - Better Business Bureau
    - Merchantcircle
    - Yellow pages
    - Client testimonials
- What do you do better and differently from your competitors?
- What special giveaways do you offer?

- Do you have a customer loyalty or rewards program?
- Why should someone buy from you?
- Why should someone come to your event, show, concert, or exhibit?
- Have you invented or patented a process or technology?
- Are you first to do what you are doing?
- Have you been in business a long time? How long?
- Have you been practicing your craft for a long time?
- Have you served a lot of clients, delivered a lot of speeches, or performed a lot of concerts? If so, how many?
- Do you have any celebrity (or reputable) endorsements?
  - If you authored a book, did any VIPs, celebrities, or reputable people endorse your book?
  - If you are a speaker or trainer, did a Fortune 500 or Fortune 100 publicly traded company, VIP, or reputable entity give you a positive survey or review?
  - Has a food critic reviewed your restaurant and given you a positive review?

Who Is Your Audience?

This is such an important question that you need to be able to identify the answer as soon as possible. I am a business owner myself. I know you might feel like saying, "Everyone or anyone," but that is too broad of a stroke. You should not take a shotgun approach to your business. A precise focus on your targeted audience is very important.

- **Who are you trying to attract?** This is going to be very different from business to business and situation to situation. But I am going to list a couple of examples with principal questions that can be applied to your specific situation.
- **Car salesman** (sells Chryslers in Swedesboro, New Jersey)
  - What are the demographics in Swedesboro, New Jersey, and the surrounding area (20–30 miles)?
  - How large is the population?
  - Who buys your cars?
  - What is their average income?
  - Are they men or women? (Women have over 80 percent of buying power.)
  - What kinds of cars are they buying? New or used?

- New? Which model(s)?
- Used? What year, make, and model(s)?
- Are there any large companies in the area for "macro" selling?
- Are there any military bases?
- How far are you from a major city?
- Who spends the most money?
- Who is the best repeat customer?
- Who provides the most referrals?
- **Jujitsu academy** (martial art school in Philadelphia)
  - Who wants to train in martial arts/karate?
    - Hardcore fighters or brawlers
    - Fans and enthusiasts of UFC/MMA
    - People trying to lose weight and stay healthy
    - People interested in self-defense
    - Women for rape prevention
  - People who love competition and competing
  - People trying to be active and social with a group of other like-minded individuals
  - Parents who want to put their children in kids' classes because:
    - They want them to be able to defend themselves from bullies
    - They want their kids to develop discipline and self-control
    - They hope their kids will be active and healthy (to get them off of video games)
    - They want them to develop self-confidence
    - They want them to interact with other kids and develop social skills
  - People who are looking for work/life balance
  - People who need to vent and need some stress release
- **Professional speaker** (keynote/workshop):
  - What do you speak about?
  - What is your niche?
  - Are you a motivational speaker?
  - Do you speak about leadership and management?
  - Do you specialize in digital marketing?
  - Do you get bookings from speakers bureaus (or would you like to)?
  - What industry are you in?
    - Automotive sales
    - Real estate
    - Education

- Hospitality
- Entertainment
- Medical

Where Is Your Audience?

After you have identified who your audience is, you now need to know where your audience is—whether you want to break it down by:

- Demographics
- Geo-targeting
- Niche
- Industry
- Associations or organizations
- Gender
- Interests

It doesn't really matter. Once you identify who they are, it will then be relatively easy to find out where they are. The question now becomes, do you want to go after them, or have them come to you? You might be confused by this question and tell yourself that this doesn't make much sense, or that it just doesn't seem possible. How can "they," my potential audience, come to me? That is exactly what this book is going to teach you. I call it *reactive selling*. Let them come to you. Why exert more energy for minimal return when you can exert minimal energy upfront, for a stronger (more gross) and easier close later.

Cold-calling someone is a much harder close or a much harder sale compared to someone (an individual, company, association, bureau, etc.) coming to you for your product or service. If you are being approached, it says the person is (1) interested, (2) a serious buyer, and (3) looking to purchase relatively soon. Picture yourself going fishing. You've got your fishing gear on, fishing pole in hand, and bait all ready to go. (If you are not the fishing type, humor me. Trust me, there is a point here.) Imagine two ponds in front of you. You can choose to fish in either one. The first pond is empty, but you have the opportunity to draw the fish to you with your selected bait. The second pond is already full of fish. All you need to do is throw your fishing line into the water and boom . . . you've got your fish. What pond are you choosing? I would bet it is the one full of abundance, possibility, and opportunity. You have access to such a pond, right at your fingertips, literally. This pond is called the *Internet*.

Once you analyze the data in regard to conventional advertising and marketing versus digital marketing, you will see that reactive selling is the smartest, most powerful, transparent, and cost-effective strategy you can adopt for success.

Conventional versus Digital—Which Is Right for You?

Major controversy has developed over whether it is more beneficial to invest your time and money into conventional marketing and advertising mediums like radio, television, and print, or to place your focus, energy, and resources into digital marketing efforts. Digital marketing and advertising are the clear choice and here is why. Conventional marketing and advertising are intrusive—meaning that it is where and when people don't want to be bothered. The reality is that people no longer wait for the Sunday newspaper to hit the front doorstep so they can search for ads to help make a buying decision. People don't gas up the car, get the family all buckled in, and drive down Route 66 looking for your billboard, in hopes of getting some pertinent information that will make them feel more comfortable in their decision to purchase a product or service. Sure, they may take notice of it, but they are not intentionally searching for it. In fact, with all of the new "no texting while driving" laws recently put in place, it is obvious that people are too distracted to look at the road, let alone take the opportunity to look up. Furthermore, people don't watch CNN or even *Keeping Up with the Kardashians* in eager anticipation of the commercials so they can get excited about a product or service.

Conventional media and advertising have lost the dominance they once had. And if you are not willing to change your thinking patterns and marketing philosophies and processes, you are risking extinction of your product or service. If you are not constantly in a state of evolution, you are then in a state of regression. Believe me—the world will not wait for you to catch up.

People are tired of being bombarded by the "shotgun," "spray and pray" approach of conventional advertising. Some conventional marketing advocates reading this may be offended by what I am saying, but I am only speaking the truth and more importantly speaking from experience. As a business owner of several multimillion-dollar companies, I have experimented with both conventional and digital methods and at first was somewhat reluctant. But I saw in advance where the future was headed and made the decision to trust; for return on investment (ROI) reasons, I have chosen to participate strictly in digital mediums, and, wow, has it paid off! I believe it is fair for me to assume that some part of you, or maybe all of you, must agree with me or feel the same way. This is why you agreed to invest your time in reading this book, because you realize the importance of partaking in the digital age, even if that realization lies somewhere deep down. I understand that change can be scary. I also understand change can be uncomfortable. But this is not the first time we have been down this road, and it surely will not be the last. Think of the evolution of cell phones. They started off as large cinder block–looking devices with modest options, but they served their intended purpose, a purpose we were all quite astonished by. Wait, I don't have to be connected to a landline to speak to someone? I don't have to wait by the phone at home in anticipation of a phone call? I can make or take a phone call on demand, while running errands? As the size of the phone began to dwindle, the functionality of the phone began to increase exponentially, leading to the development of the smartphone. Not everyone was sold on the idea, and not everyone transitioned without hesitation. Quite honestly, the new capabilities were downright scary and intimidating for a decent majority, yet fast-forward to today and practically everyone has a smart phone, and our kids are just about born with them. The point is that, like a cell phone, digital advertising is not a fad or a phase. It is a permanent structure that is rooted deeply into our culture and will only evolve further. Even companies that once offered or still offer conventional marketing services are adapting and growing to accommodate and fulfill the wants and needs of today's buyers. Take a look at the yellow pages, for instance. We once depended greatly on this five-inch bible of information to determine what companies were available to conduct business with. Today, that same bible of information is conveniently located at www.yellowpages.com. Yellow pages didn't choose to fade away—they chose to adapt and evolve. Just like we must do. We must go where the fish are if we want to not only survive but also thrive. And that is why I chose to title this book *Winning the Game of Googleopoly* and not *Winning the Game of Comcast, or Radio, or Billboards, or Newspapers*.

Some may not even agree with my assessment and may not consider traditional advertising intrusive or annoying. They may even consider it a form of branding. But the reality of the situation is that conventional advertising no longer has the effect it once did, and statistics prove it. These numbers show that conventional advertising is declining year after year, and traditional ad sources are losing revenue at alarming rates. And why? Simple—because people are tired of the noise! They are tired of having things that they don't want or need constantly forced in their line of vision. And they are finding ways to negate them, to go around them, to avoid them, and to block them. It is kind of like the cat-and-mouse game between a highway patrol officer and a motorist who owns a radar/laser detector, looking to speed with the comfort of not getting a ticket. This very concept is happening with advertising. Americans are arming themselves with the radar detectors of anti-intrusive advertising.

You know these detectors as and most likely possess:

- Satellite radio
- DVRs
- Video-on-demand
- Pay-per-view
- Hulu
- Netflix
- Social media
- The Internet

Did you know that an astounding 77 percent of viewers use another device while watching TV?[1] Let's allow that to marinate for a few seconds. This means that if you have 100 people in a room watching television, 77 of them would be head down, eyes down, focus split, logged onto their computers, smartphones, iPads, or whichever electronic mind candy they choose. This tells me that your potential audience is listening to the television, rather than watching the television.

Prospects, consumers, and shoppers alike are all tired of the old-school tactics and antiquated strategies of the past. We live in an on-demand universe where people want, no, *expect* information, when and how they want it—and quickly too! Hence the term *on-demand*. It is evident that our patience for retrieving information has diminished. This is why we often see phrases like "Click here for a quick quote," or "Get your credit approved in 60 seconds or less." And if you fail to

---

[1] *Source:* Jim Lecinski, *Winning the Zero Moment of Truth* (Google eBook, 2012).

provide the information they are seeking, with a tap of a finger or click of a mouse, they will certainly move on. I discuss this in greater detail later in the book.

So we've established the fact that conventional marketing and advertising are indeed intrusive for the consumer, where and when people do not want to be bothered. But did you realize they also lack transparency for the marketer? In other words, there is no true way to calculate a return on investment (ROI). Yes, each of the mediums can articulate circulation, viewers, and listeners (how many fish are in the pond), but how can someone possibly identify out of all of those viewers, listeners, or readers which folks are legitimately interested, in-market prospects? You can't! It is very difficult—next to nearly impossible—even to quantify it. Obviously, if you are running an ad in the newspaper, television, or radio and someone comes into your business or calls you on the phone and states it is a direct result of the ad, you can quantify some value. But does that value surpass the monetary investment? Probably not. The problem as I see it is you must ask yourself the following. Can you identify exactly how many people actually saw the ad? No. Can you identify out of the people who did see the ad if they were even in the market for your product or service? No again. How about this: can you identify out of the people who did see the ad whether they even cared? Definitely not. Let's just say that we did have a means to generate that statistic and you found that some did care about your product or service: Can anyone assist you in identifying out of those who did have an interest how many people actually cared enough to take action—in other words, how many people called or visited you or your business? You might say yes, or you believe so, but that brings on a whole new set of challenges. You see, in order to measure a true ROI, you must have a viable tracking system to manage lead generation and prospects. This might include call monitoring and tracking software and/or a customer relationship management (CRM) solution. If you do have these tools, the question becomes, are they set up the right way with the right content and strategy? Are you and/or your team fully trained on these tools and maximizing their effectiveness? And if you possess these tools, are they set up the right way? Are you using them for each and every action item, every single time, without exception, without fail, the correct way? If you cannot answer yes to these questions, you have a problem. You see, in order for you to be able to quantify true ROI, you need to have an accurate tool of measure, housing accurate data and resulting in accurate field intelligence. Otherwise, "garbage in, garbage out." The last time I checked, garbage won't buy you anything. In fact, it can cost you.

Conventional advertising and marketing cost a fortune for a majority to afford. If you are a sole proprietor, actor, musician, speaker, singer, car salesman, karate instructor, or personal trainer just starting out, how on earth are you going to afford a conventional marketing spend? Or maybe you're not just starting out; maybe you've been doing this for a long time now but haven't quite made it and have limited means to work with. How do you intend to pay for the advertisement source? The answer, of course, is that you can't and you won't. It is like the chicken or the egg concept with some business owners. They need an audience to purchase whatever it is they are selling in order to earn money. But if you have no audience, you cannot make a monetary return. You need to make yourself visible—make yourself seen. And in order to do that, you must pay to play, and conventional advertising is the most financially challenging way to go. I am not trying to deter you from your dream of mainstream media notoriety; I am just trying to give you a reality check. Unfamiliar with the cost associated with conventional advertising? I will give you an example in the Philadelphia market. Television would need a budget of at least $3,000 per month for at least three months to have an even slight impact on the audience. That is quoting you direct numbers from my Comcast rep in Philly. I personally ran TV commercials for a very popular independent recording artist, promoting a hot new single on the radio with a major label feature with Meek Mill of Maybach Music Group. As a matter of fact, her TV commercial for her new track was even played on the highly anticipated Kardashian wedding episode: $9,000 in 90 days for about 60 TV commercials. Was it worth it? It depends on how you define "worth it." It provided some notoriety and credibility, but did it provide ROI? No, definitely not. Maybe if we had a million-dollar budget and were able to commit to a full campaign, but it was too expensive to keep up the initiative on TV. Same thing for radio ads—we were spending thousands of dollars for radio ads on Clear Channel. But the way that conventional media works is through frequency and repetition. You would spend thousands of dollars per month to air a 15- or 30-second commercial, and for what—brand awareness? It just doesn't make sense, not when there is a much cheaper way, a more effective way, with lasting results.

There are numerous problems with relying entirely on a conventional advertising or marketing campaign:

1. First, you have to hope that there is an audience watching, listening, or reading your commercials or ads and hope that they actually have an interest in you, your product, or service. It doesn't matter if you reach 1,000 or 10,000 viewers, readers, or listeners if they don't care about you, your product, or service. You might as well be invisible.

2. You'd also better hope that if there are people watching TV or listening to the radio they don't change the channel when your commercial comes on, or they don't use the commercial time to go use the bathroom, jump on the Internet to check on their social media, or use their cell phones. Remember that 77 percent of people use another device while watching TV. Imagine what that number rises to when a commercial is being aired.

3. It is also important to have a well-thought-out strategy in mind:
   - I have seen a lot of people save up money or use money they did not have to advertise on television or radio because they thought it was a sure shot for maximum exposure and they had substandard content created. I'm not saying *they* were substandard, but their actual video or audio production was of poor quality. That was counterproductive to the overall mission and a huge waste of financial resources.
   - I have also seen these same people use their very last-chance money and squander it on conventional media. They invested in TV or radio air time and got it, but it was on an overnight schedule or it was a random inventory, meaning their commercial was played in a spot the radio/TV channel didn't sell a time slot to. In other words, since they didn't have a real budget or strategy, they were receiving only the bottom-of-the-barrel ad space. They never had prime-time slots or desired segments.
   - Cable seems like an awesome, cost-effective solution, but a lot of people don't understand that cable is not even on the Nielsen rating, meaning that there could be fewer than 1,000 viewers watching a particular channel. So, just because something is cheap when it is usually really expensive, don't assume it is a deal. It is priced that way for a reason.

You may be on the complete opposite side of the spectrum and not fall under the same category mentioned earlier. You are not a small business, an individual person, or a startup. In fact, you are a large company with a large advertising budget, who can easily afford TV, radio, and print. That is great! But the fact that you can afford to use these conventional advertising opportunities doesn't mean that you should use them. Affordability shouldn't give you the license to spend irresponsibly—not if you want to grow your net profits. You do not want to just exist in the black; you want to dominate in the black and continue to evolve.

You must put first things first—that is, put the most important things at the top of your list. These are the items you must act upon quickly. More importantly, you need to be careful of distractions disguised as opportunities. This is a very important strategy and a strategy that you should always employ when designing a marketing plan initiative. As I discussed earlier, there is so much noise in the world, so many shiny objects lurking in our paths, fighting for our attention. There is so much sensory-overloaded content that it is easy to become confused and distracted. There are so many options, so many directions to take—from blow-up gorillas to airplane banners. Which way do you go? How do you pick the right strategy? The answer is simple . . . pick the *best* strategy, the proven strategy, backed by hard data—a strategy that will give you the largest ROI on both your time and your money. There is nothing, and I mean nothing, in advertising and marketing that can even come close to the power of the Internet.

Here are some important facts to consider:
It took . . .

- Radio 38 years to reach 50 million people
- Television 13 years to reach 50 million people
- The Internet 4 years to reach 50 million people
- And it took Facebook *only* 2 years to reach 50 million people! That's right—2 years!

The Internet is the most powerful marketing mechanism ever created on planet Earth. Conventional advertising outlets, such as television, radio, newspapers, magazines, and billboards, have been rapidly losing reach and revenue to the point that major entities like newspapers and radio stations have been sold, consolidated, or gone bankrupt. And the simple reason is the Internet. It has completely changed the game on so many levels. The Internet allows consumers (content consumers) the opportunity to consume the content when and where they want. They are no longer slaves to conventional media. At one point, if you liked a recording artist or a certain song, people would glue themselves to the radio waiting for their jam to come back on. The same went for a favorite TV show. People would rearrange their schedules so they wouldn't miss a TV show or a soap opera. Nowadays, people only need to go to Hulu or Netflix to watch their TV program. They can record the fight, the news, or whatever else they want to see on their DVRs and watch it later on, at their leisure. As for radio, there is Pandora and iHeartRadio, and even better for music enthusiasts are Vevo and YouTube, due to the visual component. People can consume as much as they want, whenever they want, and best of all . . . for free!

THE TRUTH SHALL SET US FREE!

As a business owner, I walk in the same shoes as you do, and I find comfort in knowing that Internet/digital advertising provides advertisers, marketers, business owners, professionals, artists, and so on the opportunity for transparency that we so greatly deserve. Instead of just throwing stuff against the wall to see what sticks, as we have done in the past, the data provided by the Internet is completely transparent and traceable, down to the penny. Even with Internet advertising you must put first things first, but you are no longer flying blind. You can see and determine which Internet tactics are the most effective for you and the market you are trying to penetrate. If you spend money on:

- Pay-per-click
    For transparency you should identify:
  - Via Google Analytics, exactly how much did each and every click cost you?
  - How many keywords did you buy and what were those keywords?
  - How much did those keywords cost you per click, per campaign?
  - Which keywords worked better than others?
    With this information, you can evaluate your ad budget-to-visibility ratio and adjust accordingly. If you find that certain keywords just aren't producing results, you simply eliminate them. This way you can

dedicate a larger portion of your ad budget toward the keywords that are most effective for your targeted campaign and that are illustrating success and, most importantly, results. What is great about this is that this evaluation can occur in real time and with the ability to alter the campaign rather quickly, unlike a television or radio campaign, where you commit to a specific length of time and wonder what the results were. You do not have the option to change stations or time slots until your contracted campaign runs its course.

- Display ads/banner ads
     For transparency you should identify:
  - How many impressions did you get?
  - What was the cost per impression?
  - What was the cost per campaign?
  - How many click-throughs?
  - What was the cost per click-through?
- Social media ads (Facebook/Twitter)
     For transparency you should identify:
  - How many impressions or views did you get?
  - What was the cost per campaign?
  - What was the cost per impression or view?

As mentioned before, conventional media is limited to providing only an estimate of what their viewership, listeners, and readers are and have no way of identifying exactly how many people will see the ad, care, or, most importantly, act on it. On the other hand, digital marketing has the capability to supply the marketer or advertiser with these answers. It can tell you exactly:

- How many people saw the ad
- How many people cared
- How long the person stayed on the page, landing page, ad, etc.
- Whether he or she read it
- How many click-throughs occurred
- How many leads occurred
  - How many emails were sent
  - How many phone calls were made
  - How many saw the digital ad and went directly to the business or bought the product or service or downloaded the song

- How much it cost
  - The cost per:
    - Click
    - Impression
    - Phone call
    - Email
    - Sale
  - The gross profit from the campaign
  - The net profit from the campaign

Again, would you rather throw your bait into a pond and hope that a fish swims by and happens to notice, or would you rather throw your fishing line into a pond full of fish that are specifically looking to chew? They are hungry and in search of what you've got. All you have to do is make yourself available as a choice, and when done correctly, the dominant choice.

The bottom line is that the majority of the world uses the Internet for just about everything. The Internet is the first place people go before they ever step foot into a business, pick up the phone, hire a trainer or consultant, or buy a service or product.

Regardless of whether you are an individual, small business, or a large corporation, the most powerful and cost-effective form of advertising is the Internet. There is absolutely no other advertising medium that comes even close for effectiveness, affordability, reach, and ROI.

ADDITIONAL RESOURCES

For more information about how important it is to be visible online, and how digital marketing can drastically improve your ROI from advertising, please visit http://www.googleopolybook.com/understanding-online-visibility.

CHAPTER **2**

Reality Check:
Google Is a Monopoly

At this point you understand that visibility is key. If you are not visible, you are invisible and will not be able to sell your product or service or develop a fan base. Or it will be much more difficult. So the question becomes, "What is the best way to be visible?" I established that the answer is "the Internet." The Internet is the most powerful form of marketing and advertising with the highest ROI. The next question is, "What is the most powerful form of Internet/digital marketing?" The answer is unequivocally "search engine domination," specifically through the "oracle" itself, Google. Of course there are other major players in the search engine space that exist, such as the following:

• Bing: 350 million unique monthly visitors as of 2014
• Yahoo!: 300 million unique monthly visitors as of 2014
• Ask: 245 million unique monthly visitors as of 2014
• AOL: 125 million unique monthly visitors as of 2014[1]

While these statistics may be shocking, none of them comes close to Google. Google is the leviathan in the search space. Google receives over 1.1 billion unique visitors per month. There are 7.046 billion people on planet Earth and 1.1 billion of them uniquely search Google monthly. That is just about equal to all of the other major search engine providers combined! Comscore ranks the search engine market share as follows:

1. Google: 67.5 percent
2. Bing: 18.7 percent
3. Yahoo!: 10 percent

---

[1] *Source:* www.ebizmba.com/articles/search-engines.

4. Ask: 2.5 percent
5. AOL: 1.3 percent[2]

To be crystal clear, all of the other search engines combined don't equal even half of Google's reach. If that wasn't enough reason to believe, let's add YouTube into the mix. YouTube is also a search engine, and it is actually the number two search engine, not Bing. The reason it wasn't included in the top-five list is simply because it isn't a traditional search engine. It is a video search engine, but it is a search engine nonetheless. Consumers go to YouTube to search for answers just like they go to Google. The only difference is they are specifically requesting a video response to their specific search.

Here is an amazing breakdown of YouTube:

• There are over 3 billion searchers every month
• Over 1 billion unique visitors per month
• 100 hours of video are uploaded every minute
• Bigger than Bing, Yahoo!, AOL, and Ask combined
• 6 billion hours are viewed every month

And the most incredible aspect of YouTube is that it is owned by Google! That is right! In 2006 Google acquired YouTube for $1.65 billion.

Let's put this into perspective. Google already is the preeminent search engine entity on the planet.[3] Google is bigger than the other four competing search engines combined. Now when you add in the dynamic that Google also owns the number 2 search engine, YouTube, it becomes no question that Google dominates (practically monopolizes) the search space.

Consider these stats for Google and YouTube combined:

• Over 2.1 billion unique visitors per month
• Over 103 billion searches per month

I share this with you because it is very important to always be careful of distractions disguised as opportunities. There are so many

---

[2]*Source:* http://searchenginewatch.com/article/2345837/Google-Search-Engine-Market
-Share-Nears-68.

[3]*Source:* www.mushroomnetworks.com/infographics/youtube---the-2nd-largest-search
-engine-infographic; http://phandroid.com/2014/04/22/100-billion-google-searches/.

shiny objects in digital marketing and Internet advertising, so many choices, so many search engines, and so many solutions promising to be the ultimate answer to your visibility needs. You have to put first things first and ask yourself how you are going to get the biggest bang for your buck and the biggest return for your time. After all, time is money. It is the most precious commodity we possess. Once it's gone . . . it's gone. So you need to be careful not to allow companies, people, or backseat drivers the opportunity to sway your thoughts and coerce you into investing your attention, time, and resources into "B" player options. Their arguments may be compelling and sound something like this:

- B player: Bing has 350 million unique users and almost 20 percent of the market share.
- I say, so what! As impressive as that may sound, it still doesn't compare to the potential exposure Google has to offer.
- B player: If everyone is focused on Google, then there is less competition on the other platforms.
- I say, so what! Again, remember our goal is to be where the most fish are, not just where a fair amount are.
- B player: I don't like Google or even use Google.
- I say, so what! That makes you the minority, not the majority.
- B player: You should diversify and maximize your opportunity and minimize your risk.
- I say, not a good idea. I spoke about spreading yourself too thin and diluting your effectiveness by trying to implement various strategies simultaneously. You want to conquer one action item or opportunity at a time and make sure to put first things first. This way you can make sure the most important action items pertaining to your marketing strategy are targeted and executed first.

Google is synonymous with search and search engines, the same way Q-tips are synonymous with cotton swabs, Kleenex is synonymous with facial tissues, and Rollerblades are synonymous with inline skates. Q-tips, Kleenex, and Rollerblades are companies, not objects! But their brand and corporate names are so powerful that they have become interchangeable. The brand names have outweighed the name of the products themselves. It's no wonder that the name *Google* has turned into a verb that is so commonly used in people's day-to-day speech. I'm sure you've heard someway say, "I need to Google that," or "I Googled that," or "Google says." If people are looking to satisfy a curiosity or have a question, they simply turn to Google in order to search for their desired answers. It is surreal, but true, that people find and have found their:

- Husbands
- Wives
- Pets
- Furniture
- Directions
- Advice
- Automobiles
- Homes
- Fitness regimen
- Health and beauty tips
- Recipes
- And everything in between

. . . all on Google.

In 2011 Jim Lecinski of Google wrote an eBook called *Winning the Zero Moment of Truth*, otherwise known as the ZMOT. It changed the way people and companies thought about and approached advertising and marketing. It altered our paradigm, the way that we viewed and understood the consumer buying process. It revealed that there is a space between stimulus (something that elicits an action or response) and the "First Moment of Truth" (coined by Procter & Gamble). This new space between consumer stimulus and response is the ZMOT. This is where consumers are influenced by what they see, read, and find online. The days of a consumer seeing a product or service and immediately whipping out the credit card to complete the purchase are over. There is now a space of time consumers utilize to do research before making a decision to purchase. It doesn't mean weeks or months necessarily. It may take only a few hours, or minutes even, but regardless of the length of time, there is that predecision research being conducted. Google's ZMOT eBook goes on to say that over 80 percent of all transactions start on search. From something as inexpensive as a paperback book to something as expensive as a jet plane. Yes, folks, those are actual transactions! A consumer is going to drop the item or service of interest into the Google search field and review what pops up.

Let's look at the automotive sales industry as an example. The second-largest item that the average American will ever purchase in his or her lifetime is an automobile (right behind a home). JD Power & Associates states that 92–99 percent of Americans will go online to do some form of research before they ever step foot into a dealership. Whether this research is due to pricing, availability, service, trade-in information, credit application, insurance, or just to make the process and experience more convenient, people are influenced by what they see online. After all, perception is reality.

I am going to give you a strong example of Google's ZMOT, which happens to be a personal true story.

One early morning, my wife and I were at the gym working out, running on the treadmills side by side. (Side note: Karina is a huge fitness buff and is all about everything and anything fitness- and wellness-related.) So, picture us side by side on the treadmills, with our headphones on, listening to our favorite workout jams via our iTunes on our iPhones, when a TV commercial comes on for the Ab Rocket Twister. Karina immediately looks up with this smile, because it seems that she is the unofficial tester of all of these "As Seen on TV" fitness products. She points to the Plasma and mouths to me, "I want it!" I look over at her like, "Woman, are you crazy? Whatever you want, honey, please just let me be. I am having a hard enough time just trying to keep my focus and stay alive on this treadmill." I tell you, in less than 27 seconds, as she is running on the treadmill, she Googles "Ab Rocket Twister" and sees that it has only 2.5 stars (Google review) out of 5 stars. And *boom*! Just like that she went from a state of excitement to a state of disappointment, exited her Safari browser, and went back to listening to her iTunes tracks. She dismissed the product from her thoughts. She put her trust into the recommendations of others who tried the product before her, and she identified that it wasn't a product that she was willing to spend (or in this case risk) her money on. Once again, the amount of time from point of interest (the time from when she was exposed to the infomercial) to the Zero Moment of Truth (the time she decided against moving forward with the product) was less than 30 seconds! Try to imagine all of the time and cost that went into that infomercial for the Ab Rocket Twister, and just like that, it was obliterated in less than 30 seconds by Google reviews. It no longer mattered that the models casted in the infomercial possessed "six-pack" abs, the object of man's envy. In fact, they lost all credibility in her eyes. They were no longer credible examples of the product's results, but simply actors attempting to take advantage of people, despite the product's lack of effectiveness. This visual combined with her strong shopper impulse were no match for the words she read across her cell phone screen from other consumers. Their dissatisfaction with the product was powerful enough for her to change her mind and decide against purchasing the product. And that is the power of ZMOT.

But it doesn't end there. You may possibly be thinking that Karina is only one opinion and one story, and question whether that is enough to make a difference in a world filled with over 7 billion people. But to assume that would be wrong. Sure, in this case she is one voice, but listen to what happens next.

Every Sunday at the Bradley home is family night. This is where we get together for food and entertainment with immediate and extended family members. That first Sunday following the gym incident, Karina and her sister were sitting down talking in the family room when, sure enough, the infomercial for the Ab Rocket Twister comes on. Karina had just given birth to our fourth child, and her sister was pregnant and expecting her third. Naturally, they were discussing their fitness status, wants, goals, desires, and wishes. So what do you think happened when her sister got that same excited look on her face when she saw the infomercial? Karina, of course, shared her Google review findings with her sister, which quickly put an end to any desire to purchase the product. You see, it becomes a ripple effect. Karina goes online and reads the reviews for the Ab Rocket Twister. She then decides not to buy the product. Her sister gets excited over the same product, and Karina quickly puts that impulse to rest. Now if Karina's sister comes across someone who mentions the product, she too will advise against it and so on and so on. This is why it is so important to have a strong Google review presence.

Google has warranted credibility. People feel that if it is on Google, it must be real. It is considered to be a factual resource for anything and everything. If we have a question, it has an answer. It is the oracle of our time. Many years ago, this same phenomenon occurred with the invention of the television. People believed that if it was on TV, it must be real. The same situation has occurred with Google. People feel that if they Google something, the answer they seek will magically pop up. With that in mind, it is important to note that while the perception in the past was that everything seen on television had to be real, there came a time when people realized that they couldn't believe everything they saw or read in the newspaper or magazines. Well, unlike those previous examples, Google is always hard at work to make sure that the information it presents to searchers is as relevant and accurate as possible, therefore ensuring that there will never come a time when people stop relying on the search juggernaut for their quests for information.

Most people don't understand the mechanics of how Google results work , but they don't think twice about questioning its validity. And they still trust and believe it to be so—just like most people don't understand how or why electricity works, nor do they care, so long as it works. They just know that it does and that it allows us to have a source of power for appliances, electronics, and even automobiles. They love to use it, they need to use it, and they depend on it. Just the same goes for Google.

It is for this reason that your search engine focus should consist purely of Google efforts. Once you come to the realization that Google is indeed the leviathan of search engines, the next step is to truly understand Google. Once you understand Google, then you can formulate a powerful strategy to dominate Google through the Googleopoly strategy you will learn herein and create an unfair competitive advantage.

Originally, Google was limited by the type of content it could supply a person when a Google search was conducted. This has all changed with the formation of *universal search*. Back in 2007, Google announced that it would unify content found on the web from a variety of sources, such as news websites, video, images, and book search engines. The objective was to ensure a more streamlined search process so that it was easier to find relevant information on a specific topic. The evolution of traditional search to universal search has upgraded the search game. At one time people had to go to specific search engines for specific forms of content. For example, images were found on websites like Flickr and Photobucket, and videos were found on websites like AOL Video, YouTube, Metacafe, Viddler, and so forth. Years ago you couldn't Google something and see images, audio, or video show up on the first page of Google's results. Today we count on this unity of information.

Universal search is the consolidated and blended search returns from:

- Video
- Images
- Maps
- News
- Local
- Shopping

Some interesting facts related to universal search:

- Video shows up for 65 percent of the keywords (people prefer to watch video over static text)
- Images show up for 40 percent of the keywords
- News feeds show up for 16 percent of the keywords
- Shopping shows up for 6 percent of the keywords
- Maps show up for 1 percent of the keywords[4]

What this means is that because of universal search, no matter what someone is looking for, no matter what someone Googles, they are now able to find all forms of content in one place, under one search. A simple search can yield results for videos, images, and articles all on page one of Google, seen in all combinations. Yet again, search engines have evolved to make the user search experience a more convenient and more productive one by turning up results in all forms, under one umbrella, without having to visit video-specific, image-specific websites.

UNLOCKING PAGE ONE OF GOOGLE

Now I am going to talk about Google's layout and what a consumer can expect to see when eliciting a search. A Google page is specific and broken down into different sections. Each section has its own algorithm with its own purpose, strategy, and focus. Figure 2.1 shows a highlighted graphic identifying each area of the Google search results page. I will break these different sections down into further detail shortly.

Before I break down the various components of a Google page, I must first share with you another interesting but vital fact about Google that, if you weren't aware of already, will change the way you look at Google, alter your Google strategy, and help you understand how to win the game of Googleopoly. *Only* 5 percent of people go past page one of a Google search. Another way of saying this is that an overwhelming 95 percent of people do not go past page one on Google (or any search engine for that matter).[5]

---

[4] *Source:* http://searchengineland.com/study-google-universal-results-show-85-searches-videos-65-maps-1-194477.

[5] *Source:* www.brafton.com/news/95-percent-of-web-traffic-goes-to-sites-on-page-1-of-google-serps-study.

FIGURE 2.1   The Google Search Results page is broken down into many sections, including pay-per-click, organic results, Google+ Business, news, Google Maps, Google's Knowledge Graph, and finally, the organic top 10 results.

It is very important to understand the significance of that statistic. Essentially, it doesn't matter how many times you show up as an option in search (fourth page, ninth page, even second page). If you are not on the first page, you are statistically invisible. You can think of page one of Google like a one-page menu at a restaurant that consists of some appetizers and desserts that are chosen less than the also-listed 10 organic "main entrée" options. If you are not even listed on the menu as an option, how can someone possibly choose you or your product or service? It's like the lottery. You have to be in it to win it. Another wife story comes to mind. My wife, Karina, will catch wind that the lottery is up to an exuberant payout and suggest to me excitely that we should play. She starts to rattle off all of the items we would buy if we were to win. She speaks about the glorious vacations our immediate family members, extended family members, and friends would take, the home improvements we would make and the charities we would donate to. She begins to paint a picture for me of how our lives would be forever different, yet Karina never buys a ticket! I say to her, "Karina, if you want to win the lottery, you have to actually play. It is not going to magically happen for you just because you speak of it." Again, you must be in it to win it.

You now know that only 5 percent of people go past page one. So it is obviously imperative that I discuss the components of page one of Google, its level of exposure and relevance, and how you can strategically utilize its various components to create a custom strategy to dominate online. These components consist of:

- Pay per click (PPC)
- Local search (Google + Business)
- Knowledge graph
- (Organic) Top 10 lists
  - Images
  - Video
  - News feeds
  - Maps

Pay per click (PPC) is Google's primary revenue stream. In 2013 Google reported $50.5 billion in ad revenue and in 2014 reported $13.9 billion in the first quarter alone. This means that Google is due to track over $55 billion in ad revenue for the year 2014. That is approximately a

10 percent increase from 2013. Google's advertising revenue has been on a massive increase for the past 10 years and is showing no signs of slowing down anytime soon. I preface this section with these metrics before I give a reality check about Google's PPC program.

The truth is that **only 6 percent** of people click on pay-per-click (PPC) ads![6]

That means that the majority of people, 94 percent of people to be exact, skip PPC and go organic. The numbers are staggering but telling. It reinforces that people are more knowledgeable than we, as marketers and business owners, may give them credit for and that regardless of where or what form they are displayed in, people are tired of having commercials forced onto them. This is true even for commercials shown online—even if they are Google commercials. People realize that the top three rows of search returns, as well as the right-hand vertical row of search returns, are essentially Google-sponsored commercials, and they understand that the only reason they are ranked higher is because their position was paid for. Being ranked in those top sponsored positions doesn't make them the best results or most credible results; it just makes them the paid results. The first listings are even labeled with a little yellowish-orange box with the word *Ad* written in it. It doesn't become any clearer than that. The vast majority of people have no desire to give these ads the opportunity for their business. They simply skip past them and go directly to what they perceive are the real and valuable listings, the organic top 10 results.

This does not mean that Google PPC is not a powerful or viable form of digital marketing. It is, but putting first things first, there are more powerful elements of digital marketing with a higher ROI than PPC on Google.

PPC should behave only as a supplement and complement to organic search, not as the primary initiative. Regardless of budget, no one should put all of their eggs in one basket and use PPC as their only strategy for exposure. But you should especially not if you have only a limited budget. If this is the case, PPC should not be considered a tier-one initiative—that is, organic optimization should be the primary

---

[6] *Source:* http://searchenginewatch.com/article/2200730/Organic-vs.-Paid-Search-Results-Organic-Wins-94-of-Time; https://econsultancy.com/blog/10586-ppc-accounts-for-just-6-of-total-search-clicks-infographic; http://adwords.blogspot.com/2011/08/studies-show-search-ads-drive-89.html; www.youtube.com/watch?v=hGVMdtRxZH4.

choice and then PPC can add some additional advertisement value, but only after you have mastered a viable organic strategy first.[7]

Google Local Business

Google Local Business (formerly Google+ Local) helps people find local destinations and businesses, and consolidates a suite of services for local business to be found. Google has a five-star review rating system. This enables a person to review and evaluate a business, product, or service online before they choose to purchase a product or service and before visiting an establishment. This is what ZMOT is all about. Google Local Business is one of the most powerful and relevant pieces of field intelligence for a shopper, buyer, prospect, researcher, or surfer. Zagat-style summaries for Google reviews have a huge impact on people, eliminating bad choices. That's right—a lot of people actually utilize the Internet specifically as a research tool with the intent not of finding a product or service but eliminating a bad choice from their options.

Businesses can customize the following aspects of their Google Local Business page and create powerful content, such as the following:

- **Graphical header:** Businesses can customize the header for consistent branding of their corporate identity and to make the page look and feel more professional.
- **Pictures:** Businesses can upload images of themselves, their staff, their customers, and their inventory. You can upload any and all relevant images.
- **Videos**
  - You can upload video(s) of:
    - Facility walk-through
    - Video testimonials/reviews
    - How-to videos
    - "Why buy from us"/Value package proposition videos
- **Coupons**
  - Freebees
  - Discounts
  - Buy one, get one free

---

[7] *Source:* https://investor.google.com/financial/tables.html.

- Referrals
- Check-ins
- Text content
  - About the business
  - Why buy
- Hours and directions
  - Business hours
  - Contact info
    - Email address
    - Phone number (with click to call)
  - Map
    - Directions
- Reviews
  - Client reviews
  - User reviews
  - Fan reviews
  - Product reviews
  - Service reviews
  - Venue/facility reviews

A review, whether positive or negative, is an opportunity to interact with the public and show your human side. Let's face it—you cannot make everyone 100 percent happy, 100 percent of the time. There may even be a time where you make an honest mistake. It happens to the best of businesses. But it is how you react to those negative reviews or complaints that determines your level of integrity and how your business is perceived in the public eye. Turning a wrong into a right can yield some serious positive consequences. Some of the worst beginnings can result in the best endings if handled correctly. I have seen the power of wrongs made right firsthand and have seen cyberterrorists turn into the ultimate cheerleaders and advocates for the exact business they originally cyberattacked. Regardless, you have the opportunity to thank your clients and fans, as well as an opportunity to make a disgruntled person happy.

Google Knowledge Graph

The Google Knowledge Graph is a system that Google launched in May 2012 that understands facts about people, places, and things and how these entities are all connected. When someone Googles something like

"Ford," for example, you will notice this large square on the right side of the Google search page that is filled with a lot of information, like the following (see Figure 2.2):

- How many people are in Ford's Google+ Circle
- Giving you the ability to follow Ford on Google+ right there on the Knowledge Graph!
- Company bio
- Stock price
- Ford's phone number for roadside assistance
- CEO's name with hyperlink to more information about him or her
- Ford's headquarters information with hyperlink to more details
- Ford Motor Company's founder information with hyperlink to more details
- Most recent news blurb
- A section at the bottom that shows what other searches people were performing in addition to "Ford"[8]

The Google Knowledge Graph is largely powered by software written by Metaweb in the mid-2000s called Freebase, which bills itself as "a community-curated database of well-known people, places, and things."[9]

Once Metaweb's Freebase became powerful enough to begin to threaten Google's standing as the only "oracle" data set to find information on the web, Metaweb and Freebase were acquired by Google in a private sale in 2010.[10] It is important to understand that Google is a content- and data-driven search engine. The simple fact is that Google is constantly consolidating information from multiple sources into one neat and concise section called the "Knowledge Graph," which completely aligns with Google's primary objective from its conception, which was to provide a more organized web.[11]

If there are very few people searching for a certain person, company, service, or widget, it is doubtful that Google will create a Knowledge Graph for that particular search query. One of the reasons Google's

---

[8] *Source:* www.google.com/webhp?tab=ww&authuser=0&ei=coL-U5T5PIf3yQT9sYEQ &ved=0CAcQ1S4#authuser=0&q=ford.

[9] www.freebase.com/.

[10] http://en.wikipedia.org/wiki/Freebase.

[11] https://developers.google.com/freebase/.

FIGURE 2.2   This is an example of a well-developed Google+ Business Page. The contact information is complete and accurate, the profile photos are clear and relevant, and photos have been uploaded. Additionally, there are a number of reviews and a clear description of the business.

Knowledge Graph was developed was because when there is an abundance of search queries on a certain keyword, person, place, or thing, it wanted to be able to provide the best and most accurate information in the most powerful format possible. It also wants to encourage you to dig deeper into a topic by presenting you with information that comes from search data acquired by the billions of searches that happen on a daily basis. For example, a search for "Da Vinci" will provide a Knowledge Graph that shows information about Leonardo Da Vinci's birth date and death date, burial place, famous inventions, and an image library of his famous paintings. Presenting the information in the Knowledge Graph format encourages you to learn more about Da Vinci, but can also help you learn more about other related topics that you might find interesting.

I believe Google Knowledge Graph is the future of search. Think about it. Google aims to provide people with the information they are looking for as quickly and efficiently as possible. Imagine not having to click through to a website to get more information because it's shown right there in front of you with all of the information that you'd ever need about a particular person, place, or thing.

Having said that, there is still a long way to go before there is enough information to show in a Knowledge Graph. For example, right now if you do a Google search for "Ford," you will see a bunch of interesting information about the Ford Motor Company, including a brief description of the company, its customer service telephone number, current stock value, and the current CEO, but consider how much more relevant information is still yet to be shown there!

Even though the Knowledge Graph represents a significant advancement in search technology, I don't believe we have even scratched the surface of what Google has in store. Think about how cool it would be to have contextual search considered by Google in the Knowledge Graph. That way not only would a search for a "Ford F-150" provide you with information about Ford Motor Company, but also you might see model comparisons between the Ram 1500, Toyota Tundra, and Chevrolet Silverado. Remember that Google's aim is to provide you with the most relevant information based on what you're searching for, and the Knowledge Graph has demonstrated that Google wants to get you specific information without even having to click through to a website.

To further my prediction that Knowledge Graph is the way that search is headed, consider that every time someone has to click through and drill down to get information, you lose 24 percent of your audience. There is no question that people want information fast. Remember my discussion about the lack of patience that exists today, the concept of on-demand information, and what will happen if you do not supply the consumer with the requested information in a quick manner.

In addition, the Google Knowledge Graph gives people exactly what they want, how they want it, and as already mentioned—fast! Why even bother to waste time with ranking a static page someone has to click into and search for a phone number or a piece of information? With the Google Knowledge Graph, right there on the first page of Google you can have a convenient list of the most relevant and searched pieces of information. Referring back to the Ford example, one of the pieces of information in the Knowledge Graph is Ford Motor Company's phone number for roadside assistance! How convenient is that? All you have to do is type the word *Ford* into Google, and there it is! The first page shows the Knowledge Graph with the phone number for roadside assistance, and better yet, if you are searching on a mobile device, which you probably are, you can "click to call." This is extremely convenient, especially if you are having an emergency with your automobile. You do not have to search within Ford Motor Company's main site or try to find the website for Ford's roadside assistance program. As a matter of fact, you don't have to do anything but type one word—"Ford"—into Google, and then it magically gives you exactly what you need (see Figure 2.3).

Google has now become the go-to tool for those looking to find a business or service. Most people don't use the yellow pages or phone book anymore because they have been replaced by Google. And with the masses of people who have the ability to access Google from their smartphones on demand, it has become the most convenient alternative or, better yet, more advanced replacement.[12]

Organic Listing "Top 10"

The nonpaid listings that appear on Google below and to the left of all the paid advertised listings are known as organic listings. It should go without saying that the "first-position, natural Google" (organic)/top 10 list is the holy grail of optimization placement for webmasters and search

---

[12]*Source:* http://searchengineland.com/google-launches-knowledge-graph-121585.

Ford Motor Company

Go Further

3,324,438 followers on Google+

The Ford Motor Company is an American multinational automaker headquartered in Dearborn, Michigan, a suburb of Detroit. It was founded by Henry Ford and incorporated on June 16, 1903. Wikipedia

Stock price: F (NYSE) $17.38 -0.06 (-0.32%)
Aug 19, 1:46 PM EDT - Disclaimer

Customer service: 1 (800) 392-3673

Roadside assistance: 1 (800) 241-3673

CEO: Mark Fields

Headquarters: Dearborn, MI

Founder: Henry Ford

Founded: June 16, 1903

Recent posts

Help us >> http://bit.ly/celebrateFocus << Have you been a part of the #FordFocus journey? We want to hear your stories. Share them using the #CelebrateFocus hash ... Aug 17, 2014

People also search for

View 15+ more

TOYOTA

NISSAN

RENAULT

Chevrolet   Toyota Motor Corporation   Volkswagen Passenger Cars   Nissan Motor Co., Ltd.   Renault

FIGURE 2.3 **The Knowledge Graph appears automatically on a Google Search Results page and contains a collection of data gathered from around the Internet, including phone numbers, company information, Wikipedia content, social media posts, and even related searches.**

Source: Example link www.google.com/?gws_rd=ssl#q=ford.

engine optimization specialists. This is your "Boardwalk." Those coveted top 10 placements are what everyone is chasing. Google is constantly changing its algorithms (which I will explain shortly) with the intent to make it hard to achieve first-position, natural Google, especially if it is for a keyword or phrase that is highly searched and has a lot of competition. Don't misunderstand—I'm not trying to frame Google as the bad guys by saying that its intent is to make it hard. It does so in order to make the web a better (and more organized) experience. One of the best ways to make sure that spammy and irrelevant sites stay away from rankings is to create a strict set of guidelines for webmasters to use. Further, it's like anything else, achieving something is only the beginning. Maintaining it is the true goal and should be your long-term strategy. Sustainability is key when it comes to search engines. Google is certainly not an exception.

There are some things that you need to be aware of in order achieve and maintain a top 10 organic/natural placement with Google. First, you need to understand the process that Google goes through in order to get your website or universal search content ranked according to its specific engine. The following pieces of information will help you understand some important key items pertaining to the process that Google uses, and also how its process works.

1. Once a website, video, image, MP3, news feed, press release, blog post, social media, or any form of content is published to the Internet or submitted to the directories, the process of indexing begins by the search engine. This is typically done by uploading a sitemap.xml file inside your Google Webmaster Tools account or equivalent software provided by other search engines.

Sitemaps are a standard protocol that webmasters use to inform search engines of URLs that are ready and available for crawling. If, for whatever reason, you are suspicious that your website is not showing up in search engines, having access to your Google Webmaster Tools account is an absolute must, because you will be able to identify if a sitemap file has even been uploaded and if there are any errors regarding your website that Google wants you to fix.

2. Once Google verifies that your sitemap.xml file is valid, Google's search "spiders" then crawl the content and read, listen, scan, and compare all of it to other website content that is trying to rank for the same keywords and search engine results page (SERP) placements. Based on Google's most up-to-date search algorithm, your website will be ranked

according to its relevancy as compared to other sites. If your content meets Google's search algorithm specifications, it will be ranked favorably and hopefully show up within the top 10 placements in the SERPs.

3. Not many people know this, but Google actually updates its search engine algorithms in excess of 500–600 times per year. Isn't it fascinating to think about how much it wants to create phenomenal user experiences through its search engine? Think about it. That is just about twice a day, every day, all year long! Most of these changes are slight. However, from time to time, Google will drop a major update, such as:

- Penguin

    Google's search algorithm update code-named "Penguin" dates back to April 2012. Its primary focus was to catch sites practicing "black hat" search engine optimization tactics, like buying links or being part of a link farm or link-generating network, designed primarily to boost Google rankings. Black hat SEO refers to practices designed to trick and cheat Google's ranking considerations in order to get higher placements.

    The biggest takeaway for this update is that Google does not appreciate nor does it want you to cut corners or attempt to cheat its engine. That goes expressly against what it is trying to accomplish by making the web a more organized place to find relevant information.

    As of this printing, the most recent rollout to date of this algorithm was Penguin 5 (a.k.a. Penguin 2.1), which was released on October 4, 2013.[13] This goes to show that Google is always identifying new ways that websites are attempting to cheat its system, which is the exact reason why it has to be consistently updated. Remember, Penguin is the spam destroyer.

- Panda 4.0

    Google launched Panda 4.0, on May 19, 2014, in order to crack down on spammers.[14] Previous iterations of the Panda algorithm were released in February 2011, which is just over a year earlier than the Penguin algorithm update. The main difference between the two algorithms is that Panda's focus was on downranking websites that contained too much advertising or too little content. This is where sites

---

[13] *Source:* http://searchengineland.com/library/google/google-penguin-update.

[14] *Source:* http://searchengineland.com/pr-newswires-answer-google-panda-troubles -penalize-press-release-spammers-195259.

like PR Newswire and eBay took a massive hit. Early reports show that eBay lost as much as 80 percent of its organic search rankings because Google significantly penalized it for housing so much value-less, spammy content. After all, Google's official mission statement is to "organize the world's information and make it universally accessible and useful"—the keyword being *useful*.

In order to play nice with the Panda 4.0 algorithm, your focus should be on creating high-quality content, not high-quantity content. With every algorithm update that Google releases, the search engine becomes smarter. It's fascinating to think that a computer program (because that's what an algorithm is) can understand enough about your website content to know whether it is high-quality.

- Hummingbird

    Another update, Hummingbird, named so because of its precision and speed, was the first algorithm overhaul in nearly 10 years. Google literally stripped out the whole engine and rebuilt it from scratch! With this algorithm update came greater understanding of not only the key-words placed in the content of your web pages but also the context behind those keywords. As you can see, with each algorithm update comes a smarter search engine. Ten years ago nobody would have been able to imagine computer programs that could understand the context of written words. What makes this even more fascinating is the fact that language is so ambiguous.

    Previous to Hummingbird, writing content for your website was very systematic. For example, you could write keyword-rich content, such as, "If you're looking for a 2012 Ram pickup truck for sale in Newark, NJ, come and visit our pre-owned trucks dealership to get the best deals," and with some confidence know that following the formula would increase your chances of ranking well.

    Keyword-specific verbiage is no longer as effective or well received by Google because Hummingbird is looking for greater contextual rel-evancy. Instead, you must now really focus on providing high-quality content to frame your keyword theme. Referring back to the 2012 Ram pickup example from earlier, if the focus of a particular page is the 2012 Ram pickup truck, you'll find greater success in providing con-tent that is relevant to the truck itself rather than just writing, "2012 Ram pickup truck for sale in NJ" a bunch of times on the page min-gled in with meaningless content. Instead you would want to write a full paragraph about the vehicle and its details with greater-quality information, rather than writing solely with keywords in mind.

Further regarding understanding the context of the content on a particular page of your site, Hummingbird also looks at and understands each word in a user's search query and aims to align that contextual search with content that best represents the user's intended search focus. Hummingbird will weigh the context more favorably over a repetition of specific keywords. It looks at every single word in the search query instead of just cherry-picking the most prominent keywords or phrases. This means that keyword data is not as valuable as it was in previous algorithms because Google is looking at the meaning behind the words and is rewarding high-quality, *natural* (human-like) contextual content surrounding a topic, rather than the sites that have the right keyword density.

You may have heard the phrase "Content is king." Hummingbird agrees with that statement and will reward you if your content is awesome.

- Pigeon

On July 24, 2014, Google released a new nameless Local Search algorithm update, which was quickly nicknamed "Pigeon" by the content curators at www.searchengineland.com. In nontypical Google fashion, very few updates were published by Google's search engineers about what was included in the update, though we do know for sure that it has affected local search listings and map listings in Google.[15]

Some business owners have observed that SERPs that previously appeared in the map pack (the map listings that accompany the organic SERPs) inexplicably have vanished or been replaced by global sites, like Expedia or Hotels.com.

Having said that, SERPs are still appearing to be quite sporadic in their display of map pack listings. It's still too early to tell if any dramatic changes to your web strategy should be made. If your website, business, or brand has been affected already, it is going to be a bit of a painful wait while SEO specialists wait for the algorithm to level out so that we can get a good handle on what has actually changed.

---

[15] *Source:* http://searchengineland.com/worried-pigeon-just-keep-truckin-200219.

The best practice at the time of writing this book is to strongly focus on making sure your website covers the consideration sets of the other clearly defined and documented algorithms (Penguin, Panda, and Hummingbird).

On-Page Elements

Early on, some alluded to the fact that on-page elements—meta-title, description, URL, H1, and so on (to be discussed in depth in Chapter 4)—weren't going to be as important, but I'm finding them just as relevant as ever. There is a very thorough review article posted on Search Engine Land that validates the importance of on-page elements.[16]

I have mentioned the word *algorithm* several times so far. If you are wondering what exactly a search algorithm is, allow me to explain. It is a mathematical program or formula that sorts out the trillions of web pages, pictures, videos, articles, and all other forms of content, and based on these formulas, ranks content on priority in relevant order. Algorithm programs look for clues in content and context and try to give searchers exactly what they want in the exact format they want it in. Search engines are so advanced that they possess:

- Speech recognition
- Facial recognition
- Pixel recognition
- (Virtual) Logic
- Assumption
- Correlation
- Comparison
- Regional search (geo-targeted)

Google's algorithms rely on more than 200 "clues" or unique signals that make it possible to guess what a searcher is truly looking for.[17]

Chapter 1 focused on the importance of visibility and showed that the most powerful and cost-effective way to be visible is the Internet and

---

[16] *Source:* http://searchengineland.com/adapting-googles-2013-algorithm-shake-ups-navigate-win-todays-seo-188427.

[17] *Source:* www.google.com/insidesearch/howsearchworks/algorithms.html.

digital marketing. Chapter 2 explains how to stay focused with the most powerful entity and resource on the Internet—Google—and why Google is the most important strategy for digital marketing today. Chapter 3 will break down the components of page one of Google and how it can be viewed with the same principles and objectives as a Monopoly board. It will cover the whole concept and strategy of "Googleopoly."

ADDITIONAL RESOURCES

Learn more about how Google works, how search results are gathered and displayed, and how you can utilize such features as Business Pages, Knowledge Graph, and more at www.googleopolybook.com/googles-secret-strategy.

CHAPTER **3**

Creating a Googleopoly: Google Page One Dominance Strategy

Dictionary.com defines a monopoly as the exclusive possession or control of something. You may recall playing the board game Monopoly as a kid, or maybe even recently. Regardless, just like the game, you can consider page one of Google to be your own personal Monopoly board—a board we would all love to gain exclusive possession of or complete control of for our desired visibility and lead-generation goals. For those of you who are familiar with the game, let me refresh your memory and for those of you who aren't, let me give you a quick synopsis. In Monopoly, the objective of the game is to make as much money as possible, as quickly as possible. The main way you can do this is by buying real estate on the Monopoly board. Essentially, the more real estate you own, the greater the chances are that people will land on your properties and be required to pay you rent. The higher the property value, the higher the rent. The more people who land on your real estate, the more rent you get to collect. The more rent you collect, the faster you get to bankrupt your opponent(s) and earn bragging rights. So ultimately, you want to obtain as much real estate as possible, preferably those highest in rank (value), and develop them with assets to increase the real estate value for a larger payout.

Chapter 2 revealed that only 5 percent of people click past the first page of Google results.[1] Take, for example, a Google search for "automotive Internet sales." There are over 147 million results, meaning that there are over 147 million listings that have some or all of the combination of words *automotive Internet sales*. Out of those 147 million listings,

---

[1] *Source:* http://searchenginewatch.com/article/2276184/No.-1-Position-in-Google-Gets -33-of-Search-Traffic-Study; www.google.com/?gws_rd=ssl#q=automotive+internet+ sales+.

the vast majority of people (95 percent) will view only what is on the first page of Google. It doesn't make a difference whether there are 1,000 results, a million results, or a billion results. Ninety-five percent of people will not go past page one. Therefore, the first page of Google is the Monopoly board—hence the phrase and philosophy behind this book, "Googleopoly." Each Google result listing is a piece of real estate, a property. First-position, "natural" Google is the equivalent of Boardwalk. It holds the prime real estate position with prime visibility, which generates the highest rent payout. The same logic applies to real-life real estate. I was born in the city of New York. If you are at all familiar with real estate in NYC, you know that it is extremely costly. The more prime position the property, the higher the value property and rent payout. The same goes for page one Google results. The higher the result listing, the more prime the result listing is.

The same holds true for the business that holds first position organically. Holding first-position, natural Google means your business is first to be seen, which means it is first to be clicked, and if the place the person is being sent to is designed to convert well, the payout will be significant. A quick side note: if you are going to spend a lot of time and resources making yourself visible online, make sure that the place you are sending people to, such as your website, is set up to represent you, your product, or your service to the best of its ability, otherwise it is all a waste. Make sure you create an awesome online brand (logo, graphics, and message). At the end of the day, being ranked in the first position on Google is just an opportunity to do business. It guarantees visibility, not that people are going to buy from you. That part is left to you. Think of the most well-known musicians in the music business. They are given a large opportunity to be backed by major labels and given major visibility opportunities. But at the end of the day, the musician must have talent. Record labels cannot force the public to become fans or purchase music or merchandise. The talent must exist, otherwise the visibility they are granted will be for naught. So I cannot stress enough that you need to make sure you are represented well. I have personally seen dealers who spend a fortune driving traffic to their website, but fail to convert sales and have an outrageous bounce rate. Don't let this happen to you.

Back to Googleopoly . . . first position is Boardwalk, second position is Park Place, third place is Pennsylvania Avenue, and 10th position is Indiana Avenue (the final position and opportunity for visibility). It's not worth as much as Boardwalk, but it is still valuable nonetheless and has the potential to take over top real estate. It's simple . . . the more times that *you* show up on the first page of Google, the fewer times your competitors, third-party providers, ads, and so on, can show up. What makes the game even more interesting is that you can increase your property value even further and in turn increase your chances of generating more revenue by developing it with the addition of houses and hotel pieces. As it pertains to Google, you too have ways to increase your "property value" even further. This can be done with the utilization of videos and images, for example. When played strategically, some properties worth less "naked" can become worth more than even Boardwalk if developed correctly. There are certain things you are going to learn in this book that will show you how to combine tactics to create the ultimate monopoly with Boardwalk and Park Place loaded with hotels. For example, Chapter 5 covers video search engine optimization, which is one of the most powerful tools you can use to gain additional real estate and property value and ultimately win the game of Googleopoly.

Going back to the example of automotive Internet sales, when you review the results for search terms *automotive Internet sales*, you will see that there are only nine pay-per-click ads, one video, and the Google top 10 list—a grand total of 20 listings on the first page of Google. For this specific example, out of 147 million listings, almost everyone will look only at the first 20 listings, as I discussed.

You cannot win the game of Monopoly with just Boardwalk. As a matter of fact, it will be difficult to win even if you had both Park Place and Boardwalk, as well as hotels on each of those properties. The same goes for Google! You can't have just one website and expect to win the game of Googleopoly. It doesn't matter if you had the most awesome website. It is still only one website with one domain and can rank only one time on the first page of Google.

You might be thinking, "How can I own Google real estate?" Simple—you have to have content that ranks on the first page of Google. You need to understand that dominating Google is way more than just having a website. To be specific, there are two types of search engine optimization (SEO):

1. Onsite
2. Offsite

Onsite SEO is the optimization of everything on your website:

- Title
- Description
- Meta-tags/keywords
- Site navigation
- Anchor text
- Keyword density
- Alt tags
- Images
- Videos
- Sitemap(s)
- Video sitemap(s)
- Load speed
- Relevant content
- Unique content
- Structured data/rich snippets
- Adherence to Google algorithms and updates

By properly optimizing your website, you will be able to have your website rank and get prominent placement on the first page of Google (that is the goal).

Here is the problem with that. Even if you have the most incredible website with the most incredible SEO, you are only one rowboat in the ocean of the Internet—meaning you have only one opportunity to show up on page one of Google and inhabit one real estate space. Having a website alone, even an awesome website, is not enough to dominate Google and drown out the competition, all of the pay-per-click ads, top 10 organic listings, images, videos, news, and so on. To accomplish this, you need to be more than a rowboat—you need to become the naval fleet, the Spanish Armada. You do that with offsite SEO.

Offsite SEO is the optimization of *everything* else:

- Social media and social media optimization
  - Facebook
  - Twitter
  - LinkedIn
  - Instagram

- Google+
- NING
- Images/pictures
  - Flickr
  - Photobucket
  - Pinterest
- Video and video search engine optimization
  - YouTube
  - Vimeo
  - Any video search engine
- Focus sites/microsites
- Online reputation
- Blogs
- Mobile marketing
- Press releases and news
- Music/audio
  - ReverbNation
  - Vevo
  - SoundCloud
  - iTunes
  - Beats
  - iHeartRadio

People are surprised to find out that all of those categories have search engine value. That's right—social media isn't just a place for you to go and chitchat with your friends. Social media optimization is a very powerful opportunity to earn real estate on page one of Google, in addition to providing the consumer with another form of information. Part of Google's algorithm is content that is connected or linked to another site. To be exact, a more powerful site that gets tons of traffic will add instant credibility to that content. Let's take Facebook, for example. Facebook has over 1 billion users on its network and has hundreds of millions of views per month. So, if you have content on Facebook, that content is properly optimized, and there is engagement on the Facebook page and on individual posts, then there is a very strong chance that the Facebook page and/or that post on Facebook will rank and possibly be on the first page of Google! Social media, specifically Facebook, in this scenario will act as an SEO incubator for the content.

Another example is images and image optimization. Let's use Flickr.com or Pinterest.com for an example. Both sites can be classified as social media sites and/or image search engines. Either way, individual pictures can be uploaded to Flickr or Pinterest, and once they are on those sites, they can be fully optimized. Once optimized, the individual images will have their own unique URLs and each image will also have the opportunity to rank on the first page of Google. Let me be crystal clear here. I am not merely saying that if you optimize pictures on Flickr or Pinterest, your Flickr or Pinterest page will rank. I am stating that if you upload individual images to sites like Flickr and Pinterest and those pictures are search engine optimized correctly, then those individual images can rank and achieve first-page placement.

The same scenario is valid for video and video SEO. Each individual video that is properly optimized can show up on the first page of Google. Video, for example, is the most consumed form of content—period. Google prefers video content over static content. So if you have video content properly optimized, it can and will rank faster and more prominently than a traditional website!

Think about how powerful that could be for you, your business, and your overall strategy. If someone is searching for you, they will find not only your website, but also on the first page of Google your:

- Videos (one to three of them!)
- Images
- Social media (your Facebook, Twitter, LinkedIn, etc.)
- Your blog
- Your customer reviews on Google+ and/or Yelp
- Focus sites/microsites

Do the math. That is six to eight out of the top 10 listings and 60 to 80 percent of the first page of Google! Remember, the more you show up on the first page of Google, the less your competitors, third-party providers, ads, and so on show up.

Another way of explaining this strategy of content diversity is like investing money. Let's say you have $10,000 and you can invest it all in one stock and hope that the stock does well. The reality is that it might or it might not do well. That is a lot of money to invest in a hope. Another option is to take that same $10,000 and invest it into mutual funds, spreading the funds out. Basically, a mutual fund comprises several stocks—for this example, let's say 10 different stocks. So instead of putting the entire $10,000 into 1 stock, you are putting $1,000 into 10 different stocks. That is 10 opportunities to make something happen. The benefit of a mutual fund is the ability to maximize the investor's opportunity while simultaneously minimizing the risk.

Most people do not realize this, so they only buy or build a website and expect that their website is going to take them to the promised land of clients, fans, business, and opportunity. The reality is that a sole website is not enough. As a matter of fact, onsite SEO or a website should be only 25 percent of the strategy. That means that 75 percent of your visibility/digital marketing strategy should be dedicated to offsite SEO.

You need to diversify your digital marketing strategy to maximize your visibility and minimize your risk(s).

In the previous chapter, I dissected the different elements of page one of Google. You have pay per click (PPC), and you have the organic top 10 list. When you are creating your Googleopoly strategy, you want to remember to put first things first—meaning that you want to focus on dominating page one of Google in a priority order. You want to spend your time and in some cases money where you get the biggest bang for your buck. That, of course, is going to be with the organic top 10 listings. Some people skip that and just try to create a PPC campaign without a viable organic presence or strategy. This is a complete waste of time and money. People who make their money in PPC are going to be perturbed by my philosophy, but deep down they too know the truth. Remember Google, not Sean V. Bradley, CSP, tells us that only a minority of people actually click the PPC ads. The vast majority of people skip the PPC ads and go to the organic listings.

The counterargument to me is usually something to the effect of, "Wait a minute, Sean—if this is "pay per click," then I only pay per click. What is the problem? You pay only when someone actually clicks your ad. If no one clicks, you don't pay anything. I get that, but here is the problem. If you only have a $1,000 or $10,000 advertisement spend, or whatever amount of budget, and you allocate the majority or all of that budget to PPC, that is only 6–12 percent click-throughs. Why would I eat up most or all of my digital marketing budget on a 6–12 percent opportunity? Why not invest that money in the organic opportunity, which represents an 88–94 percent opportunity? Furthermore, once someone clicks a PPC ad, there is nothing to show for it—game over. On the other hand, with organic SEO, whether it is a website, focus site, social media sites, online reviews, images, or videos, they are there organically. Click, after click, after click, with no budget to exhaust. And with a proper organic SEO strategy, those pieces of content will permanently hold their first-page positions and the more content you create, the more you can saturate the engines and become more prominent.

It just makes logical sense to first invest your time, energy, and/or money into the opportunities that have the biggest reach, with the longest residual value, organic SEO. There is absolutely no question. And one of the most important reasons and the best part about why organic SEO is the best strategy is the fact that it is *free*! That is right—especially if you take everything you learn from this book, you will be able to create a very powerful and free SEO strategy and have more impact than most people or companies that are spending thousands or tens of thousands of dollars per month on PPC.

Some food for thought and something to keep in mind is that Google is one of the most powerful companies in the world. Google is a multibillion-dollar publicly traded company. That means it does not share the same mission as the Red Cross. It is a for-profit corporation. Google makes the majority of its money in ad revenue, specifically PPC ads, retargeting, pre-roll, etc. Google is not going to advocate to the public how to beat its system. Google wants to keep the secret strategy of its search engine quiet—hence the updates discussed in Chapter 2, like Hummingbird and Panda 4.0. Does a state trooper want every speed-crazed motorist to have a radar or laser detector? Heck, no! Google, on the other hand, will promote the benefits and awesomeness of PPC and all of its monetized advertising strategies. And it is right! All of Google's strategies have value. They can make sure you are visible. I do not want to insinuate that Google peddles snake oil. I merely want to be clear that you need to put first things first and make sure you focus your attention and money on the most powerful efforts that will yield you the most powerful results with longevity. That is one of the most important aspects of the Googleopoly strategy.

To be specific and in this order, I will lay out the strategy for how to win the game of Googleopoly and unlock the secret strategy of the Google search engine:

- You want to focus on dominating all of the organic opportunities on page one of Google. The following is a brief list, which will be discussed shortly:
  - Your main website
  - Video SEO
  - Image SEO
  - Google+/Social Media
    - Local listings
    - Maps
    - Google reviews
  - Knowledge Graph
  - Online reputation/business directories
    - Yelp
    - Merchantcircle
    - Angie's List
    - Yellow pages
  - Press releases/news feeds
  - Focus sites/microsites
- Then you can focus on the pay-to-play opportunities, like:
  - Pay per click (PPC)
  - Retargeting
  - Display ads
  - Mobile ads

Just as I said in the beginning of this chapter, you can't win the game of Monopoly with only Boardwalk. Even though it is the single most valuable property in the entire game, it is not enough. The same holds true in the game of Googleopoly. You are going to need a complete synergistic strategy between both the organic and paid strategies to win the game of Googleopoly.

Do you remember the example I mentioned earlier of automotive Internet sales? If you Google those keywords you will find the following on page one of Google (see Figure 3.1):

- 147 million results
- Nine PPC ads
- Ten organic listings
- One video

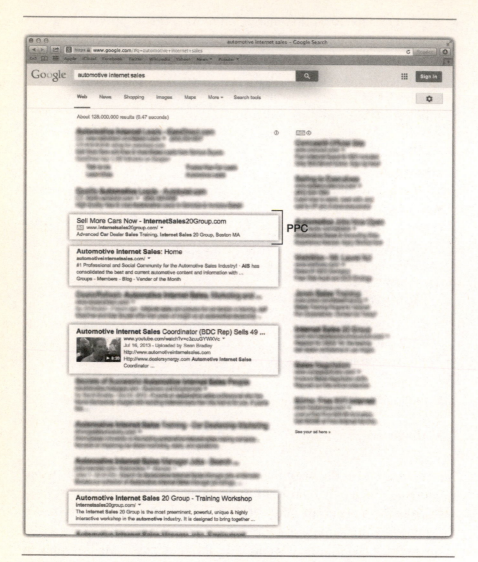

FIGURE 3.1 This a breakdown of where Dealer Synergy Inc. shows up in a keyword search for "automotive Internet sales." Three of the listings are organic: one for the online community Automotive Internet Sales, one for the owner's YouTube channel, and one for a conference that is hosted by Dealer Synergy. The fourth listing is a Pay-per-click ad for the conference.

- A grand total of 20 listings on page one of Google
- (*Only* 5 percent of people go past page one of Google)

Guess how many of those 20 listings out of 147 million belong to me?

Four! That is right—four listings are owned by Dealer Synergy Inc. Let me break down where the four come from:

- One PPC ad campaign
- One video (optimized)
- One listing for www.automotiveinternetsales.com, which is a social community created for Dealer Synergy clients
- One listing for www.internetsales20group.com, which is a three-day workshop put on by Dealer Synergy Inc.

What is crazy is that the company's main website is www.dealer synergy.com, and it didn't even rank on the first page of Google! It slipped to page three! Now that is in part because there is fierce competition for the keywords *automotive Internet sales*. Google changes its algorithms 500–600 times a year! So, things happen. SEO is a constant process, constant tweaking, constant evolution. My point is that if my multimillion-dollar company *only* had www.dealersynergy.com and someone was Googling "automotive Internet sales," I would be invisible, like the vast majority of people and companies online. However, since I am a Googleopoly master not only did I show up on page one of Google, but also I did it first-position, natural Google, as well as three additional times. I didn't merely show up on the first page of Google out of 147 million listings once, twice, or even three times. I showed up organically on page one of Google *three* times organically and once "paid." That is a grand total of four times on page one of Google out of 147 million results. That, my friends, personifies the Googleopoly strategy!

It can even get better than that! The example I just shared is a very extreme example to impress you and show you the true power of the Googleopoly strategy. The reality is that most of you reading this will not have to compete with keywords, phrases, and searches that have 147 million results. I own a national training and consulting company focused on the multibillion-dollar automotive sales industry. There are over 17,500 franchised dealerships in the country and over 250,000 automotive sales professionals. The keyword search I used as an example was a national search in a very large industry. If I was able to create a powerful page one dominance (POD) strategy like that, can you imagine what you can do in your industry? Can you imagine if you weren't national or didn't need or want to start national? If you only wanted or needed local traffic or local business? It would be so much easier and so much faster. Now combine that reality with the comfort of knowing that most people have no idea how to do this and how to dominate Google. And even some of these so-called experts and consultants and SEO gurus have no idea of this powerful Googleopoly strategy. Most people do not use a diversified approach to engage, tackle, and dominate page one of Google. If you use the strategies that I am outlining in this book, not only will you create a POD strategy, but you will also create an unfair competitive advantage in your market. You will crush your competition and conquer their prospects and opportunities for you and your organization. You will win the game of Googleopoly.

Now that I have explained the concept of Googleopoly, I am now going to break down each and every section of the Googleopoly strategy by chapter. The remainder of this book dives deep into each of the important and critical areas necessary to diversify your visibility and maximize your potential for search engine dominance. We are going to unlock the secret strategy of Google.

ADDITIONAL RESOURCES

To find more information about all the different aspects of the Google search results page and how you can begin creating page one domination (POD) strategy for your business, please visit www.googleopoly book.com/page-one-domination.

CHAPTER 4

Creating the Ultimate Onsite SEO Website Strategy

Your website is your anchor. I understand that I stated previously that onsite SEO for your website should only account for 25 percent of your overall SEO or digital marketing strategy, but please do not allow that data to underestimate its value. In fact, your website should be one of the most important visibility resources you possess, manage, and continually develop and evolve. Quite frankly, your website is a crucial asset and paramount to your overall mission. This is because almost all of your offsite SEO and digital marketing strategy will either be linked to your main website or have the responsibility of ushering traffic to your main website. Therefore, it is extremely critical to create the ultimate website.

When considering that your website is the hub of all your traffic generation efforts, it's no wonder that Google places emphasis on including specific elements on your website in order for it to rank more effectively. Google is always on the lookout for websites that best comply with its high standards, so it's essential for you to understand which elements to include, so that you can optimize your website accordingly.

Onsite SEO is the strategy of optimizing your website for maximum search engine visibility, so it has the best opportunity to be ranked properly and gain premium page one dominance (POD).

Depending on the level of exposure you have had to the concepts I am going to introduce to you in this chapter, it's quite possible that this information may appear to be complex, and that is quite all right. My encouragement to you is that you will refer back to the information in this chapter regularly, and use it as a cross-reference for further education so that you will be further empowered to conquer the web with greater knowledge and understanding of how Google uses these key elements to your website's advantage.

Whether you are creating your own website using any of the popular content management systems out there, such as Wordpress, Joomla, or

57

Drupal, or you are working with a team of professionals to help create your ultimate website experience, the principles and concepts in this chapter will empower you to confidently approach onsite website optimization from a vantage point poised for success, instead of aimlessly trying anything and everything to get your website in the good graces of the search engine.

Let's take a look at just a few of the elements that Google is looking for when considering how to rank your website. This chapter is all about the "onsite optimization" aspect of your website and what you can do to make sure that your website is search engine–friendly. Keep in mind that there are many factors to achieving a successful web presence with Google, but I am going to discuss the must-have elements that no website should exist without.

Before jumping in, it is also imperative to note that there are several other important factors to achieving website success, outside of having incredible visibility in Google. For example, let's say you are receiving a high volume of traffic to your website and you are achieving massive visibility, but there are no calls to action or mousetraps in place to convert the traffic and leads into sales. What was the point in attracting and driving all of that traffic if you are going to fail to convert it into profitability or brand awareness?

There are multiple factors to take into consideration that must coexist simultaneously, in order to make your website truly powerful. These factors make up, in part, the framework of Google's search engine algorithms. They are the elements of your website that Google looks for in order to identify its relevancy on a specific topic, as compared to the hundreds of millions of other websites out there that may also be trying to rank on page one for the same search terms. Some of these factors are as follows:

- Graphic design
- Symmetry
- Strategy
- Calls to action
- Distinguished and unique content
- Interaction
- Spelling and grammar
- Functionality

- Value
- Relevancy
- Credibility
- Consistency
- Organization
- Subject matter expertise
- Differentiator
- Examples/portfolio
- Reviews/testimonials
- Fun
- Exciting
- Interesting
- Needed (the demand for it)

These are just a few of the factors that Google considers when ranking your website, but we're not going to cover any of them in this book. That's not to suggest that they aren't important; however, Google admits that there are over 200 signals (factors) that it looks for when determining how to rank your website, some of which come with heavier weight as compared to those that I've mentioned in the list. This chapter will focus on the most crucial site-ranking factors that are tried, tested, and proven to work.

Don't get me wrong. The way that your website is presented (both visually and organizationally) to your site visitors absolutely has bearing on its potential for success. However, there have been website technologies that have come and gone, which serve as an example that beauty and experience aren't the most important elements of a website.

In the mid-1990s to early 2000s Adobe Flash and the websites built upon its framework enjoyed tons of hype, and a craze that swept the web developer world. The website experience delivered by Flash was unparalleled. It introduced animation and movement to what were pretty static and boring websites. But there is a reason that Flash-designed websites by Adobe ultimately failed. It isn't because they weren't effective. People loved interacting with Flash websites. It wasn't because they weren't beautiful. Flash websites failed because Google could not read and index them.

The Flash coding language translated to stunning websites and user interfaces on-screen, but since Google's algorithms weren't built in a way to read the language, there was nothing really there. In Google's eyes, Flash websites lacked the content and code to be properly crawled and indexed. It was, in essence, an "SEO ghost" that Google could not read properly.

This proves one important fact about your website. No matter how amazing it appears to the human eye, if it's not built with the search engines in mind—in a way that makes it friendly for Google to crawl, read, and rank—your website will suffer the same fate as Flash. It will be a ghost, it will not work, and, more importantly, it will not deliver you the results that you expect based on your business marketing objectives.

When Larry Page and Sergey Brin started Google, there was already so much content and information on the web. Their whole mission was to create a better way to organize and display relevant information based on what searchers were seeking out. In the humble beginnings of the search juggernaut, their ability to crawl the web for bulk data collection was very crude. From about 1996 to 2002, the technology was able to count the words and links on the page but was unable to understand meaning or the intent of those words.

Further, Google's algorithm relied on counting the number of times a keyword appeared on the page and awarded heavy weight to the words that appeared in the title tag of the page, any heading tags, and the anchor text of links on the page.

Since 2002 Google has continued to improve the ways in which it collects, organizes, and understands the data, authority, and language of your website.

Thanks to incredible leaps in processing technology and many years of crunching linguistics data in every language, Google's machines can now understand the content of your site and will either reward your website if deemed more relevant than other competing websites or penalize your website's pages and/or domain when they detect overoptimization. Overoptimization occurs when Google finds there to be an overt attempt to game or cheat its system.

Uh-oh: "Chance Card"—go directly to jail. Do not pass GO, do not collect $200. Because Google's search algorithms are consistently being updated, as discussed in Chapter 2, it is important to understand that the tricks of the trade that worked incredibly well back in the early 2000s would place your website at high risk of being penalized today and, in some cases, even removed and banned from Google's index. Imagine how harmful it would be to your business or brand if your domain is banned by Google—meaning that every page is removed from Google's database and can never be found for any search ever again, not even if you searched for your own name. You can imagine how detrimental this would be. This is why it is so important to remain informed.

If you think of a traditional Monopoly board game, think of your website as Boardwalk or Park Place and proper onsite optimization like putting hotels on your property. To win the game of Googleopoly, you need to first secure your Google real estate. One of your first Google real estate assets to acquire and develop would be your main website for your product, service, business, art, music, and so on.

As mentioned, Google is constantly changing its algorithm in an effort to evolve the user experience, while simultaneously attempting to eradicate spammers and manipulators of its platform. However, there is a foundation to a great onsite optimization strategy. Let's take a look at the factors that must be considered on your website, in order to make it more visible and rank higher for relevant searches with Google. In this chapter, I have outlined the main areas to focus on for proper search engine optimization, in priority order, when you build your website; if you have someone build it for you, you can hold them accountable. Do not skip any of these areas of SEO focus. If you do, you risk jeopardizing your Google visibility and your overall success in selling your product or service or developing a fan base.

DOMAIN NAME

Your domain name serves multiple purposes, from traffic generation to branding. More important than those factors, however, is that there is both SEO relevancy and SEO value in the domain name that you choose for your website. It's crucial that you select a domain name that you're extremely happy with and that accurately reflects your business because your domain can be an equitable digital asset that will pay you dividends in the form of high-ranking performance on Google for relevant searches.

You might be surprised to know that when you build, design, and optimize a website, all of the hard work that you put into the content, graphics, structure, and traffic generation of the site gets credited back to your domain. It's similar to a newly built or renovated house. When you add value to the interior or exterior of the house in the form of new finishes, woodwork, flooring, or paint, all of that extra value gets retained by the house as a whole, not any one particular element. Any value that is contributed from within the website is awarded back to your domain itself.

Building equity in your domain is not an overnight process. It is something that happens as you build your website upon a solid foundation and consistently maintain it with new (fresh) information that is relevant to your target audience.

Here are some best practices when working with URLs that work extremely well and will position your web presence for success:

- **Create site URL guidelines:** Be aware of the URL format that your website uses and stick with it throughout your entire website. This will make it easy for users (and maybe even future developers) to have a clear understanding of how your website is structured.

- **Keep it simple:** As I mentioned earlier, your domain serves multiple purposes, two of which have to do with branding and traffic generation. Therefore it's important to try to keep your domain as brief as possible. For your own sanity, consider having to write out your domain on the back of someone else's business card, or read it over the phone. Wouldn't you yourself want to make it as simple as possible to share with others?

- **Be descriptive, not technical:** This goes hand in hand with keeping it simple. Isn't it frustrating when a URL has "?," "&," or hundreds of numbers? If you are able to choose, pick a URL that is simple and memorable. For example, choose "www.yourdomain.com/fashion/women/" instead of "www.yourdomain.com/115/fashion&women=79829374?223/." Moreover, if your URL contains multiple words in the form of a phrase, consider separating each word with a hyphen—for example, www.yourdomain.com/affordable-art-supplies-in-manhattan.

- **Remember, URLs are CaSe SeNsItIvE:** Never, *ever* in a million years allow your URLs to have uppercase characters. Not only is it confusing for your visitors but also it just makes for poor URL structure practice. If your website currently has uppercase characters in your URLs, consider creating 301 redirects to lowercase versions of the same page.

- **Beware of subdomains:** Subdomains are somewhat of an appendage to the main domain. I see them regularly when companies include a blog on their website (e.g., blog.yourdomain.com). Since we're talking about building domain equity, it's important to note that subdomains may not be treated as equally as primary domains when it comes to rewarding link value or credibility from a search engine perspective.
- **Geo-targeted domains can be helpful for branding:** Where most small to medium-sized business are concerned, including geo-targeting in your domain can be helpful for your visitors to help them identify your location and area of service.
  - For example: www.MarltonKarate.com, www.LandscapingCherry HillNJ.com, www.PhiladelphiaDentists.com or www.UsedCar Dallas.co

The scope and objective of your online business will ultimately determine how you proceed with a domain name. For example, if you serve a local market area and your primary goal is to dominate local-related searches and obtain Google page one dominance, then you must have a domain that is geo-targeted to the city or market area that you service. Doing so will give you an extra edge over sites that are not geo-targeted and will make it easier for potential customers to recognize that you are in the same area as them.

Suppose that someone was searching for a karate school in Marlton, New Jersey, and they typed into Google "karate schools in Marlton, New Jersey." What do you think would show up if you owned www.MarltonKarate.com or www.KarateMarltonNJ.com and those sites were properly optimized? Think about how you would rank versus a karate school named "Cobra-Kai Martial Arts" with a domain of www.CobraKaiMA.com (located in Marlton, New Jersey). Yes, with a geo-targeted domain you would have an advantage to achieve premium placement on Google, again for locally relevant searchers and their search queries.

This is not to say that merely purchasing a geo-targeted domain will guarantee you premium Google placement. Such is not the case. There are many more factors to consider when optimizing your website besides a geo-targeted domain. However, I am suggesting that if you have two different websites that were optimized well and one of them happens to have a specific and relevant geo-targeted domain, it will enhance that website's ability to show up higher and receive premium Google placement over the other site that uses a generic domain.

On the other hand, if your business does not serve a specific market area or city and the scope of your business is broader and more far-reaching, utilizing a geo-targeted domain may not have much more influence over your ability to receive premium Google placement. Whatever domain you choose to go with, be sure to select a domain that is relevant to both your business and your brand. It should always be something that will last with your business and be easily remembered and recognized by your intended target audience.

So what's the best strategy for selecting a domain name that will, as mentioned, fit your business objectives and resonate with your intended target audience? Here are some tips and software tools that can assist you in getting the most out of your domain name and dominating Google for relevant searches.

Exact Match Domains

Exact Match Domains are what they sound like. They are typically domain names made up of two to three keywords that match exactly a user's Google search query (Two hypothetical examples of Exact Match Domain are www.atlantacarloans.com or www.cheapmanhattanplumber.com).

Though there has been some controversy in the past over the effectiveness of using exact match domains, those who utilize them as a single aspect of an overarching onsite SEO strategy have and continue to experience great success. As it is with most onsite SEO elements, they must be implemented properly in order to get the maximum benefit possible.

With that in mind, I wouldn't fear using exact match domains especially if they fit in with your online business model and, as already mentioned, with your overall business objectives. Likely one of the largest benefits to using exact match domains is that they make it much easier to develop targeted keyword anchor text from authoritative websites. I will get more into this when I talk about links later on.

I have experienced huge success with exact match domain names. Earlier in the book I shared the example of "automotive Internet sales." If you Google that keyword phrase, www.AutomotiveInternetSales.com shows up prominently, in the first position out of a whopping 147 million results! This is the ultimate goal when trying to achieve Google page one dominance, wouldn't you agree?

In order to ensure the effectiveness of your exact match domain, it is important to note that you should never purchase one of them without having the intention (and actually taking the action) of optimizing your website along with it. This book is all about the factors (or rules) that Google considers as it determines how to rank your website, so it's absolutely vital for you to follow them so that your site will achieve top rankings with Google.

As a secondary rule for not only exact match domains but also for any domain in general, be willing to spend a little extra money if it means that you can acquire a top-level domain (TLD) (e.g., .com, .net, .ca, .org, .co.uk, .com.au).

Domain Software

There are technology resources that you can use to assist you in making the best possible decision in choosing your website's domain. Here are a few of my favorites:

- www.moz.com (formerly SEOmoz.com)

  What originally started as an inbound marketing consulting firm cofounded by Rand Fishkin and Gillian Muessig in 2004 quickly became one of the most prominent SEO and inbound marketing software agencies in the world in 2008. The MOZ platform has a wide array of tools that can help you understand many aspects of your website's health, including domain relevancy and strength.

- www.wordtracker.com

  Wordtracker is an essential tool in your SEO toolbox, especially if you want to uncover keyword opportunities and see what your competitors are doing. A tool like this is especially helpful when considering exact match or partial match domain names.

- www.adwords.google.com/KeywordPlanner

  Though this tool must be accessed from within a Google AdWords account, signing up for one not only is free but also will give you access to Google's keyword tool that it built to help advertisers get the most out of their online advertising. I consider this going straight to the source when looking to get insights into keyword data that you can use when considering what domain name to use for your website.

Years ago there was no software to assist us in making an intellectual decision regarding which domain name is best suited for us and our marketing goals. It is an incredible feeling to know that there is actually software that can assist you in picking the best possible domain for your website(s). With that being said, there is absolutely no need for you to shoot from the hip when it comes to selecting a domain name that will best represent your business and your brand, and help your website get the traction it requires in search engines, in order to be successful.

The software products that I've mentioned, especially the Google Keyword Planner, are primarily designed to help you find success with your PPC campaigns, but they have become powerful resources for those who wish to use an exact or partial match domain for their website. Because these products assist with creating a basis for competitive keyword research, they can help you identify what keywords will be most beneficial not only in your PPC strategy but also for your domain name. With powerful tools at your fingertips such as these, why wouldn't you conduct research to help you identify the viability of the keywords you wish to use in your domain?

Using keyword software to help you find the best exact or partial match domain can give you powerful insights into the following:

1. *How many people typed a specific keyword into Google locally in the past month?*

With the abundance in raw information about local user search queries, being able to see how many people are searching for specific keywords in your region can help you gauge the popularity of that keyword as it pertains to your market. You can also see historical data on that same keyword preceding the 30-day period in order to learn whether it has had sustainable search activity for a longer period of time. Knowing whether your desired keyword is merely a short-term trend will help you understand the sustainability of your sought-after domain name.

2. *How many people typed a specific keyword into Google globally in the past month?*

Many local searches are influenced by global trends. Understanding the global search trends for your desired keyword will help you gauge the sustainability of your domain name on a much broader scale.

3. *What are similar keywords to the ones that you picked?*

Depending on the keywords that you initially chose, the software I mentioned earlier will also help you identify keyword opportunities. This can help you see where there are openings to dominate online by showing you where there isn't as much competition but good and often—even great—search volume.

4. *How many people typed those similar keywords to the ones you picked into Google in the past month?*

Similar to points 1 and 2, learning about the search volume for the similar keywords can help you understand how wide or how narrow the potential for your desired keywords are.

5. *What is the estimated competition on that keyword or phrase? . . . and much more!*

Keyword competition is often rated "high," "medium," or "low." When there is high competition, that generally means that it will take much longer for your keywords to rank in search engines, and that there will be much more work involved in building and maintaining your website. When it comes to PPC, high competition always means that you're going to pay much more for each click than medium or low competition.

With medium and low competition, you may not have as much search volume per month as a highly competitive keyword, but you will be able to rank much faster for your chosen keyword. Medium-competition keywords still get decent amounts of traffic, which can translate to success for your business, and they won't require nearly as much work to get ranked.

As you can see, there is a bit of a trade-off when determining what level of competition you're going to aim for with keywords, but ultimately you have to decide based on your business or personal objectives.

Each of the five points we've just discussed can be summed up in one term: keyword forensics. Typically when it comes to SEO, *keyword research* is a much more common term; however, keyword forensics refers to much more than just gathering data about specific keywords to determine which are best to use. Keyword forensics focuses on surveying key phrases as they have been entered by users in an effort to identify their behavior.

Keyword forensics is user-centric, whereas keyword research is keyword-centric. The reason that understanding user behavior in search is much more powerful than just tracking ranking factors is because when you know more about your target audience's search behavior, you can ultimately deliver a better online experience for them through your website, and, at the end of the day, that should be your top-level online marketing goal.

Software products can help you understand more about user search behavior (aka keyword forensics) because they automate the acquisition and analyzing of so much data and then present it in a way that's simple to comprehend. With so much information, there would be absolutely no reason whatsoever for you to rely on guesswork when trying to identify the right exact or partial match domain to use.

Why would you ever choose to buy and build a website around a keyword or key phrase that doesn't receive any search traffic? Would it not make much more sense to use something that fits in with your business objectives (geo-targeted or not) and gets thousands of searches per month, every month, on a consistent basis?

To me it makes a lot more sense to create a domain out of a relevant and popular keyword or phrase. PPC companies or strategists use this tactic before they bid and buy keywords for PPC campaigns. I say you should use the same strategies and tactics utilized for PPC campaigns for organic, onsite SEO initiatives, like creating the *best* domain using the most searched keywords or phrases. This will give you an unfair competitive edge. Think about it: how many people have any clue that there is something called *keyword forensics*? How many people know that creating a domain that has organic SEO value will give them a competitive edge? The answer is very few people, which means that this is huge for you!

There are numerous tools and technologies that can assist you in keyword forensics. Some of these tools you have to pay for, but some are free, like Google's Keyword Planner tool. Basically how it works is that if you have an idea about a keyword or phrase, you can type it into the tools and it can tell you how many times that keyword or phrase was typed into Google both locally and globally. Additionally, tools give you suggestions for related keywords and phrases. This is good because sometimes those awesome keywords or phrases are not available and you need other ideas or suggestions.

Please understand that these tools are not to be considered scripture. They are resources to assist you in making decisions about the best words to use as a domain, as well as the best keywords and phrases to optimize on a web page. There are a couple of real possibilities regarding the data you will receive from these tools.

- You might use a keyword research tool like one of the ones that I listed in this chapter and find that the data you give does not match correlating data from another resource. Let me be specific:

- Let's say that you use Google's research tool Keyword Planner; you search for how many people are typing in "karate school Marlton" and see that the tool says there are *only* 100 keystrokes (meaning that there were only 100 times that someone typed in "karate school Marlton"). However, if you reviewed the Google Analytics from www.MarltonKarate.com for the referring keywords (meaning what people typed into Google to get to your website), it says there were 1,500 people who typed in "karate school Marlton." Even though both Google Analytics and Google's Keyword Planner are Google products and services, they can and a lot of times do contradict each other. There are theories why, some wild and some simple—for example, the conspiracy theory that Google does not want to give the public all the information because then Google is arming people (SEO specialists and marketers) with information that will empower them to achieve better organic results, thus reducing their need for paid search/PPC, and so forth. It's like a school teacher handing out the final exam with the answer key attached. It wouldn't be beneficial to the college, which is being paid to educate. I am not sure if people are paranoid or they are on to something. Another theory is that with the crackdown by the government on privacy, Google is limiting the type of data it collects about people. I can see how people would be freaked out if they knew Google was keeping track of *everything*—like exactly what people type into search engines and how those searches lead them to specific websites—and saving that data, as well as sharing that data so other people can use that data to create strategies for better engaging those people to get them to buy their products or services or try to convert them into a fan or prospect.

If you use Google's Keyword Planner, you see "Bracket not provided" a lot (about 84 to 96 percent of the time). So, use the tool as a guide, not as gospel.

TITLE TAGS

Title elements, also known as "title tags," are one of the most important aspects of onsite SEO by far. They define the title of a document or web page. Title tags are used on SERPs (search engine result pages) to give a synopsis or a preview of a website or web page. In other words, the title tag is meant to give a useful and specific description of the content on a web page. This is imperative to both the onsite SEO and the user's experience. It creates value in three main areas:

1. SERPs
2. Relevancy
3. Browsing

Google usually displays 55 characters of a title tag. So, if you keep your title tag characters at 55 or less you can expect 95 percent of the time to have your full title tag displayed (correctly) on a Google search results page.

Using keywords in your title tag will give you a competitive edge. As a matter of fact, if someone searches for a specific keyword that happens to be in your title, Google will highlight that keyword in the title tag in the search result. This means that you will get a higher click-through rate and of course better visibility.

There are two main components of title tags:

1. Search engine optimization: You want to use relevant and righteous keywords in the title tag so the title tag/web page becomes prominent on page one of Google. Title tags are the most visible and prominent on Google's search results page.
2. Click-throughs: You want to make sure that you write the title tag so it is compelling or interesting enough to make someone want to click through.

Always remember that it isn't all about getting ranking—it's also about getting click-throughs. There is a cause and effect relationship here. You need to be visible for the opportunity to do business. So, once you have visibility you need to convert that visibility to a click. Once that click is accomplished and that person winds up on your website, the strategy now changes to generating a lead, or a sale. This means that once a prospect is on your website, you want them to pick up the phone and call you, or you want them to contact you via email or a contact form on your website. That way, once you have engaged the prospect in live communication, you have an opportunity to present your value package proposition (your message about why to buy from you) and sell them on yourself or your product or service. The other possibility from a click-through is that you have an ecommerce website or a shopping cart on your website that would bypass the need for an email or a phone call and they can go directly to buying your product or service from that click-through on the search results page on Google.

These best practices for title tag creation will yield you low effort and high SEO value:

- **Consider readability and emotional impact.** You want to create a title tag that will emotionally engage and captivate the searcher. This will ensure more visits from Google's search results. The title tag is the first interaction with the searcher/prospect. You know what they say: "You only have one shot to make a first impression." So, you should use that first impression wisely. Make sure that you articulate a compelling reason for them to click through.
- **Be cognizant of your title tag length**. Remember that Google will truncate (shorten) your title tag if you exceed 50–60 characters. That might not be conducive to your overall strategy. With that being said, you shouldn't obsess over title tag length. Title tag content and the ability to entice a prospect to click are more important.
- **Make sure you place the keyword(s) close to the start of the title tag**. This secret tip will prove powerful for ranking, and the prospect will be more likely to click it on Google's search results page.
- **Remember your brand is important!** The strength of your brand will dictate where you place the brand's name in the title tag. If you have a dominant or popular brand, then the strategy is to put the name of the brand in the beginning of the title tag. This is because it might make the difference in a person clicking the link. However, if you have a fledgling brand, product, service, or company, then it would make more sense to put the relevant keyword in the beginning of the title tag and the brand name at the end of the title tag, because the keyword will have more of an impact on the prospect clicking through versus an unknown or new brand.
- **"Exact match" title tags are** *bad* **unless it's the name of the website.** Google started to penalize for this because it said it was overoptimization.
- **Use natural language.** Make sure that your keywords are in the title tags, but make sure that they are part of natural language. You don't

want to just drop random keywords that have SEO value but don't have logic or conversational value.[1]

Here are some examples:

- A martial arts school in Marlton, New Jersey, named Full Circle Martial Arts with this domain: www.FullCircleMartialArts.net
    The proper title tag would be:
    - Full Circle Martial Arts—Martial Arts School in Marlton, NJ
    - Under 55 characters, so it will be displayed properly on a Google search result
    - Semantic indexing
    - Geo-target for local business is extremely important
    - Relevant keywords in title tag
- A car salesman in Philadelphia, Pennsylvania, that specializes in bad credit car loans with this domain: www.AutoCreditApproved.com
    The proper title tag would be:
    - Get Your Auto Credit Approved in Philadelphia PA—Call 215-555-1212
    - Under 55 characters, so it will be displayed properly on a Google result page
    - Semantic indexing
    - Geotarget for local business is extremely important
    - Relevant keywords in title tag
    - Solid call to action
    - Proper use of a phone number in a title tag!

A lot of people use Google like a phone book. They search for something, and if they find a phone number in the title tag, they can click to call right from the search results page. This will reduce abandonment. You will be able to provide prospects with the information they need faster and reduce redundant clicks!

- An Italian restaurant named Tour of Italy, located in Brooklyn, New York, with a domain of www.TourOfItalyBK.com
    The proper title tag would be:

---

[1] *Source:* http://moz.com/learn/seo/title-tag.

- Best Italian Food in Brooklyn—Tour of Italy Restaurant—Reserve Now
- Under 60 characters, so it will be displayed properly on a Google result page
- Semantic indexing
- Geotarget for local business is extremely important
- Relevant keywords in title tag
- Solid call to action
- Multiple relevant keywords and phrases within the title tag

Don't get lazy and not do enough. On the other hand, do not try to do too much with the title tag. Make sure to use unique title tags for each page and, most importantly, make sure that they match the content theme of the page they are on. Specifically, you do not want to stuff too many things in a title tag or "keyword stuff." For example, regarding the Full Circle Martial Arts school in Marlton, New Jersey, Marlton is a respectable town; however, the town right next door is Cherry Hill, New Jersey, and it is an even more popular and prestigious location. As a matter of fact, it has a booming economy, one of the best malls in New Jersey, and an affluent community. Most people who search Google with a geo-targeted location will usually choose a town, city, or county that has the most possibilities. For example, Cherry Hill is a more "happening" place and has more perceived options. So, searchers might choose Cherry Hill over Marlton, even though they live in Marlton. Cherry Hill, New Jersey, is only five minutes away from Marlton. Another scenario is that someone lives in Cherry Hill, New Jersey, and is interested in a martial arts school or karate school. Mathematically speaking, there are more possible students that live in Cherry Hill, New Jersey, versus Marlton because there are more people who live in Cherry Hill. So, should Full Circle Martial Arts settle only for students that live in Marlton? Of course not! Especially when Cherry Hill is only five minutes from Marlton. So, logically the owners of Full Circle Martial Arts will want to target Cherry Hill. The problem is that you do *not* want to add numerous geo-targeted keywords in the title tag. Specifically, you do not want to have "Cherry Hill," "Marlton," and "Medford" in the same title tag for several reasons:

- As mentioned earlier, you don't want to dilute the search engine relevancy and spread your title tag too thin. Have a focus. If you have a main primary market area (PMA), then focus that geo-target on the home page's title tag. If you want to conquer other geo-targeted locations, then simply create additional pages with unique title tags that focus on those geo-targets

- Remember that Google displays only 55 characters (sometimes even less), so you don't want to have a run-on title tag that has ellipses—that is not a good look. So, you need to put first things first and make sure you do not exceed the character limit in the title tag.

Here is the example of how Full Circle Martial Arts School should properly handle the title tag situation if they want to conquer opportunities from the nearby and bigger town of Cherry Hill, New Jersey.

- Brand a totally new page (this page will have a relevant subdirectory, or an extended URL) and create a totally new title tag for that page (focus).
  - Example of the URL and subdirectory:
    - www.FullCircleMartialArts.net/Karate-School-Cherry-Hill-NJ
- Example of the title tag: Martial Arts—MMA Karate—School in Cherry Hill—NJ
  - Under 55 characters, so it will be displayed properly on a Google search result
  - Semantic indexing
  - Geo-target for local business is extremely important
  - Relevant keywords in title tag
  - This title tag's keyword strategy is to conquer prospects that are not in the business's primary market area. The objective is tactically designed to convert other martial arts schools' clients and prospects to Full Circle Martial Arts.

By now you should realize that a website does not have to have only one title tag. In fact websites need to create as many title tags (and web pages) as they need to articulate their value package proposition and highlight all of their profit centers. Here are some tips:

- Including "call to actions" on some of the title tags is a good practice.
  - The About Us page
    - Learn about How Full Circle Martial Arts Trains Karate Champions

- Phone numbers in the title tag are debatable . . . there is no right or wrong way to do it. There is *value*. I suggest that you not use phone numbers in all of your title tags. Use numbers only in pages/title tags that make sense, like the example I gave earlier in the chapter.
- If you use all caps in your title tag you won't get ranked. Google does not like it.

HEADING TAGS

As their name suggests, heading tags are used to identify clear separations between the heading text of a page and its associated content. They are among the more important on-page SEO elements because they are used to represent sections in website content and help Google understand how relevant the written content on the page should be in comparison to its heading.

In SEO, heading tags are powerful because search engine spiders use them to check the relevancy of the heading tag with the context of the page content associated with it. If your heading tag and the subsequent content are misaligned, you risk confusing search engines and losing search engine ranking opportunities.

There is a sequential hierarchy to heading tags, ranging from H1 all the way to H6. There are several factors to understand about heading tags so that you implement them properly on each page of your website. From H1, you must follow the sequential order of the heading tags on your site without breaking the order. You cannot create an <H1> tag and skip over the <H2> and go straight to an <H3>. Similarly, you can't begin your page with an <H2> tag without first including the <H1> tag.

H1 is without question the most important of all the tags and should exist on every page of your website because search spiders check it to get a basic description about what content should be on the page. After the <H1> tag, every proceeding check that the search engine makes is in cross-reference to the <H1> tag for relevancy.

There are lots of different opinions on the best strategy for utilizing heading tags for proper SEO ranking. I am going to focus on what Google wants. As mentioned in Chapter 2, it's all about Google. No egos, no distractions, just focus on exactly what will appease Google, and you will be successful. I have found that the best Google strategy is a pyramid-style approach.

FIGURE 4.1   This pyramid shows the proper structure to create an effective header tag strategy.

Pyramid Strategy

In order to make sure you are creating effective header tags, you need to create a proper hierarchy. The best way to think of header tags is in a pyramid, like the food pyramid. Take a look at Figure 4.1 to see the pyramid strategy for header tags. At the tip of the pyramid is the <H1> tag. You should have only one H1 tag. An H1 tag will consist of more than one keyword; it will be a keyword phrase. An <H2> tag contains two to three key phrase tags. <H3> and <H4> tags can have even more keyword phrases, just as the base of a pyramid will be wider. The same goes for the heading pyramid strategy.

When it comes to the actual keywords or phrases inside the heading tags, you want to focus on three important variables: consistency, relevancy, and user experience. Google's search spiders evaluate the keyword consistency and the keyword relevancy between all of the heading tags and the rest of the content on the page, as well as content associated with it. Since Google places a lot of importance on overall user experience, it is important that the heading tags be properly created to give the user the best understanding of what the page content is about.

Think of creating a powerful SEO strategy like writing a thorough outline for an article, book, or idea. You want to create outline headings and then bullet-point thoughts or ideas by drilling down intelligently. Let's just pretend that I was writing a book (darn, where's my wink emoji?). It is much easier to focus your direction first by creating an outline and then going back and filling in the details. I would first start with a concept, and then I would outline the entire book's focus, section by section. I would then create chapter titles, drill down with chapter descriptions, and then further drill down with bullet points for the details. I would review my outline numerous times, making sure to include all supporting information and, if necessary, modifying it. Then finally I would structure my final book outline. This outline would work as my blueprint for my book. It would be an important guide to ensure that everything makes sense and also to make sure that I stay focused on the end goal in mind.

Here is a perfect example of the proper use of headings for the ultimate SEO strategy that will enable you to achieve page one dominance on Google.

Example

<H1>Los Angeles Honda Dealer - Sean Bradley Honda</H1>
<H2>Selling New Honda and Pre-Owned Vehicles</H2>
<H3>Honda Accord</h3>
<H3>Honda Civic</h3>
<H2>Serving LA County and the Surrounding Areas</H2>
<H3>Honda Dealership Near Glendale, CA</H3>

The example shows the hierarchy of a car dealership and how its homepage might be structured. You'll see that there is only one H1.

The number of headings should be limited to the need. In this example, there are two general needs: location and item. The location can be relatively wide in the local area; people are willing to drive to a dealership 50–100 miles away in order to get the right car. If you have a different type of local business, like a restaurant or a barber shop, proximity plays a much higher role. People aren't going to drive 50 miles to get to a particular barber shop, so you will need headings that only represent the immediate local area. Also, a barber shop offers limited services beyond cutting hair, so there's no need to put in too many headings for multiple products or services.

The items for the car dealership are individual models, so I included an <H2> that discusses new and used cars and broke it down further to include <H3> tags for individual models.

Here's an example of a heading structure for a more complex type of business.

Example

<H1>Dallas Lawyer - Sean Bradley, Esquire</H1>

<H2>Top Litigator in the Dallas Area</H2>

<H3>Ft Worth Attorney</H3>

<H4>Fort Worth Personal Injury Lawyer</H4>

<H4>Super Lawyer in Ft Worth<H4>

<H3>Plano Law Offices</H3>

<H2>Specializing in Multiple Legal Disciplines</H2>

<H3>Divorce Attorney Dallas</H3>

<H3>Class Action Lawyer Dallas</H3>

The easiest way to think about heading tags is to put them in the way that you would personally search. One might think that a restaurant has many different items on their menu, but people will rarely search for "Los Angeles macaroni," for example. They would search for "LA restaurants" or "Los Angeles steak houses." How do you search? Let that guide your headings.

One last mention about heading tags: they should not be used for styling text—use CSS for that. Don't put a heading tag around some part of the content just because you want it bold or bigger. Use <strong> or ask your designer what CSS calls you can make for styling text. [2]

---

[2] *Source:* http://blog.woorank.com/2013/04/how-to-use-heading-tags-for-seo/; www.searchenginejournal.com/2014-important-h1-tag-seo/106613/.

Meta-description, also simply known as **description**, is the second most important focus when optimizing a web page. However, the importance is not primarily for SEO—it is for obtaining click-throughs or for the user experience.

Meta-description is defined as Hyper Text Markup Language (HTML) attributes that explain in specific detail the contents of web pages. Descriptions are utilized on SERPs to showcase a synopsis of a web page.

Just as for title tags, there is an optimal number of characters for the description. So it would behoove you not to exceed 155 characters if you want to appeal to the search engines.

The most important thing to remember when you are creating the meta-descriptions is to utilize keywords strategically. But you do not want to keyword stuff or randomly sprinkle keywords. Google frowns upon this this and will penalize you for it. You need to write your descriptions using compelling ad copy that will entice searchers to click through. Uniqueness and relevance for each page's meta-description are imperative.

If someone searches for something and types in a keyword or phrase like "divorce lawyer Atlanta" or "who is the best divorce lawyer in Atlanta" and one of those keywords or phrase is in the description of a website ranked on a search engine results page, Google will **bold** the keywords or phrase. These **bolded** keywords will increase click-throughs, so make sure you write your meta-descriptions accordingly.

For example, if you Google "best divorce lawyer Atlanta" (https:// www.google.com/#q=best+divorce+lawyer+in+atlanta), you will see this rank organically on the top 10 list (see Figure 4.2):

Georgia Super **Lawyers - Top Lawyers** in GA **(title tag)**

www.superlawyers.com/georgia **(URL)**

Find **top** rated Georgia **lawyers**, **lawyer, attorney, attorneys** at Super **Lawyers** – GA **Lawyers**. . . . Find **Top** Rated **Lawyers** in Georgia . . . **Atlanta** magazine. List(s) . . . (Description)

This is a perfect example of an awesome description that is engineered to appeal both to Google and to the individual searcher looking for the "best divorce lawyer in Atlanta." But when you put together the awesome title tags with the awesome domain name and combine it with the awesome description, then *boom*! You have a recipe for Google success. Think about this example a little more deeply. Put yourself in the shoes of people who are very distraught: they are having severe marital

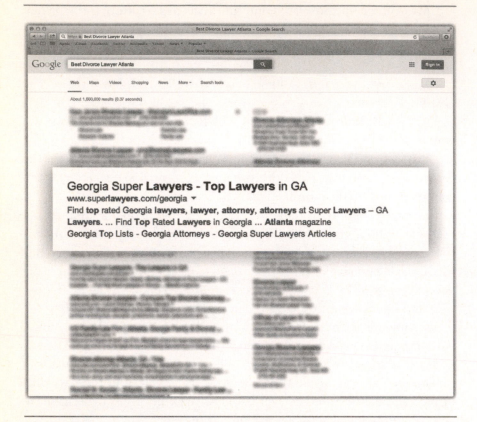

FIGURE 4.2   This image shows a great example of how you can use meta-description to represent your business, and how it is displayed in a Google search.

problems to the point that they are seeking a divorce. They have a lot to lose here:

- Custody of the children
- Assets
  - Home
  - Cars
  - Real estate investments
  - Retirement fund
  - Jewelry
- Cash

Then compound the situation with all of the emotions, like fear, anger, frustration, and sadness. Can you try to imagine all of these things running through your head, and you are thinking, "I *need* a divorce lawyer ASAP, and I need the *best* one before I get railroaded!" Now you turn to the mighty oracle, Google, the answerer of all questions, and you type in, "best divorce lawyer in Atlanta." Google provides you with only 21 listings (on the first page), 11 PPC ads, and the top 10 list. Remember only 6 percent of people click PPC ads. So, that leaves us the top 10 list. You look through the top 10 list and see the words *Super Lawyer*, *Top Lawyer*, *Georgia*, and *Top Rated*. You also see this numerous times in the title and the domain, and you see numerous **bold** keywords in the description. You must be thinking, "Wow, the Google oracle must be right again!" And then you click through. And that's how it works, folks!

Let me give you a different scenario with a different industry. Let's say you were looking for a cleaning company or housekeepers in the Tulsa, Oklahoma, area.

If you Googled "reliable house cleaning Tulsa," you will find the following in first-position, natural Google:

Tulsa, OK Cleaning Service | Total Care | House Cleaning . . . **(title tag)**

totalcaremaintenance.com/tulsa-ok-home-cleaning-service/ **(URL)**

For a **reliable Tulsa** OK cleaning service, call 918-851-9338 today! You won't find a better **house cleaning** service in **Tulsa**! **Home cleaning** services **Tulsa**, OK. (Description) [3]

The description is awesome! If you were seriously in need of a cleaning service or housekeeper in the Tulsa, Oklahoma, area, and you asked the mighty Google oracle where can you find a *reliable* cleaning service, and Google showed you this listing with that perfect description, chances are you would call the phone number right inside the description or you would click the link. Most people would take some sort of action if they were truly in the market. The description sold you on why you needed to call or click them. Plus it had *your* desired keywords in **bold** text. You asked Google for a "reliable" cleaning service, and, dammit, that is exactly what Google found for you. And Google wanted you to know that it heard

---

[3] *Source:* http://tinyurl.com/qblbenx.

you loud and clear with your specific request for a "reliable" cleaning service, so it **bolded** all of the keywords you specified in the description.

A couple of important things to be cognizant of:

- Be careful not to duplicate meta-descriptions on different web pages. Just as it is not good to duplicate title tags, the same goes for the description. Google is very clear that it likes unique and relevant content, descriptions, and title tags; everything must be customized and unique for each and every page.
- Double quotation marks will get your description truncated. To prevent Google from cutting off your meta-description, do not use double quotes in your meta-description. If for some reason you feel compelled to use quotation marks in your description, make sure that you use only single quotation marks.[4]

LINKING

Before I get into the details of linking, back linking, inbound linking, and so on, I want to share with you the backstory of Google and why linking is so important.

In 1996 Larry Page and Sergey Brin hooked together a ton of old Stanford University computers that the university would have thrown away and built the first "citation" or link-based search engine. At the time the only way to search through Stanford's database of professors' research projects was via a contextual search that returned thousands of results ordered by the count of the keyword searched in the actual document. The problem was that hundreds of documents that won the keyword count game pushed the more relevant and authoritative papers off into obscurity.

They decided that a better way to return the docs for a searcher would be to combine the word search with a citation count on the assumption that the papers and documents that were the most cited resources were the most valuable to researchers. They were right!

They offered this new link-based technology to Yahoo! and Microsoft at the time and were laughed out of the buildings, so they raised venture capital and did it themselves, creating Google and hundreds of billions of dollars of wealth in the process.

---

[4] *Source:* http://moz.com/learn/seo/meta-description.

Google was built on link-based technology. It makes sense to understand linking and how to do it properly to maximize your website's opportunity to achieve Google page one dominance.

The old adage goes, "Show me your friends, and I will tell you who you are." That quote says it all. That is how Google feels, too! Part of Google's algorithm is that if you are linked by a known site that is relevant and gets a lot of traffic, then you will get "link juice" and be rewarded by its credibility. It makes perfect sense. Google is trying to ensure that searchers find the most relevant source, and if a recognized authority links back to you, then you are considered credible. This type of link is called an *external link*.

External Links

An external link on your website could be an outside website or resource that links back to your website. However, if you link to an outside source, that is considered an outbound link. External links that are from a larger, more established source that links to your website will have the strongest value for your website's SEO credibility.

A website's primary objective in achieving high SEO ranking (and Google page one dominance) should be to secure as many external links as humanly possible. The theory is that external links are much more difficult to scam, spam, or manipulate. If your website has a lot of external links, Google has confidence that your site is truly popular and thus needs to be ranked favorably.

The two main reasons that external links are important are:

1. Relevance
2. Popularity

Google finds external links tremendously valuable in correlating relevance to web pages. In addition to relevance, there is the aspect of popularity. If there are a lot of people or websites that are linking to your website, especially if they are similar, Google recognizes this. If popular (bigger) sites link to you, then it tells Google that you are important and need to be considered and ranked accordingly.[5]

---

[5] *Source:* http://moz.com/learn/seo/external-link.

Internal Links

The level of credibility a site possesses is the key to getting a website ranked on Google. How does your site gain credibility with Google? External links are crucial, especially from sites that are well established themselves. However, links from within a website are crucial for Google to evaluate the relevancy of the site and ultimately decide how to rank the site.

There are numerous ways for a website to utilize internal links:

- Website navigation
- Links in the content, anchor text
- Links on the pages
- Site map

Here are some best practices for linking that will help you achieve your Google page one dominance:

- Don't put too many links in the body of your text content. No more than five or six links.
- Keep your total links (including navigation) on any page under 100 and you will be in great shape. Remember that fewer links means more link juice!
- Have a link strategy:
  - Links that are in the body of your content will have a higher relevancy to Google's algorithm.
  - Make sure that you link from one section in your website to another section that is relevant.

    For example, your website is www.autocreditapproved.com (a bad credit/no credit website for people who need a car loan), and you are writing copy for the home page, talking about how your company can help anyone get approved—all they have to do is Apply Now. You can make "Apply Now" a hyperlink that goes directly to your credit application.
  - It is a great practice to add a link to new content or old content as an update to an article or blog post.

There are so many ways to build and entice other websites to link to your company it is absurd. In fact, there are so many ways that you really must decide which ones are worth your time and investment. Not all of these are recommended, but here is a very long list of ways to get links that can move you into the top spots for your most important commercial search terms.

Keep in mind that if it's easy and seems too good to be true, it is. Appropriate link building takes effort, and in general the more effort it takes, the higher the quality of the link and the harder it will be for your competitors to replicate what you are doing.

Here is the list:

www.linkbuildingbook.com/link-building-resources.html

There are more things you can do to build links than you'd ever want to attempt. If you are a local business, you should focus on local links like charities, local online journals, local newspaper sites, local radio station sites, local politics, chamber of commerce sites, and so forth.

If you are a national or international business, you'll need to focus on the more authoritative sites in your industry. Think about associations, existing vendors, partners, bureaus, government affiliations, university affiliations, large charities and national newspapers and media authorities. Be prepared to spend a significant amount of money to compete for valuable commercial search terms—you are not the only fish in the sea. However, if you are competing on a local level, creating the proper strategy can be very inexpensive or free. You just have to put in the time and patience to cultivate your strategy.

Get an idea of what it's going to take before you enter, make your strategy first, and then evaluate your budget. You are not going to win the number one spot for "pay day loans" by spending $2,000 a month, no matter what you do. Use keyword planning tools and consult with an expert if you are unsure about what it will cost to become visible for valuable search terms. Otherwise, you may find yourself on an uphill battle that will only lead to frustration.

Plan ahead and plan to win. The number one spot gets 70 percent of the traffic and page 2+ gets nothing. Organize your content correctly and then link, link, link. With the right strategy and assets you can win for anything. Avoid easy automated link-building "solutions" as they are typically ineffective or provide only a temporary boost and are always dangerous. Nothing will ruin your day like a Google slap, and sometimes the only way to get away from the penalty is to change your domain! Just like everything else in life, hard work pays off and shortcuts can ruin everything. Choose wisely and do it right the first time to avoid the hassle of cleaning up a huge mess. You can tell when it's too good to be true and in link building the easy route hurts, so do the work, make it happen, and have fun.

Figure 4.3 shows an example page of correctly optimized commercial content.

The content is worthy of study because despite the fact that the dealership is very small and located in tiny Alachua, Florida, more than 20 miles outside of Gainesville, Florida, this page outranks the big boat dealers that are physically located in Gainesville. A quick link analysis shows us that no inbound links have be built to point at this page at all, yet this page ranks number one in Google for commercial terms such as "outboard boat motors Gainesville FL," "Yamaha outboard motors Gainesville FL," and "Mercury outboard motors Gainesville FL."

So let's take a closer look.

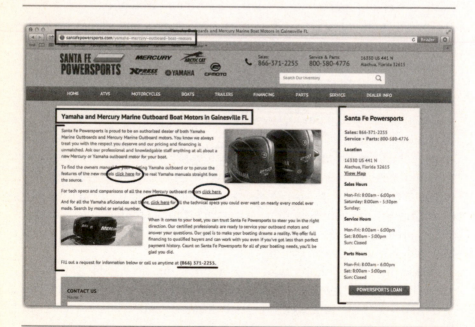

FIGURE 4.3   This screen capture shows a fantastic example of a correctly optimized site with proper headers, supporting content, and backlinks.

Source: http://santafepowersports.com/yamaha-mercury-outboard-boat-motors.

The heading tag incorporates the important keywords and clearly describes the content.

Yamaha and Mercury Marine Outboard Boat Motors in Gainesville FL

The paragraph content is in proper English, reads well, and includes utility for the user.

Santa Fe Powersports is proud to be an authorized dealer of both Yamaha Marine Outboards and Mercury Marine Outboard motors. You know we always treat you with the respect you deserve and our pricing and financing is unmatched. Ask our professional and knowledgeable staff anything at all about a new Mercury or Yamaha outboard motor for your boat.

To find the owner's manual for your existing Yamaha outboard or to peruse the features of the new models, click here for the real Yamaha manuals straight from the source.

And for all the Yamaha aficionados out there, click here for all the technical specs you could ever want on nearly every model ever made. Search by model or serial number.

When it comes to your boat, you can trust Santa Fe Powersports to steer you in the right direction. Our certified professionals are ready to service your outboard motors and answer your questions. Our goal is to make your boating dreams a reality. We offer full financing to qualified buyers and can work with you even if you've got less than perfect payment history. Count on Santa Fe Powersports for all of your boating needs, you'll be glad you did.

Notice that keywords are incorporated but not overused, and everything on the page is true and verifiable. The webmaster has included valuable links off the page to authorities on the topic of outboard motors.

To find the owner's manual for your existing Yamaha outboard or to peruse the features of the new models click here for the real Yamaha manuals straight from the source.

The link in this paragraph links to www.yamahaoutboards.com/owner-resources/owners-manuals.

And for all the Yamaha aficionados out there, click here for all the technical specs you could ever want on nearly every model ever made. Search by model or serial number.

The link in this paragraph links to www.yamahapubs.com/index.do?pg=search&category=4, which is a complete database of tech specs for each and every model of outboard motor Yamaha has ever made.

These types of resources can be found with simple Google searches, and including these links to authoritative and topically relevant resources

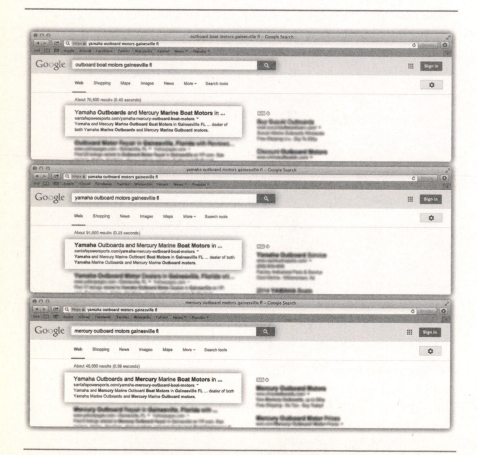

FIGURE 4.4   This image shows how different keyword searches bring up the same optimized company website.

gives your page added value that Google consistently rewards with preferential treatment in search engine results (see Figure 4.4).

There are a couple of other examples of best practices on this page. When you are viewing the page, roll over the images to reveal the image alt tags. Alt tags are meant for visually impaired and blind web users. Thanks to the advent of alt tags, blind people can still absorb graphical content on the web via their software or braille-enabled devices describing the images to them. This is a great place to include keywords but should not be spammed or stuffed. When writing your alternative tags for your images, imagine that you are blind and ask yourself how you would like this image to be described to you.

On this example page, this image has the following alternative description:

Yamaha Outboard Motors

While this does include the targeted keywords, it also clearly describes the actual image.

What follows would be considered an inappropriate use of image alt tags and may cause a Google penalty against your page and/or domain:

Gainesville FL Yamaha Outboard Motors for sale Yamaha Boat Motors Cheap Yamaha Outboard Boats for sale in Gainesville FL Florida Boat Motors in Gainesville FL Outboard Yamaha boat motors boat engines Gainesville boats for sale boat motors Florida Yamaha boats motors FL Yamaha Gainesville FL Yamaha

If you were blind and reading through this page, which one would you rather hear as a description of the image?

The first is a great quality indicator that both visually impaired people and Google will reward you for; the second would be considered spam and would entice Google to slap you with a penalty.

It is important to remember that Google values and rewards utility. When writing content for your website, it is best to have a light touch with the keywords you want to rank for. Describe your product or service clearly and provide as much utility as you can with appropriate authoritative links to useful data or tools, clear H1 category headings, and relevant images and videos.

CONTENT

Bottom line is that content is king. There are a lot of great strategies for Google domination, but the bottom line is that there is no tricking Google. That is the secret; you need to understand exactly what Google wants and then just do it. Google wants to provide people with exactly what they are looking for when they are looking for it. You want to make sure that you create the most interesting, relevant, timely, and consistent content that you possibly can.

In addition to **relevant content** you want to make sure that you create **unique content.** There is nothing worse than duplicate content (besides content that sucks). If you have duplicate content, then you will not get ranked on Google. You can't cheat Google; you can't use or reuse the same content on multiple pages within a website. You also cannot cut and paste random content from Google or any other search engine and use it on your website and expect to get ranked. Nor can you expect to cut and paste partial pieces of content from different sources on the Internet and sew them together like Frankenstein on your website and expect to get ranked on Google. It's not going to happen. Just like when we were in school (some of you still might be in school), you couldn't hand in a term paper or book report that was plagiarized. The same goes for Google. You can't steal other people's content and think Google will give you SEO credit for it. As a matter of fact, there are lots of free and paid software programs that can check for duplicate content and or plagiarized content:

- www.grammarly.com
- www.plagtracker.com
- http://smallseotools.com/plagiarism-checker/
    This one comes with SEO tools:
    - Article Rewriter
    - Keyword Position
    - Pagerank Checker
    - Backlink Maker

- There are more sites and resources—all you have to do is Google **plagiarism checker seo**, and this will show up for page one Google:
  www.google.com/#q=plagiarism+checker+seo

Keyword Density within Your Content

As defined by Wikipedia, keyword density is the percentage of times a keyword or phrase appears on a web page compared to the total number of words on that page. Google's algorithm takes into account (in part) keyword density as a factor in identifying whether a website or web page is relevant to a specific keyword and/or phrase.

For example, if a used car dealership that specialized in "bad credit, no credit" car loans, located in Dallas, Texas, had a website called www.BadCreditDallas.com, then it would make sense for the home page of the website to have text content that included the words *bad credit* and/or *Dallas, Texas*.

A Very Important Google Tip

You want to make sure that you are *not* spamming keywords randomly on the web page or throughout the website. You can't merely sprinkle keywords throughout the site and think Google is going to like it and rank you. Back in the day you could get away with this. However, with Google's algorithm updates with Penguin, Hummingbird, Panda 4.0, and so on, Google is hitting spammers and manipulators hard and penalizing them. You need to write content as you would write ad copy—professional and captivating, with proper grammar, spelling, and logic. The content needs to be written for people. You can't "keyword stuff" content. You need to keep your keyword density to 1 to 3 percent. Anything above that and you risk Google penalizing you for keyword stuffing or spamming.

What you need to do is write awesome content that:

- Describes your website or web page
- Describes your product and/or service
- Describes what your value package proposition is (why buy from you)
- Details your menu
- Answers questions proactively
- States problems and solutions
- Includes keywords used in the:
  - Domain
  - Title tag

- Meta-description
- Heading tags
- Alt tags
- Videos
- Geo-targeted location(s)
- Targeted prospects/audience/demographics [6]
- Keyword Density Analyzer Tool:
  - http://tools.seobook.com/general/keyword-density/
  - www.keyworddensity.com

CONCLUSION

My disclaimer is that I could write an entire book on SEO and Google's page one dominance as it relates to a web page or onsite SEO. However, this is a unique book with a very unique and powerful strategy: Googleopoly. The true power of Googleopoly is in the synergy of utilizing multiple initiatives simultaneously to achieve Google page one dominance. Synergy is defined as two or more agents that come together whose effect is greater together than their individual effects. In the game of Monopoly, Boardwalk is awesome in itself, and Park Place is a great property to own, too. They provide impressive payouts, but put them together and you have the ultimate monopoly. Throw some hotels on them and forget about it!

As the power of synergy relates to this book, each of the strategies we discuss in future chapters is beyond effective and compelling on its own. As a matter of fact, a lot of people have been successful and effective with just utilizing each of these strategies alone. But if you combine each of these individual awesome opportunities, you are going to create an incredible synergistic strategy, second to none. And this, my friends, is how you are going to win the game of Googleopoly!

With that being said, I chose to go deep into this chapter for onsite SEO for multiple reasons. First and foremost, as I have said before, even though there are numerous strategies within Googleopoly and Google page one domination, your website is your anchor. And all of the details throughout Chapter 4 will prove to be invaluable for strategies in optimizing video, social media, blogs, focus sites, and so on.

---

[6] *Source:* http://en.wikipedia.org/wiki/Keyword_density.

NEXT EVOLUTION IN ONSITE SEO

Your opponent owns Pacific Avenue and Pennsylvania Avenue. He or she is rounding the corner, with eyes on the prize. What will happen next? Will he or she score the perfect roll and land on North Carolina Avenue, to secure the monopoly? Or will he or she fall short and be sent to jail? Or maybe, just maybe, he or she will overroll by one and land dead smack in the middle, leaving it all to chance—hello community chest.

I have outlined and detailed many powerful techniques, strategies, and secrets thus far to achieve Google page one domination. However, to win the game of Googleopoly, you must think four to five moves in advance. You must anticipate both what Google might change or how it might modify its search algorithms, and you must also anticipate what and how people are going to search. If you can predict or try to predict how things are going to evolve, you will not only compete but also lead the way and dominate on search engines. Making logical predictions regarding Google and its users is one of the most important aspects of winning Googleopoly.

Don't freak out and think, "How in the world can I predict what Google is going to do?" All you have to do is be cognizant of how *you* would search. What would you like answers to? If you were in need of answers, what would you type into Google? What would your children type into Google? What would your parents type into Google? Basically, just begin with the end in mind. I get it—Google can be intimidating because it is a multibillion-dollar, publicly traded corporation, but put that to the side for a second and look at www.Google.com. What do you see? I see simplicity! I see a white page with a search bar! Google has always tried to keep it simple and to the point. So, it might seem like an unrealistic goal to anticipate Google, but here is the secret advice: Try to figure out how Google can make things more relevant, more up to date, faster, and in the exact format that a searcher is searching, and you are well on your way to a proactive strategy!

Use this book, which is saturated with experience, secrets, tips, strategies, and resources, all provided to give you an unfair competitive advantage and the knowledge necessary to be ahead of everyone else. This is imperative in order for you to make the absolute best decisions regarding the way you invest your time and money in your marketing initiatives.

In order to plan for the future, though, you need to have a basic understanding of the web's past, as well as the road map for where it's headed. Most people have probably heard of the terms *Web 1.0* and *Web 2.0*, but few know details about the transition.

Web 1.0 is known as the "static" or "read-only" web. Up until the late 1990s, there was little to no interaction on actual websites. By the time the year 2000 rolled around, however, sites like LiveJournal and Blogger were giving users a simple way to publish to the web. From there, social networking sites like MySpace and social news sites like Digg formed new types of online interactions that shaped what we now call social media. This ability to interact online dramatically changed the way people used the web. Around this time, keyword-heavy content and optimization were common SEO strategies.

What's coming now is the Semantic Web, which will define Web 3.0 and act as the next dramatic change to the web. These changes will include semantic markup, hyperpersonalized search, and deductive reasoning that will provide the most relevant results for a user's search query.

Googleopoly strategists are beginning to see these changes put into practice today, as Google makes a push for sites to use semantic markup in order to allow its search engine to read the web the same way you and I do.

With its 2013 Hummingbird algorithm update, Google took the first step toward the future of Web 3.0. The reason this update was so important is because it allows Google to gauge a user's intent like never before.

For example, if I search for "2012 Nissan Altima" now, I get a broad list of results that vary from pure information to reviews to dealer inventory and third-party providers, like edmunds.com, KBB, cars.com, AutoTrader, and so on. The future of search, however, will be dominated by long, detailed queries, such as "I would like to purchase a black 2012 Nissan Altima with less than 30,000 miles." This will allow very differentiated results from someone looking to do research on the same vehicle who might search with the phrase "I want to read all of the critical reviews on the 2012 Nissan Altima."

The future of search is context—not just content and links. Google's recent algorithm updates have taken action to ensure its future results become more about relevancy, as well as to weed out bad results from sites attempting to game the system and punish sites that feature duplicate content.

Car dealers have been particularly hurt by these recent updates due to poor practices from website providers using outdated systems featuring built-in duplicate content. Modern developers and website providers that deal with inventory use the "rel=canonical" term in their code to let search engines know that a particular set of duplicate content serves a legitimate purpose.

Let's think back to that 2012 Nissan Altima. Every Nissan dealer on the planet has the same Nissan Altimas. There may be some different colors or a few different options, but when we visit an inventory page on a dealer's website, all of the information about each vehicle is essentially the same—power windows, power door locks, CD player, alloy wheels, and so forth. The long list of standard equipment and options is duplicate content. Canonicalization was created to allow sites to tell search engines, "I have a lot of these things and the purpose isn't to spam search results."

Google assigns trust, authority, and value to a page based on relationships. If a car dealership has 500 vehicles in stock, that's 500 pages of potential duplicate content. Every page on a website is linked to every other page on a website through various links and navigation. Those links create relationships between all of the pages on the site. If those relationships are poor (i.e., lots of duplicate content pages being interlinked with quality pages), then the entire site's level of trust and authority can effectively be brought down as a result.

Now, imagine what happens if you don't tell Google that your inventory isn't duplicate content spam. Those relationships become severely damaged. As a result, every page on the site is devalued by each additional page of duplicate content—all because a simple piece of code wasn't properly implemented. We see this on over 90 percent of car dealership websites today.

If a car dealership site's inventory features multiple iterations of the same product, there is an easy way to check whether your website is utilizing the canonical tag. Navigate to one of your inventory pages—making sure it's a product that you carry more than one of—and right-click your mouse button and click "View Source" (not available in the Safari web browser). A pop-up will open, full of the code that makes up the front-end structure of your website. Do a "Find/Replace" search (use Command + F or CTRL + F on your computer) and now type in "canonical."

Did that search find and highlight anything on the page? If not, your product pages are not using the proper markup, which means your site is telling Google, "Hey, we're duplicating content all across our site, despite the fact that it violates your guidelines!"

There are many other types of markup, such as those detailed by Schema.org, that this book won't go into; however, this will give you an idea of red flags to look for and/or topics to discuss with whomever is providing your business's website.

ADDITIONAL RESOURCES

Google's search algorithms are changing all the time. For the most up-to-date information and the most current SEO strategies including title tags, domains, and linking, please visit www.googleopolybook.com /website-seo-strategy.

CHAPTER 5

Video and Video SEO

We are going to transition in the rest of this book to the other 75 percent of your Google page one domination (POD) or visibility strategy, aka "offsite SEO." Going forward, each chapter is going to go into detail for each of the diversified strategies for offsite SEO. Again, putting first things first, as it pertains to the other 75 percent of your Google POD strategy, I will focus on video and video SEO.

I want to say this here and now that there is *nothing* that you can do that will have as much effect on winning the game of Googleopoly or dominating Google page one as video SEO or VSEO. There is no onsite or offsite SEO strategy that will yield immediate organic SEO results like video SEO. The bottom line is if you want to seriously have an unfair advantage in creating a Google POD reality or utterly crushing your competition, pay close attention to this chapter. Take a lot of notes and then when you are done, re-read this chapter. This is the part of the book that is going to change your business immediately. I am talking about immediate gratification. If you decide to execute nothing else from this book, be certain to execute this strategy. My clients pay me top-dollar rates to teach them these very strategies and techniques I am sharing with you for the very low price of a book.

Before I dive into VSEO, let's go over some very important information, facts, and statistics about video in general:

- We have all heard that saying, "A picture is worth a thousand words." Well, according to Dr. McQuivey, vice president of Forrester's Research, "**1 Minute of video is equivalent to 1.8 *million* written words**!" Based on his philosophical view of video, he has said that video combines sight, sound, motion, body language, artistry (sometimes), and full-sensory stimulation, all focused to convey, articulate, sell, or convince someone of something.[1]

---

[1] *Source:* www.videobrewery.com/blog/18-video-marketing-statistics.

- People prefer to watch video more than they engage in other mediums:
  - More than writing letters
  - More than writing emails
  - More than talking on the phone
  - More than texting
  - More than reading books
- As mentioned in Chapter 2, YouTube is the number two search engine on the planet. YouTube has more monthly views than Bing, Yahoo!, AOL, and Ask combined. YouTube is second only to Google, which owns YouTube.
- In December 2013, 188.2 million people in the United States watched 52.4 billion online content videos. The average American spent more than 19 hours watching online video![2]
- In 2013, 72.1 million U.S. smartphone users watched video on their devices at least monthly. This is expected to rise to 86.8 million, more than a quarter of the U.S. population, in 2014.[3]
- Over half of 25–54-year-olds share video online.[4]
- Ninety percent of consumers watch online video.[5]
- Seventy-one percent of consumers say that video is the best way to bring product features to life.[6]
- Mobile shoppers are three times as likely to view a video as desktop shoppers.[7]
- Internet video traffic will be 69 percent of all global consumer Internet traffic in 2017.[8]
- Prospects are 53 times more likely to click a video versus a static link. Let me be specific: if there is a video thumbnail on Google page one, a searcher is 53 times more likely to click that link versus any other listings that are ranked.

---

[2] *Source:* comscore 2013.

[3] *Source:* emarketer 2013.

[4] *Source:* emarketer 2013.

[5] *Source:* mediapost 2013.

[6] *Source:* multichannel merchant 2013.

[7] *Source:* onlinevideo.net 2013.

[8] *Source:* cisco 2013.

If that wasn't enough to blow you away, let's break down the science of communication:

- Fifty-five percent of communication is visual perception and body language.
- Thirty-eight percent of communication is tone and inflection.
- *Only* 7 percent of communication is text or the words that we use.[9]

What does all of this mean? It means that Google gets it! People—that is, searchers—want video! I am going to repeat that: searchers prefer video content more than any other content. And as discussed, Google's main goal is to give people exactly what they are looking for, when they are looking for it. So, the public's need, want, and desire for video content have influenced Google's algorithm. Google's algorithm favors video content. What does this mean? It is simple: If you have a website that is optimized properly, it will take anywhere from 30 days to 90 days for that website to get ranked by Google. Let's say you have a website that has keywords or phrases with moderate competition; you would be lucky to have a website rank in 30 days (at least). On the other hand, a brand new video that also has moderate competition that was properly optimized can rank within hours or a couple of days. Let me repeat that: A conventional web page can take 30, 60, or even 90 days, but a video properly optimized can rank and achieve Google page one dominance in hours or days!

Part of the reason this is possible is because relevant and optimized video is such a high priority for Google. There are way more web pages on Google compared to videos, simply because in the beginning of the Internet there were no videos—there were only web pages. All of the web pages started to pile up. So, when videos started to come into existence, obviously there would be more traditional content versus video. However, since the world prefers video, so does Google. So, if you have the right combination of relevance and optimization of good-quality video (audio and lighting), your video content will surpass the nonvideo content. Google will award you with a favorable chance

---

[9]*Source:* http://en.wikipedia.org/wiki/Albert_Mehrabian.

card : "Advance to Go, Collect $200." You will blow past the competition while eliminating your risk of landing on their properties for a rent payout.

Are you excited yet? You should be! But before I get to explain to you how exactly you are going to be able to achieve this, step by step, I want to get you a little more excited! Video SEO has another incredible and practical application: conquesting (see Figure 5.1). For example, please Google the following:

- Toyota Corolla Torrance
  - What you are going to find in first-position, natural Google is a video for a Honda dealership! Let me repeat that. If you Google Toyota Corolla Torrance, you are going to get a video of a Honda Civic, in first-position, natural Google. This is the ultimate Google POD strategy personified! Why? For starters, Toyota's U.S. manufacturing headquarters are located in Torrance, California, and one of the top selling Toyotas in California is a Corolla! So, you would expect when you search for a Toyota Corolla Torrance, you would find a Toyota dealership . . . . Nope! In first-position, natural Google is a *powerful* video on the Honda Civic and why it is a *better* choice than the Toyota Corolla! Seriously, think about what I just said. That is crazy! As previously discussed, people perceive Google as the almighty oracle. People search for their husbands, wives, pets, furniture, cars, and homes. They trust Google. They ask Google all sorts of questions, sometimes all day, every day. So, if someone searches for that Toyota Corolla in Torrance, California, and the "Google oracle" says, "No, you do *not* want that Toyota Corolla . . . you *really* want and need the Honda Civic, people will believe Google! It is after all . . . Google!
  - Let's say you search for something as simple as "Miami Rav4." Out of over 1 million results, first-position, natural Google will be a video for Rick Case Honda! Again, that is beyond surreal. In addition to the first-position, natural Google ranking, the video of the Honda dealership is a full-blown, conquesting assault against the *all* Toyota dealers. The video is of high quality, as well as strategically created to truly sell the value of *not* only Honda over Toyota but also specifically why "Rick Case Honda" is clearly the *only* choice for *any* of your automotive needs.

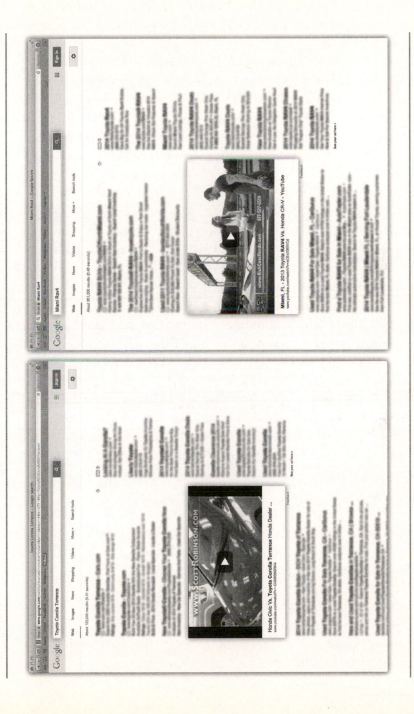

FIGURE 5.1 Two incredible examples of how a conquesting video can dominate a Google search page. In the first example, the search term was for a Toyota Corolla but the result was for a Honda Civic, and the second example is a search for a Rav4 and a video promoting the Honda CRV comes up first.

101

Let me put this into perspective. Not only can you dominate Google page one when people are looking for you or your type of product or service. But with video SEO, you can additionally dominate your competition! If you are "Sprite" and someone is searching for "Coke" or "Pepsi," you can appear all over page one of Google. Can you imagine how valuable that is? In the automotive sales industry, for example, Google did a study in conjunction with Compete and Polk[10] that says that 72 to 79 percent of automotive shoppers are "cross-shopping" other brands. What that means is that if someone is searching for a Ford F-150, chances are that between 72 and 79 percent of people are looking at other trucks, like a RAM 1500 or Chevrolet Silverado. Why is this information important to you? Simple . . . if almost *all* of your prospects are searching your direct competitors and you do *not* show up when people are searching your competitors, you are leaving a lot of money on the table—too much money. So, you need to make sure that "conquesting" is a huge part of your overall marketing and advertising strategy and the best way to "conquest" your competition is to create a video SEO strategy.

Okay, now that I have you on the edge of your seat, and have you consuming each and every word of this new video SEO strategy, I am going to explain to you step by step how you can do this yourself for free or how you can hire someone (outsource) to do it for you and hold them accountable. Either way, this is seriously going to impact your initiative.

You might be shocked to find out that there are a lot of similarities between a web page or website that is properly search engine optimized and a video that is properly search engine optimized. Both a website and a video have the same genetic (metaphorically speaking) components (see Figure 5.2):

- A website has a URL (website address) . . . so does a video.
- A website utilizes HTML code . . . so does a video.
- A website has meta-descriptions . . . so does a video.
- A website has text content . . . so does a video.
- A website has links / back links . . . so does a video.
- A website has meta-tags or keywords . . . so does a video.
- A website needs unique and relevant content . . . so does a video.
- A website can be geo-targeted . . . so does a video.

---

[10] *Source:* www.thinkwithgoogle.com/research-studies/new-vehicle-cross-shopping.html.

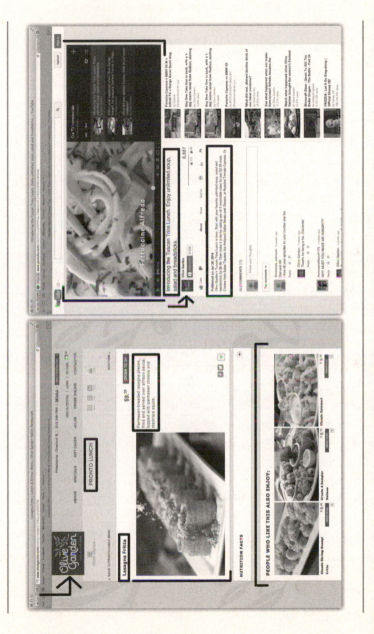

FIGURE 5.2 This image shows the comparison between a standard website and a properly optimized YouTube video page. Both pages have many of the same components, such as images, descriptions, headers and the option to include meta-descriptions, tags, and keywords.

103

- A website needs to be properly search engine optimized and adhere to Google's algorithm(s) if it wants to properly rank and achieve Google page one domination. Yup, you guessed it—so does a video.

If you understand Google, what Google wants, and why, as well as how to properly optimize a website or web page, and you apply that to creating and cultivating your video SEO strategy, you are way ahead of the curve. I created the instructional design of this book a certain way. I structured the curriculum in a priority format, in which each chapter builds onto the next chapter, and synergistically it becomes even more important and valuable as a resource the deeper you get into the book.

There is a lot of confusion when it comes to video. Unfortunately, a lot of people do not realize that video can and should be thoroughly search engine optimized. They think that all you need to do is upload it to the Internet and it's "all good." That is far from the reality. I think most people are going to be shocked as they read this chapter to find out that there are so many similarities in value and strategy for video SEO and traditional website SEO. But there is a big difference, and that difference is that video far exceeds the value of a traditional web page. Furthermore, there is a multiplicity effect of easily being able to create additional supplemental videos and easily uploading them to a myriad of video search engines like Vimeo, YouTube, Truveo, Metacafe, and so forth.

Try to imagine having the ability, resources, and money to create numerous, even hundreds of full-blown websites. Creating numerous search engine optimized videos is exactly like creating numerous full-blown or main websites for yourself or your business. Jackpot! You just landed on free parking!

Let's remind ourselves of the game objective and what our primary mission is for the battle of the best-positioned real estate: Googleopoly. Video would truly make sense because it is fast, easy, and cheap—an indisputable combination! Additionally, if you want to secure Google real estate, there is no other real estate better for mass creation with profound and immediate results like video.

Think of video SEO like "video on demand" television commercials! For example, you can optimize video so if someone that lives in Medford, NJ, or the surrounding areas was hungry and in the mood for Japanese or Hibachi and they Googled "Hibachi Medford NJ," they are going to see on the first page of Google two videos with thumbnails for a new

Hibachi restaurant. Those two thumbnails stick out, and I guarantee you that the majority of people are going to click those videos and watch them. Most of them will click those videos first and never even look at the static content on the rest of the Google search page. When people click either of those videos that are on the first page of organic Google, they are going to be blown away, because they are going to see family and friends in the video, clapping and smiling as the Hibachi chef wows and awes them with his culinary skills and theatrics. It is an *amazing* video for anyone who is looking to decide on what restaurant to choose for dinner.

Let us dissect this a little further . . .

There are 5,600 results showing for "Hibachi Medford NJ." As just stated, it is great that if someone local is searching for a Hibachi in Medford, New Jersey, Jasmine shows up numerous times but especially with two video thumbnails that rank on the first page of Google. It is like having a TV commercial on demand. What I mean by that is that TV and radio, for example, just spam people with commercials, regardless of whether they are interested in a particular product or service. However, video SEO is different. People are going to the mighty Google oracle and asking for a Hibachi in Medford, New Jersey, and not only does the mighty oracle provide listing options but also it goes a step further and returns two beautiful, multimedia "web-mercials." These web-mercials have *real* people, real families, actually at Jasmine's Hibachi. The web-mercial shows the actual restaurant with the actual chef, demonstrating live his culinary and Hibachi skills. This is relevant and captivating video . . . and it is on demand. It answers the searcher *exactly*, not spamming with a "spray and pray" approach.

I have an even more incredible example of video SEO:

What if someone in the state of New Jersey was interested in eating Hibachi, but not just any Hibachi—they *only* wanted to eat at the *best* Hibachi restaurant in the state of New Jersey. So, they Googled "Best Hibachi New Jersey." You are going to find one of Jasmine's videos on the first page of natural Google, out of 230,000 results. This example is so powerful because it is not limited to only a geo-targeted search within a town in New Jersey. The video shows up prominently for a search of the "best" Hibachi restaurants in the state of New Jersey. What is also amazing about this example is that it is the *only* video that shows up on the search return—meaning that it is different from all other listings.

It stands out, and people will click the video over all of those other result returns.

Example

www.google.com/search?es_sm=91&sclient=psy-ab&q=+hibachi+ medford+nj&btnG=

www.google.fr/?gfe_rd=cr&ei=rg7sU-P-C-2A8Qe37oHwBw#q=best+ hibachi+new+jersey

Let's go over the video SEO outline and then go back to each point and dissect each one with step-by-step details and examples:

- Strategy
  - Search engine enlightenment
- Start-up/resources
  - Equipment
    - Camera
    - Software
    - Audio
    - Lighting
  - Video search engines
    - YouTube
    - Vimeo
    - Truveo
    - Metacafe
    - Viddler
    - Revver
- Begin with the end in mind
  - Create a list of keywords or phrases that you want to show up on the first page of Google
    - Create campaigns
    - Prioritize them
    - Outline them
- Video content creation
  - Audio
  - Lighting
  - Equipment
  - Editing

- Optimizing
  - Title
  - Description
    - Contact information
    - Unique content
    - Destination mapping
    - Back links
  - Category
  - Meta-tags/keywords
  - Root file optimization
  - Location (geo-targeting)
  - Date
  - Closed-captioning
- Syndication
  - Different video search engines
  - Social media
- Supplemental uploads
  - Strategy
  - Calendar
  - Resources

HOW TO PROPERLY CREATE A VIDEO SEO CAMPAIGN

Strategy

The first step in proper video SEO, is having a strategy. I am shocked and appalled that there are so many people who have no strategy and no idea what they are doing and are simply shoving video after video online with no optimization. Basically most people are flooding the Internet with irrelevant (to Google) video content or spam video. Some people don't realize they are doing this, while others do know but do not care. I am here to tell you that you don't need to swim upstream. You can thoroughly optimize videos with profound immediate effect as well as long-term residual effect.

In order for you to create the best possible strategy for yourself or your product, service, company, or whatever you are trying to gain visibility for, I am going to let you in on some very interesting facts and details that if you use them to your advantage will give you a huge competitive edge.

Did you know that search engines, specifically Google, have:

- Pattern recognition search technology (facial and image recognition)
- Voice recognition search technology (speech and audio)

PATTERN AND VOICE RECOGNITION SEARCH

Obviously Google and other search engines do not see videos, images, and faces of people and things the same way we do, because they are computers and software versus real, live people with sensory perception. But they do "see." To the search engines, video, images, and pixels are just data—forms and patterns. Google has sophisticated technology that allows it to see these patterns, pixels, and images clearly. Through time, experience, and evolution, Google has trained itself to recognize patterns with images, faces, etc. The technology is *pattern/facial recognition software*. There are different levels of sophistication in this technology. Some of the most advanced examples of this technology are military and government facial recognition technology that is utilized to find terrorists and other criminals on the CIA's or FBI's most wanted list.

Some commercial examples are social media and mobile apps that allow users to tag their friends online through technology called *facial detection*. Another awesome example of facial detection technology is how Google protects the public's privacy on services like Street View. This is how Google detects and then blurs out the faces of any person that was in proximity of a Google Street View car when it was capturing footage. Facial detection is also the technology that empowers Google+ to be able to prompt you to tag images and videos. Unlike facial recognition, facial detection won't tell you who the pictures or videos are of. However, it will prompt you to find them in your photos or tag them.

How many times have you logged into Facebook to find you have been tagged in an image from a friend? Or how many times have you uploaded a picture onto Facebook and been prompted to tag a friend? Exactly!

Let's look at this a little deeper here. First, the fact that there is technology like this is truly awesome. Now let's get real here and understand what this means. All of these pictures, images, logos, videos, pixels—the data—are being stored in databases for Google (including Google+ of course), Facebook, Instagram, Pinterest, Flickr, PhotoBucket, Yahoo!,

Bing, YouTube, and more. All of this data is collected, stored, categorized, and organized. As all of this data keeps piling in, it starts to form patterns for the recognition and detection software as well as the search engines. For example, if you have images of President Barack Obama that were uploaded to numerous websites, social media platforms, and search engines, and in the title tags, H1s, H2s, meta-descriptions, anchor text, meta-tags, keywords, alt tags, and so forth was "Barack Obama," it wouldn't take too long for facial recognition/detection/search engines, including Google, to correlate the image of "Barack Obama" with the text or words *Barack Obama* or *Barack* and *Obama*.

Let's go a little deeper with how powerful this is and how intricate it truly is. Most of these social media sites can be connected with each other. Some have partial integration, while others have full integration. This also is true with iTunes and Android apps. If you want to use a particular app or integrate a social media platform with a different social media platform or if you want to use an API or an app on a social media platform, these apps and social media platforms ask you to give them permission to access information, details, and friend lists from those *other* social media platforms or apps! Sometimes these apps or social media platforms ask for crazy privileges on your other platforms or apps. And it blows me away that most people just give it to them. So, not only are all of these different companies and technologies collecting all of this data from you, but also they are sharing with each other. Sometimes with your permission, and sometimes they buy or sell it (sometimes even that is with people's permission). I tell you all of this for only one reason—to understand there is so much information that is gathered, stored, organized, categorized, bought, sold, or shared that when enough people, websites, images, or videos label something similar and it is consistent, it then becomes so. It becomes what it is now known for.

Another example of this is a logo for a business, like the Nike Swoosh or the "H" logo for Honda. Both of these examples are logos for huge companies. I am sure there are thousands and thousands of pictures, images, sketches, pixels, and video for the Nike logo and for Honda's logo. As a matter of fact, a quick Google search for "Nike logo" shows that there are 135 million pages and documents in its index that include the words *Nike logo*. The first things that show up are numerous images and versions of the Nike logo. If you refine your Google search to images, it will display thousands of graphical images in different colors and formats!

How does this happen? Google has learned that the Nike logo, both with and without the words *Nike* in the logo, is still the Nike logo. Let me be clear: Google and other search engines recognize the "swoosh" as the Nike logo, even if the letters or words are not in the logo. That is very powerful for image recognition and detection.

Let's keep that spinning for a while, and let us focus on voice/audio recognition search technology. Similar to the power of facial and image recognition and detection is speech/audio recognition technology and software. Have you ever uploaded a video onto YouTube and added a song from your favorite band or a single that was buzzing on the radio? Well, chances are that if you did, YouTube would have informed you that it has matched "third-party content." Basically, YouTube is saying, "Wait a minute—this is not your song, you do not own it, and we know that you do not own it." Did you ever wonder how in the world YouTube could know within seconds of you uploading a video to its platform that the accompanying song does not belong to you? It's simple—because YouTube uses a very powerful speech and audio recognition and detection technology. Audio or MP3 files contain search engine metadata. Similar to how I just explained that pictures and images can be optimized, you can also optimize audio files, songs, music, and sounds with keywords and tags that will identify them to the search engines. In addition to that, sites like YouTube and other video and audio search engines allow people to create "closed-captioned" documents to accompany the audio files. Certain sites allow people to upload complete lyrics to songs, transcripts to audio files, and so on. Similarly, alt tags give blind people a thorough (alternative) description, so they can fully understand what that image represents or looks like without physically being able to see that image.

Metadata within the MP3 or audio files is there to describe the audio that a deaf person cannot hear. They cannot hear the words, but they will be able to read them clearly. But voice and speech recognition software goes way deeper than that. It is so advanced that from your desktop or your mobile device you can ask Google any question you want without typing, just by your voice. As I sit here writing this book (typing), I am in Paris, France. In an effort to create awesome examples for this book, I Google voice-searched for "how tall is the Eiffel Tower," and within seconds it jumped to Google Page One search listings. And then it actually said 301 meters! Being an American, I never use the metric system and I am lazy, so I asked the Google oracle, "how tall is the Eiffel Tower in feet and inches," and without skipping a beat, the Google oracle's voice belted out, "The Eiffel Tower is 986 feet tall!"

Apple's Siri is a huge success because people love the simplicity of just talking and asking a question without the typing, especially while working, walking, driving, or whatever. It is just a heck of a lot easier to ask a question out loud versus typing out questions or sentences, sorting through the pages, and clicking links. By asking Google or Siri a specific question, not only is it easier than typing and researching "manually," but also the answer is easier, because they both will verbally answer you as well as provide you the appropriate content, whether that is a search result page on Google, an image, video, map, or other specific form of content.

Just like with images and pictures, the audio and MP3 metadata and SEO files are created, stored, organized, shared, bought, and sold. The search engines are evolving on a daily basis and have millions of categorized, credited, and validated songs, podcasts, soundtracks, sound files, MP3 files, and so on.

To sum it up, in case you did not know before reading this book, Google is so advanced that it can understand and recognize not only websites and web pages but also images, pictures, songs, audio files, and all forms of MP3 files, which means that Google can sort through images, pixels, pictures, faces, logos, music, audio, MP3 files, and so on . . . and can identify what is what and who is who.

Secret Tip

Unlike traditional SEO strategy or ability, a video has a different dimension or depth of optimization possibilities. You can optimize video with multiple additional layers or opportunities that simply do not exist in a traditional web page that has only text. I have just outlined how hypersensitive and advanced Google's capabilities are in sorting and recognizing audio, video, images, and pictures. So, if you incorporate this into your strategy you will appease the search engines all of the time.

(continued)

(*Continued*)

For example, if you want to optimize for "**Best Hibachi in New Jersey**," then you should shoot/create a specific video and:

- Make sure that you actually *say the words Best Hibachi in New Jersey*.
- Make sure that you have pictures of a Hibachi in your video or that you shoot video in a Hibachi.

Video SEO is different from traditional SEO, so if you have never heard of these strategies or you are not experienced with them, do not worry. I will be walking you through the entire process step by step. I am going to teach you brain surgery with a spoon.

Let me go back and make sure you understand what I just taught you. Based on the fact that Google holds incredible value in categorizing *everything*, like all audio, video, pictures, and images it comes in contact with, and based on the fact that Google has some amazing high-level software that possesses speech recognition, facial recognition, and pixel recognition technology, you have the opportunity to give Google *more* of what it wants! Make sure that every single video you create and optimize will possess as much detail as possible (without over-SEOing) for Google's audio and visual recognition to kick in and recognize your content.

Please remember that there are no magic beans and you cannot trick Google. All you can do is give Google what Google wants. And Google is obsessed with the details. There is a famous Japanese philosophy called *Kaizen*. Kaizen is the art of continuous improvement, which means that if you want a 100 percent change, you do not find one thing and change that one thing 100 percent. That is not realistic. What Kaizen teaches is that you should find 100 things and create a 1 percent change for each of those 100 things combined. That equals 100 percent change. I think that the Kaizen philosophy is paramount in trying to achieve Google page one domination. You can't simply do one thing and have 100 percent success or a 100 percent Google page one domination. However, if you find 100 things (not 100 literally—just as an example) you can focus on that equal 1 percent success in dominating page one of Google, and you combine them all, you will have a 100 percent Google strategy for page one dominance. There are 28 viable property opportunities to secure on the Monopoly board. You cannot win the game by simply owning one property. It is the combination of the properties that is going to give you the greatest odds of winning. The same goes for Googleopoly. One organic position isn't enough to shut out the competition. However, while it is difficult to secure all 10 organic positions (100 percent change), securing organic positions one by one and the combination of the earned positions will reap great rewards.

You still want to make sure that you adhere to the rules and strategy of traditional SEO when optimizing your video content. In addition to all of the proper optimization techniques you will use to optimize your video(s) to make them favorable to Google, you now have a completely new and unique way to further optimize and further provide value to Google.

Have you ever played Scrabble? Most people have—it is such an incredible game. It can be addicting! Scrabble has rules, and once you understand the rules and as long as you have a good vocabulary as well as good spelling skills, you can enjoy the game and have an opportunity of winning the game. Everybody was loving it—they had their strategies for how to win. People even created strategies to use Scrabble's rules to their advantage, like with triple word points, etc.

Then what happened? A new game emerged called *Upwords*. That totally changed the game. In Scrabble you could create letters only in front or in back of other letters. For example, if there was the word *hat*, you could add a *ch* at the end of *hat* and make that word *hatch*. Now in this new game, with new rules, came the opportunity to build "upwards"! That meant that just like Scrabble, you could still put letters in the front and the back of words to change them and evolve them into new words. But, in addition to that, you were now able to build "upwards." You were now able to stack letters on top of each other. For example, in that word *hat*, you could place a *c* on top of the *h* and turn that entire word to *cat*. Now, these are simple examples to explain to you the difference between Scrabble and Upwords. Both games focused on vocabulary, spelling, and creativity. However, if Scrabble was a two-dimensional game, then Upwords was a three-dimensional, maybe even a four-dimensional game. Both games were similar with the same objective, to win by scoring points, by creating vocabulary words out of single letters. However, Upwords had more opportunity to be creative as well as giving the players more opportunity to win. The same goes for video SEO. Think of traditional SEO as Scrabble and video SEO as Upwords. Both strategies are awesome, important, and rewarding (when you achieve Google Page One Dominance), but video SEO is *more*. Video SEO allows the person, company, or marketer more opportunity, more tools, more ways to be creative, and more ways to be rewarded.

Does this mean that you throw away your Scrabble board? Absolutely not! First and foremost, traditional SEO is not going away. It is needed, and it is important for you to master traditional SEO (that is why I made Chapter 4 all about traditional or onsite SEO), but you do need to acknowledge there is another game out there called *video SEO* (Upwords). Me, personally, I used to love Scrabble until I was introduced to Upwords. Upwards to me just makes more sense—it is more fun and gives you so much more opportunity to be creative and win! With that being said, I would have never been able to be great at Upwords if I had never mastered Scrabble. Upwords was the next evolution in word games, just as video SEO is the next evolution in SEO.

Getting Started/Resources

Video SEO might sound high-tech, and it might sound intimidating as far as the resources that you will need to be successful. The truth is that it is not as complex as it sounds, and it absolutely does not require high-tech equipment or software to work properly.

Here is a quick resource/technology checklist of everything you will need for your video SEO initiative:

- Video camera
- Studio lighting
- Microphone
- Video search engine
- Video editing software (optional)
- Green screen (optional)
- Computer (optional)
- External hard drive (optional)

Video camera: Your cell phone is more than adequate to create some amazing content for your video SEO campaign. As long as you have a smartphone that is fairly new, like an iPhone or a Samsung Galaxy (or any cell phone that has an HD video camera) you are fine. Modern cell phones are so advanced that you truly do not need to invest in a separate video camera. However, there are different levels of camera quality available, such as a 4K, DSLR, or even film. But again, the vast majority of people do *not* need to shoot on that high-quality camera. Music videos, reality TV shows, and full-length movies utilize those types of cameras. You will be able to dominate the first page of Google with any video camera as long as you properly optimize the video. On the other hand, having awesome video content can add to the "sizzle" aspect, the "shock and awe" aspect. But the video quality will not compromise the SEO aspect of the initiative (as long as you are shooting in high definition—above 720p).

I strongly suggest that you put first things first and instead of investing in an expensive camera or super high-quality camera, I urge you to focus on other resources you will need, like lighting and microphones. You should be content with utilizing your cell phone video camera. You might want to invest in some accessories for your cell phone to enhance it:

- **Lenses:** You can buy all sorts of external lenses for your iPhone or Android. There are telephoto, wide angle, and even DSLR-caliber lenses for your cell phone.
  - Photo Jojo (http://photojojo.com/store/)
  - Ollo Clip (http://www.olloclip.com)
  - iPro (http://www.iprolens.com)
  - Oprix (http://www.optrix.com/superior-camera-lenses/)
  - Adorama (http://www.adorama.com/ALM501003.html)
- **Tripods, mounts, and/or stabilizers:** There are so many devices that you can use to enhance your cell phone:
  - Traditional tripod
  - There are a myriad of mounting options. Some are "flex" devices, which you can mold into different forms for customized grip.
    - www.istabilizer.com/products/istabilizer-flex
- **Monopod:** These are *awesome*! A monopod enables the user to be able to take the ultimate "selfie." You can even shoot video yourself, without holding out your arm or getting assistance from another person.
  - http://www.istabilizer.com/products/istabilizer-monopod

- **Dolly:** This is just like a traditional video production team's dolly, but smaller. It is a mobile video production mount. A dolly will allow for smooth, controlled tracking shots, giving an extra touch of professionalism to the shot.
  - http://www.istabilizer.com/products/istabilizer-dolly
- **Stabilizers:** These are ideal for eliminating all of the shakiness in videos. Especially if there is movement in the video production, you don't want someone getting dizzy from watching your video. A stabilizer accessory can eliminate or minimize the shakiness of a video, even if you are running with the camera rolling!
  - http://www.igalleria.ca/product-p/12120708.htm
- There are many more options . . .
- **Audio/microphones:** What is more important than having an expensive video camera or high-tech video equipment is having great audio. Now that you understand that Google has speech recognition software/technology, it is imperative that you have clear audio in your videos. If you shoot video and the audio is horrible, then Google will have a difficult or impossible time in correlating what you are saying or capturing in your video with what is in its vast databases. Let's say, for example, you don't use an external microphone instead of your cell phone. You are going to have limited range and limited capabilities. Another problem is that if you shoot video in a noisy area, like in your office, in a studio, outside, or anywhere where it is not quiet, you risk the external noise being picked up and diluting your audio content and your audio SEO possibilities. Be careful if you are outside and it is windy. You might not realize it because it might not seem noisy while you are outside, but I assure you that when you watch and listen to your video you will be shocked by all the noise of the wind. There are several great inexpensive options that everyone should look into investing in:
  - **iRig Mic:** It is the first handheld microphone for iPhone, iPad, and Android devices. It is exactly like having a studio microphone but for your mobile device.
    - http://www.ikmultimedia.com/products/irigmic/
  - **Wireless lavalier microphones:** These are my favorite devices; they are small, convenient, and powerful—a must-have for your mobile studio. It is important to purchase both the transmitter and receiver. The total package can be a bit pricey, but the quality and maneuverability make it well worth it.

- http://www.hdhatstore.com/Wireless-Lavalier-Microphone-for-iPhone-and-iPad.html
- **Shotgun microphone:** These are designed to capture audio from a specific source. They are very good at cancelling out background noise and boosting the overall tonal quality. These types of microphones are suitable for adding wind noise reduction accessories.
  - http://www.bhphotovideo.com/explora/audio/buying-guides/shotgun-microphones

You want to have the absolute best audio you can possibly create for your video for two main purposes. First and foremost for the user experience: there is nothing worse than clicking a video whose audio sucks. If the audio is too low, or if the audio is too loud, a person might get annoyed and just abandon your video and never finish watching your message or watch it again. Remember, you have only one shot to make a first impression. There is nothing worse than ruining an awesome video because the audio was off. It doesn't matter if you have great content and most of your audio was awesome. If there is *any* bad audio, static, or inconsistencies in the audio I recommend that you scrap it and reshoot the video or repurpose the video. In any case, you should not launch a video with audio that has any problems whatsoever. The other reason, already mentioned, is the SEO factor. You want the audio to be crisp and clear for SEO recognition and validation. Almost everyone has experienced the annoying scenario of calling a company like an airliner or bank that has voice prompting and *clearly* answering the damn questions but the computer does not accurately pick up your voice commands. Or, I am sure that there are people who have tried to use General Motor's On-Star or Apple's Siri and tried to *clearly* give voice commands or voice prompts, and to your utter frustration, they didn't understand you. It drives me crazy!! Just the other day, I was repeating myself like five times to Siri. I started screaming at her and calling her dumb! What was scary was that I was calmly and clearly asking her a question with the handset on my face, not Bluetooth, and she still mixed up what I was asking her. So, my point is that if Apple and General Motors technology can flub things and specifically words from audio prompts, Google is going to have a difficult time validating and recognizing your audio content for SEO purposes if the audio is less than satisfactory.

One last tip in regard to the audio of your video: It would be a good idea to test the audio when you first start shooting to make sure it is working properly. I assure you it is better to find out in the very beginning if the audio is not perfect or if there is a problem rather than shooting your entire video, interview, or promo, and then finding out the audio was off and you can't use that video.

- **Lighting:** Equally as important as the audio integrity of your video content is the visual integrity of your video content. Just as Google has speech recognition technology, it also has facial and image recognition/detection technology. For the technology to work, there needs to be visual integrity. For example, if you upload pictures of your spouse on Facebook, over and over again, Facebook starts to recognize pictures of your wife by her name—let's say, in my case, my wife, Karina. So, let's say I have uploaded 50 images of Karina and tagged Karina in those images. Facebook "learns" and understands who Karina is and what she looks like. So, if I post images of Karina, Facebook will prompt me to tag Karina by her name. However, there are times that I will upload a picture of Karina and Facebook won't prompt me to tag Karina. As a matter of fact, there are times that Facebook does not recognize Karina. This is because there is something wrong with the picture. There is nothing wrong with Karina, only the image of her (at least for Facebook). What I mean by that is that if the image quality is compromised due to the fact that she had her eyes closed, or it was a weird angle, or the lighting was bad, then Facebook won't recognize Karina. Let's say the picture was taken at night without a flash. That could be a problem for recognition. If a picture was taken outside during the day but it was cloudy, that could be a problem for facial recognition. The bottom line is that if the picture, image, logo, object, etc. in the picture is dark, blurry, out of focus, or in any way shape or form compromised visually, you most likely are not going to be able to benefit from Google recognizing your content and correlating your content for proper (image/visual) SEO ranking.

There are cost-effective lighting kits that you can buy brand-new or you can go onto eBay and buy a pre-owned kit.

- **Lighting kits:** You can find adequate lighting kits that start at $30–$40 and upwards. You are not Steven Spielberg. You do not need a major lighting kit package. You want to make sure that your videos come out clearly and try to eliminate harsh shadows. You want to showcase your video content in the most advantageous way possible.

- http://www.ebay.com/sch/Lighting-Kits-/19591/i.html
- **Flashes:** You do not need to buy any external flashes, but you need to remember to use your flash when needed. All modern cell phones come with flashes. So, all you have to do is develop a habit of using yours.
- **Green screen:** Green screens are awesome . . . if you know how to edit them or if you plan on investing in a professional video production company to do all of your editing of green screen footage. But it is not necessary for achieving Google page one domination, similarly to how 4K, film, and DSRL footage is gorgeous on a SEO level but will not enhance optimization. Now, on the other hand, it provides the "wow" factor or user experience. You will be able to shock and awe someone if you create awesome, unique, and captivating content. Green screen is a viable option, if you know how to use it or if you have a company (or person) that you can outsource to. My recommendation is that at first focus on developing your content library with standard video content from your cell phone and start to optimize those videos. Once you have mastered the basic techniques and you are seeing results, then at that time start to experiment with using a green screen or start to look into the possibility of outsourcing your green screen footage.

The main purpose of green screen is to create captivating visual content. But green screen is not the only way you can do that. There are other ways you can create visually stimulating and artistically beautiful content besides green screen:

- Whiteboard animation: This is a unique animation style that is useful when explaining something in an intriguing and exciting manner.
  - http://www.whiteboardanimation.com
- 3D and 2D animation: This can range anywhere from simple 2D motion graphics to complex 3D cinematic effects. Either way, it can add that extra punch you need to captivate the audience.
- Stock footage: Stock footage is a good option if you are looking to include professional video clips or images but don't necessarily have the time or resources to shoot the footage. Purchasing stock footage is an easy yet effective alternative to shooting your own content, and the extensive amount of online libraries makes it very accessible.

You could even have videos with simple resources like:

- Watermarks (bugs)
- Lower thirds
- Overlaying graphics
- Overlaying text

Software: The rule you want to live by is "keep it simple," which means don't buy something unless you need it; do not get things just to get them or just in case someday you might use it. You do *not* need *any* software whatsoever for video SEO. You can literally shoot a video off of your cell phone, upload it directly to YouTube from your cell phone, and, using YouTube's Video Manager, optimize your video completely within five minutes (this is after you master the basics on how to actually optimize video).

However, if you were artistic or obsessed with enhancements, you have a variety of software programs that you can use for editing amazing video content. Here is a quick list of my top five software applications:

1. iMovie
2. Final Cut Pro
3. Adobe Premier Pro
4. Adobe After Effects
5. Adobe Photoshop

There are even editing applications that allow you to edit on your mobile device, such as Magisto and Lumify. If you want a more advanced option, the latest version of Final Cut Pro is available for the iPad, allowing for more advanced editing on the go.

Once again, you do *not* need *any* video editing software for you to achieve Google page one domination. However, if you create beautiful, unique, relevant content, it will differentiate you from the competition and allow you to "shock and awe" or "wow" your prospects. Keep in mind that the more captivating the content, the more likely someone will share and embed the video.

Video search engines: YouTube is not the only video search engine. There are a lot of different video search engines. Here is a partial list of the ones that I feel have the most SEO value:

- Vimeo
- Metacafe
- Viddler

- Dailymotion
- Break
- Revver
- Truveo

In addition to these video search engines, you have social media platforms or image search engines that can upload and optimize video content:

- Flickr
- Pinterest
- Photobucket

Secret Tip

Part of the Googleopoly strategy is to diversify your video SEO visibility by diversifying your video search engines, which means that you do *not* want to upload and optimize video content only onto YouTube. You want to diversify to numerous video engines. But the trick is *not* to duplicate content. Just like traditional SEO will not give any SEO value or SEO ranking to duplicate content, the same holds true for video content. You can't simply upload the same video to numerous video search engines and expect them all to rank and gain SEO equity.

You do not need to use every single video engine out there. I suggest starting out with three or four different video search engines and sticking with those. Build up your video asset library of optimized video content on those video platforms, and then as your campaigns mature, you can enhance your strategy by adding additional engines if you see the need.

Computer/backup hard drive: Computers are a matter of personal preference. There is no computer better than another for proper video SEO. Some people prefer a PC, and some people prefer an Apple. Other people prefer an iPad or tablet, while others prefer doing video SEO from their cell phones. My personal preference is both my Apple iPhone and my Mac laptop. But I have no reason to justify my choices other than personal preference. The reality is that you can use any device that has Internet capabilities. In regard to a backup hard drive, I highly recommend investing in a backup hard drive for numerous reasons. The first is that you do not want to save your video assets on your local hard drive. It will clutter things up as well as choke down your processors. Plus you always want to have a backup just in case something happens. Additionally, video files, such as MP4s and MOV files, eat up a lot of memory very quickly and you do not want to run out of space. And finally, your video assets are worth a lot. They are unique content; you want to protect your assets. If you store your content, you will be able to easily go back to reuse or repurpose your content for future video SEO projects.

Now that you have all of your resources and equipment ready, it is time to create your video SEO campaigns. Remember, you want to always begin with the end in mind.

You want to play Monopoly, not Candyland. With video SEO, you need to think three or four moves in advance. You need to anticipate exactly what people are going to type into Google and then maximize those keywords for your video SEO strategy. Think about who your audience is: who are the people who are going to be going online and typing in questions to the almighty Google oracle? And, most importantly, what are these people going to type into Google? If it was you looking for your product, service, company, music, information, etc., what would you type into Google? This is a very important question that you need to answer. I suggest that you ask people around you the same question, such as family, friends, peers, colleagues, to get different opinions.

Create a list of the keywords and phrases that you think people will type in order to find things that you do or sell. It is important that you create a comprehensive list. Most people never take the time out to think of all the different ways people could search to find you, or your company, product, or service. Once you have created a master list of keywords and phrases, then you will move onto creating video content.

Before getting into content creation details, let's break down an example so you can fully understand what I am talking about.

Example

Let's say you were an automotive sales professional who worked at a Honda dealership in Burlington, New Jersey. Here is an example list of keywords and phrases that people might type into Google:

- Honda dealership
  - Burlington
  - New Jersey

- South Jersey
- Cherry Hill
- Honda Accord
  - Burlington
  - New Jersey
  - South Jersey
  - Cherry Hill
- Honda Civic
  - Burlington
  - New Jersey
  - South Jersey
  - Cherry Hill
- Honda Odyssey
  - Burlington
  - New Jersey
  - South Jersey
  - Cherry Hill
- All other models of the Honda lineup
- New Honda
  - Burlington
  - New Jersey
  - South Jersey
  - Cherry Hill
- Used Honda
  - Burlington
  - New Jersey
  - South Jersey
  - Cherry Hill
- Toyota dealership (because it is the direct competitor of a Honda)
  - Burlington
  - New Jersey
  - South Jersey
  - Cherry Hill
- New Toyota
  - Burlington
  - New Jersey
  - South Jersey
  - Cherry Hill

- Used Toyota
  - Burlington
  - New Jersey
  - South Jersey
  - Cherry Hill
- All other competitors of Honda
- I need a car
  - Burlington
  - New Jersey
  - South Jersey
  - Cherry Hill
- I need a car loan
  - Burlington
  - New Jersey
  - South Jersey
  - Cherry Hill
- What is better, a new or used car?
  - Burlington
  - New Jersey
  - South Jersey
  - Cherry Hill
- Should I lease or finance my car?
  - Burlington
  - New Jersey
  - South Jersey
  - Cherry Hill
- Bad credit / no credit
  - Burlington
  - New Jersey
  - South Jersey
  - Cherry Hill
- Lowest price car
  - Burlington
  - New Jersey
  - South Jersey
  - Cherry Hill
- Cheapest car
  - Burlington
  - New Jersey

- South Jersey
- Cherry Hill
- Best price car
  - Burlington
  - New Jersey
  - South Jersey
  - Cherry Hill
- How do I not get ripped off at a car dealership?
  - Burlington
  - New Jersey
  - South Jersey
  - Cherry Hill
- Honda reviews
  - Burlington
  - New Jersey
  - South Jersey
  - Cherry Hill
- Car dealership reviews
  - Burlington
  - New Jersey
  - South Jersey
  - Cherry Hill

If you were a Honda car salesman, your audience is *anyone* who is in the market for *any* type of automobile. It doesn't matter if they are in the market for a Honda or not. As a matter of fact, your audience is *anyone* who is looking for *anything* automotive related: new or used vehicle, service, parts, aftermarket products, and even special financing. Why? Simple: You are looking for an opportunity to do business. That is all—nothing more, nothing less. It is your job after you create that opportunity to sell the value of who you are and what you do to the point that the prospect wants to buy from you (which is an entirely different book). You need to identify every single possible thing people can search that might possibly lead them to *you*! Think of yourself like beach sand. That is right—I said beach sand. Have you ever been to the beach and gotten out of the ocean and had sand particles stuck to you? Have you then gone home and taken a shower and the next day still found sand on you? *Exactly*! It is hard to get rid of all the sand. It might take days to remove all of the sand particles. That is what you want to be to the public. You want to be like beach sand. You want to show up *everywhere* they look on Google. You want people to find you not by one way alone. You want them to have many different doors that they can walk through to find you.

I hope you didn't skip a word or phrase. It might seem redundant that I put all of those examples in this book, but it's not; it is important that I show that there are so many combinations, so many keywords, and so many phrases. What is crazy is that I honestly did not even scratch the surface. I couldn't possibly put all of the possibilities in a book. But that is the point! That is exactly what you need to do—and more—for video SEO to work properly. That is also what makes video SEO special, different, and better than traditional SEO.

Traditional SEO is limited by the amount of keywords or phrases that you can have on a website. Google will penalize you for over-SEOing or "keyword stuffing." And in regard to PPC, my gosh—it could get ridiculously expensive trying to buy or bid on a fraction of those keywords, especially if there is high competition or high traffic on those words and phrases. Video SEO enables you to target and crush all of the keywords. It is simple; you just create new videos for additional keywords that you want to target. So, instead of over-saturating one video, you simply can create more videos and optimize different keywords for different videos.

Okay, now you understand that there is a tremendous amount of keywords and phrases that you can utilize for your video SEO strategy. Take your master list of all of the keywords and phrases and put them in priority order. You might have 10, 20, 50, or 100 keywords or phrases. You do not want to randomly create video content. You want to create video content for the most important or most powerful keywords. Let's use the same example of the Honda car salesman.

If you were a Honda car salesman, you work on commission. So, time is literally money. You do not want to waste time on things that are not going to return opportunity or sales. As a matter of fact, you want to do things that are not going to merely generate opportunity. You want your efforts to return the maximum possible return on your investment, whether that is your time or money. You want to sell as many cars possible so you can make as much money as humanly possible. So, you might want to think about what the hottest models are in the Honda lineup. What are the most searched Honda vehicles? What Honda vehicle does the dealership sell the most of? Well, one of Honda's biggest sellers for years has been the Honda Odyssey. As a matter of fact, the Honda Odyssey has been rated as one of the absolute best minivans year after year and boasts one of the highest resale values of any minivan on the market. So, an easy first choice for a keyword target would be "2014 Honda Odyssey." If the dealership is located in New Jersey, "2014 Honda Odyssey New Jersey" or "2014 Honda Odyssey NJ" are all great choices. Why? Simple: That is what people will be searching for if they are interested in getting more information on a 2014 Honda Odyssey or if they wanted to actually buy a 2014 Honda Odyssey. Remember what I shared with you earlier on, that when people are searching for certain products and or services, especially an automobile, they will "geo-target" their search so they can find a local business. You can put "2014 Honda Odyssey NJ" at the top of your list of video SEO content. If you were going to create another awesome choice for video content, it would be a conquesting strategy campaign. The number one competitor of the Honda Odyssey is the Toyota Sienna. Therefore, you would want to add "2014 Toyota Sienna NJ" to your list of video SEO content that you want to create. And so goes the process. You want to prioritize your "shot list." Once you have your total video search engine campaign shot list created and prioritized, the next step is going to be content creation.

CONTENT CREATION

Here is where you start to put together everything you have learned thus far. If your first campaign(s) is "2014 Honda Odyssey NJ" or "2014 Toyota Sienna NJ," you want to create compelling video content for those key-words. You want to trigger that **visual/image recognition** technology. If you were a Honda automotive sales professional, you might want to shoot the video (with your cell phone video camera) either in or next to a 2014 Honda Odyssey. You can possibly shoot the video next to both a Honda Odyssey and a Toyota Sienna. This way, you will have the visual elements of the vehicles for the video validation. Another option is that if you didn't have access to either one or both of those vehicles, you could either shoot on green screen and add them in graphically in postedit or you can simply shoot video next to a picture of one or both of those vehi-cles. Either way I would suggest that if those were your keywords that you were targeting, you would want to capture the actual visual images or actual vehicles in your video.

The next aspect is **audio/speech recognition**.

This is very important and different from traditional SEO. You want to say the actual keywords that you are trying to rank for in the actual video. But just as in traditional SEO, you can't just spam verbally random keywords for SEO purposes. You need to say the keywords in a way that is perfectly normal as well as applicable to the specific video. For example, this would be a perfect audio for the example scenario:

> If you are considering the 2014 Toyota Sienna, you should really reconsider and take a look at the 2014 Honda Odyssey. It is a better minivan. Edmunds.com rates the Honda Odyssey a far superior vehicle with a better resale value over the Toyota Sienna. And if you are in the Burlington, New Jersey, or the surrounding area, you should look at ABC Honda. Call me, Sean V. Bradley, at 555-1212, and I would be happy to answer any and all questions that you may have, or we can schedule a test drive and you will see for yourself why the Honda Odyssey is truly better than the Toyota Sienna.

You might be thinking, *wow*! That is a lot of words. Wrong! I just pulled out my trusty iPhone stopwatch and recorded myself reading that script at a moderate pace and I clocked it at only 35 seconds. Let's say you were slower than me. How much slower can you possibly be? Maybe 45 seconds. Still, 30–45 seconds is a perfect amount of time for a video SEO campaign video. Reread my script again—that is a tremendous amount of valuable, relevant, and unique information that was wrapped up and delivered in 35–45 seconds. Do you see the potential SEO value? There is plenty!

The important takeaway is connecting the visual/image recognition with the speech/audio recognition in the same targeted campaign. In this scenario, the Honda salesperson shot a video from his cell phone inside the 2014 Honda Odyssey (maybe with one of the flex mounts or monopods), and as the camera was facing the salesperson and the inside of the Honda Odyssey, he said that entire script. Let's put this all of this together:

- The goal is to get the video content to achieve Google page one dominance for either or both of these keyword phrases:
  - 2014 Honda Odyssey NJ
  - 2014 Toyota Sienna NJ
- You need to shoot video content with those keywords visually personified.
- You need to shoot video content where those actual keywords are said on camera for the speech recognition.
- This is the first step to validate to Google that this video deserves to be ranked on the first page of Google for those keywords or phrases.

After you have captured the relevant video content, the next step is going to be to upload the video asset to YouTube.

UPLOADING YOUR VIDEO TO YOUTUBE

YouTube has changed its algorithms recently, and one of its changes now makes the overall YouTube channel very important for individual videos to get ranked favorably. Before, the individual video asset was measured and evaluated based on its SEO value. Now YouTube/Google assigns relevance points for the overall value of the YouTube channel that the video is housed on. What this means is that if you create a YouTube channel and the overall channel gets views (the more the better), has subscribers (the more the better), receives comments (the more the better), or if the channel or the videos on the channel get shared (the more the better), the more the channel is recognized as a relevant content source.

To build on that even further, if the channel was set up the proper way with proper SEO strategy, the better it will be for the individual videos housed on that channel. If the channel gets activity and relevance, it will truly help the ranking of the individual videos that are housed on the channel.

Proper Setup and SEO for Your YouTube Channel

- **URL:** Just as with a main website or a focus site, the URL is also important for a YouTube channel. If you were a Honda salesperson, instead of creating a YouTube channel with your name, like www .youtube.com/seanvbraldey, you would have much more Google success if you created a YouTube channel with a URL, like www .youtube.com/hondadealermarltonnj. There is no SEO value with the domain name *seanvbradley*; however, there is a lot of geo-targeted SEO value for "hondadealermarltonnj." Think about it—if someone searched for "Honda Dealer Marlton NJ," your personal YouTube channel with the domain www.youtube.com/seanvbradley has very little shot of achieving Google page one dominance. On the other hand, you would have a much more realistic opportunity to rank on the first page of google with a YouTube channel with the domain www.youtube .com/hondadealermarltonnj. So, not only can the individual video rank on the first page of Google (discussed ahead), but also the actual YouTube channel itself (if properly optimized) can achieve Google page one dominance.

- **Channel description:** Just like a traditional website, the Meta-Description section is very important for SEO. If you were a Honda salesperson, you would want to write a description for your YouTube channel, stating that your channel is dedicated to people who are in Marlton or Burlington, NJ, or the surrounding areas, who are interested in new Honda cars, used Honda cars, and pre-owned cars in general, information about financing and/or leasing vehicles, and buying and shopping tips, etc.

- **Create a trailer video** (intro video): Create a "trailer" video or an introduction video for your YouTube channel with a full video SEO strategy. Shoot and say the keywords you want to rank for in the actual video.

- **Create channel art:** Create a graphic or a banner for the "header" of your YouTube channel. I would make sure that you articulate the name or focus of the channel in the banner. This is debatable because, unlike traditional SEO, you cannot create "alt tags" for the channel art. However, I believe that the search engines have pixel and image recognition software, so I practice consistent habits no matter what the SEO medium that I am engaged in.

See Figure 5.3 for a breakdown of a Youtube Channel page, high-lighting the aspects discussed above.

There is a whole checklist that YouTube provides you when you are setting up a channel. Just simply go down the list of tools and resources and make sure that you utilize each and every one of them. They are there for a reason. The most important are the details, descriptions, and URLs, which the search engine can read, look at, and correlate for relevance and content consistency.

Assuming that you properly set up your YouTube channel, it is now time to upload your video to YouTube. You can either upload via your cell phone or from a laptop or desktop. Either way the process is very

FIGURE 5.3   This graphic highlights the important aspects of a Youtube Channel page. Pay close attention to the cover photo and the introduction video, specifically the title, backlinks, and description.

easy. I have no personal preference in regard to which device I use to upload video SEO campaigns to YouTube. But, when it comes to actually optimizing these videos within YouTube's Video Manager, I prefer to edit using either a laptop or a desktop. I find editing on my iPhone difficult—not impossible, just difficult.

Here is a quick checklist for a proper YouTube video SEO optimization strategy:

Basic Settings

- Root file
- Title
- Description
  - Text content
  - Keyword density
  - Back links
  - Destination mapping
- Meta-tags/keywords

Advanced Settings

- Category
- Video location
- Recording date
- Subtitles/closed-captioning

Root File

When you upload a video file to YouTube or any other video search engine, the source file looks something like this:

IMG_6760.MOV (or .MP4)

There is no SEO value here if you leave it as is. So, simply rename the root (raw) file, utilizing the keywords that you are targeting for optimization.

Let's get back to the chapter's example scenario. After you shot video footage for the "2014 Honda Odyssey Is Better than the Toyota Sienna NJ" campaign and uploaded it to YouTube, your video's root file might look like "IMG_6760.MOV." You now need to rename it so that it has

SEO relevancy. Rename the root file to something like this (depending on the type of file, it could also either be an .MP4, or a .WAV):

2014_Honda_Odyssey_Better_Than_Toyota_Sienna_NJ.MOV

Tip: Use the word *video* in the raw file when you rename it.

What you are trying to accomplish is keyword and content consistency and relevancy. You are trying to let the search engines know that this video is in fact about "2014 Honda Odysseys," "Toyota Siennas," and "New Jersey (NJ)" and that the "Honda is better than the Toyota." Every detail you add to the overall campaign further validates that in fact that is exactly what this (video) content is about. And it further validates to Google why it should rank you favorably and prominently on the first page organically.

I am going to keep repeating myself. What you want to do is keep validating to Google that this video in fact is about "2014 Honda Odyssey is better than Toyota Sienna NJ." Every chance Google gives you to prove this, you must take it and utilize it. So, if you have the opportunity to name the actual root file, then name it with the exact keywords that you are looking to show up for in the search engine.

I want to be clear that naming the root file or not naming the root file utilizing the desired keyword visibility strategy is not in itself a major factor. To win the game of Googleopoly, you have to have a synergistic strategy, and the overall effectiveness lies with the synergy and consistency of the overall strategy. In essence it is details; you are being very detailed and very specific. You are allowing Google to absorb multiple factors that are all articulating that this video in fact is about what you state it is about. It is like that old saying, "If it looks like a duck and it quacks like a duck . . . chances are that it is a *duck*!" That is how Google thinks, too. Take a look at Figure 5.4 to see how a YouTube video page is broken down and appears for a viewer.

VIDEO TITLE

This is very important. You must be very clear in the title and not overdo it. I suggest that if you are a local business or if you are looking to target the local community, you should always use a geo-targeted location. For this current example for the Honda car salesman, if the dealership

FIGURE 5.4   The main aspects of a YouTube video, including the video player and the details of the video, as well as a description, backlinks, and keywords.

was located in Burlington, NJ, then you want to target "Burlington" and/or "New Jersey"/"NJ." If the dealership was located in Marlton, New Jersey, then you would want to target "Marlton," "New Jersey," and "NJ." Another strategy is to target a town, city, or state that you want to get business from *other* than the location where you or your business is physically located. Let's say that the Honda dealership was located in Marlton, New Jersey; then targeting Cherry Hill, New Jersey, might be a great idea. Cherry Hill is a larger, prominent location that is only five minutes away from Marlton. It is very likely that people who actually live in Marlton would search for Hondas in Cherry Hill. Why? Simple: because they know there are a lot of car dealerships in Cherry Hill and/or because they feel they would get a better selection or a better deal in a larger town, like Cherry Hill.

Be careful not to put numerous geo-targets in the title. I get it—you want to show up whenever someone searches anyplace that is even remotely close to you or close enough that you can service them. There is no need to stuff too many geographical places in one title. Remember one of the best parts of having a video SEO strategy is that you are not limited to just one video! If you were a Honda sales consultant located in Marlton, New Jersey, then you would want to sell cars to people who were searching for automotive needs, such as new cars, used cars, and financing, in:

- Marlton
- Cherry Hill
- Burlington
- Mount Laurel
- Mount Holly
- Medford
- Pennsauken
- Camden
- Vorhees
- Philadelphia

Instead of stuffing different towns and locations in the same video in the same title, just create additional video SEO campaigns. Specifically, create video SEO campaigns for every single geo-target from which you are looking to drive traffic and prospects. You want to make sure that you keep one focus, one strategy per video.

Do Not Dilute the SEO Potential in Your Title

You can use approximately 85 characters in your YouTube video title. However, I recommend that you use 65 or less. Similarly to the title tags on your website for traditional SEO, you will have only a certain number of characters that will display properly. The sweet spot for displaying your video title properly is approximately 65 characters or less.

Since you have a very limited amount of space to articulate what your video is about, you want to make sure that you maximize each and every word. You do not want your keywords to compete for relevance within the Google algorithm.

Here's a bad example of a video title:

2014 Honda Accord in Medford, Cherry Hill, Red Bank, Keyport, Camden, NJ

Even though that was exactly 65 characters, it is not a good example of a video title for strong SEO value.

Here is a much better example:

For The Best Selection & Prices for 2014 Honda Accords in Medford, NJ - 08055

The second video title is clearer. It has only one geo-target, Medford, New Jersey. You don't want to spread your SEO value among several different geo-targeted keywords. You want to only have one focus per video. There is absolutely no reason to get greedy and stuff different geographical locations in one video title.

Another aspect of the second video title example is that it is written like ad copy, not like a bunch of random keywords thrown in there to spam Google. Just as with traditional SEO and title tags on websites, the title is not just for SEO. The video title needs to be written in a way that will intrigue and entice someone into clicking the play button and watching your video!

Which one of the two examples accomplishes that? Of course, the second example does. If you were looking for a 2014 Honda Accord to lease or buy and typed into Google "2014 Honda Accord Marlton (NJ)" and a video with the following title appeared on the first page of Google, maybe even in first-position, natural Google, what would you think?

For The Best Selection & Prices for 2014 Honda Accords In Medford, NJ - 08055

You might think, "Damn, the Google oracle has done it again and has given me *exactly* what I was looking for . . . I was actually looking for the *best* selections available and of course the absolute *best* price . . . Thank you, Google oracle!"

One last piece of advice regarding your video titles: Don't dilute the search engine relevancy by having conflicting, redundant, or irrelevant keywords. It goes beyond just not having multiple geographical locations in your video title, to having multiple focuses. For example, you do not want to list multiple cars in the title:

2014 Honda Accord, Civic, Odyssey NOT the Toyota Camry, Corolla or Sienna (This is BAD)

As previously stated, you do not want to dilute your SEO opportunity. You don't want to spread your keyword focus thin. Plus it is just gobbledygook. It is not written for people. That example is of an untrained person throwing random keywords they hope will make their video show up if someone searches those keywords on YouTube (of course, this won't work).

There Is an Exception to the Rule

Comparison videos or conquesting videos are the exception to the rule. If you were a Honda salesperson (or dealership) and you wanted to conquest the Toyota prospect or buyer, you can compare the Honda versus the Toyota.

If you were a Honda salesperson and you wanted your video to show up for Honda Odyssey buyers or shoppers and/or for Toyota Sienna buyers or shoppers, then you would create a video campaign stating why the Honda Odyssey is better than the Toyota Sienna. You would create the relevant video content and make sure you utilized the speech and pixel recognition strategy. Here is an example of a proper title that would be powerful for video SEO:

The 2014 Honda Odyssey is BETTER than the Toyota Sienna - Marlton, NJ.

This is the exception for the rule but it makes sense. You are not trying to just keyword spam or stuff. You have a valuable piece of content here. There are a lot of people who search Google with that exact question: "Which Minivan is better, Honda Odyssey or Toyota Sienna?"

If you Google "**Which Minivan is better, Honda Odyssey or Toyota Sienna**," You will see 801,000 results. The entire first page of Google is filled with websites like Edmunds.com, Autotrader.com, US News, Kelly Blue Book, NewCars.com, Cars.com, Consumer Reports, and Motor Trend. These are all major websites and authorities that receive millions of unique visitors per month, in some cases tens of millions of unique visitors. All of these websites compare the Honda Odyssey and the Toyota Sienna, going over specs, details, options, gas mileage, safety, performance, customer reviews, and more. These third-party sites are there to give prospects, shoppers, and buyers the most up-to-date information to assist them in making an educated buying decision.

You know what else is on that same search engine results page? A video SEO campaign that I created:

2014 Honda Odyssey BETTER Toyota Sienna . . .[11]

Take a look at Figure 5.5 to see exactly how and where this shows up on the Google search page.

I wanted to create video campaigns that would show up on the first page of Google, organically. So, I tried to think of what type of questions people would ask or want to ask that would help them make a buying decision. The two most popular minivans on the market are the Honda Odyssey and the Toyota Sienna, and there are a lot of people who want to know which one is better. It is safe to assume that a lot of people would ask the almighty Google oracle that very question. So, it made sense to shoot a video and optimize it for proper video SEO power. And, as just mentioned, it worked beyond expectation. Out of almost 1 million results and all major automotive information and resource websites that generate tens of millions of unique visitors per month is my video with a thumbnail! It is the *only* video on the entire first page of Google, and it is the only thumbnail. The title reads,

2014 Honda Odyssey BETTER Toyota Sienna

Let me repeat that: A prospect types into the mighty Google oracle, "Which minivan is better, Honda Odyssey or Toyota Sienna?"

---

[11]www.google.com/#q="Which+Minivan+is+better%2C+Honda+Odyssey+or+Toyota+Sienna".

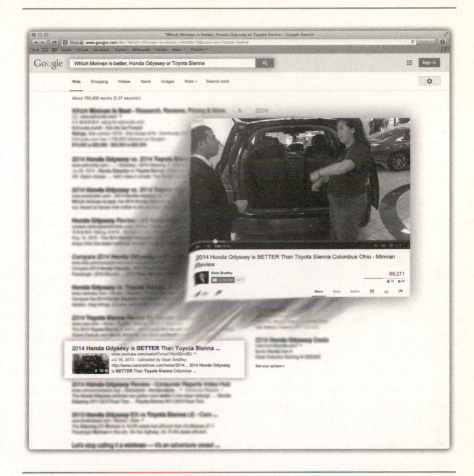

FIGURE 5.5   This is how a conquesting video posted on YouTube will show up on a Google search results page. The listing includes a title, thumbnail, and description of the competing brand mixed in with the results of the actual searched brand.

and the mighty Google oracle responds with a video with a title that says,

2014 Honda Odyssey Is BETTER than Toyota Sienna

If you click that video, you will see that it has 69,100 views (at the time this book was written) and rising. That is a lot of views for a video from a car dealership in Columbus, Ohio. That is an incredible example of the power of video SEO.

DESCRIPTION

You want to make sure that you write a unique, compelling, and relevant description for your video. I am still amazed at how many people do not put any descriptions whatsoever in their videos, or they cut and paste the same simple and sometimes crappy description from video to video.

The description section on a video is similar to the meta-description section on a website for traditional SEO. The same rules apply. The most important is that you write a unique and thorough explanation of your video.

In the description section of your video the *first* thing I suggest is that you put your contact information on the first line. It should look like this: http://www.seanvbradley.com 267-319-6776

It is very important that if you put your website or social media site in your description, you make sure you add the "http://" before the "www." If you do not do this, then your website address will not be hyperlinked. You will have only a website address that won't link anywhere. It is very important that you create that hyperlink. A lot of people use mobile devices to search Google and to watch videos. If someone Googles something, one of your video SEO campaigns pops up on the first page of Google, and they click to watch your video about you or your product or service, they can simply click a link from your video and be forwarded to your website! This is called a *site link*.

Also, you want to make sure that you put your phone number right next to the hyperlink to your website or social media. Most people on the Internet prefer to pick up the phone and call you rather than email you.

Autotrader.com states that nine out of ten people online prefer to communicate over the phone versus via email. You want to always provide a phone number for a prospect to call you. Many people who are searching Google do so from mobile devices. The "click to call" feature is amazing regarding video SEO. Let's say someone is searching Google from their iPhone or Android and they find one of your videos. They will have access to your phone number (if you provided it in the description section of your video), and they can click it to dial—hence the name *click to call*.

YouTube's description section is not that large. There are roughly four lines (or rows) that are visible for your description. Anything after that will be hidden and the video viewer will have to click a button called

Show More to see the full description. Here is the problem: If you put your contact information at the bottom of your description, you run the risk of people not realizing there is a Show More button and never finding your contact information. Some people might know it's there but not care enough to click the button to see additional information. My suggestion is that you assume that no one will ever click the Show More button. So, you want to try to put the most important information at the top of your description. The most important information is your contact information, specifically your website (hyperlinked) and your phone number.

Going back to the chapter's example, let's say you are a Honda car salesman and you are creating a video SEO campaign. You want your video(s) to show up on the first page of Google if someone was searching for "2014 Honda Odyssey" and/or "2014 Toyota Sienna." You want to make sure that you shoot the relevant video footage with the speech and visual recognition strategy in place, which means that you want to say those keywords verbally: "2014 Honda Odyssey and/or Toyota Sienna." In addition to saying those actual keywords, you want to capture the visual elements of the Toyota and or the Honda by being inside one of those vehicles, being next to them, having pictures or logos of those vehicles in the video, or creating them in postedit with green screen effects or After Effects. After you have created the video content, the next step in video SEO is writing the proper title for the video. After the title has been created, the next step is writing the description. In the description you are going to want to elaborate on the details of what the video is about. Just like a traditional meta-description, you are going to make sure that you have keyword consistency in the description. This means that whatever keywords you want to show up on the first page of Google are the same keywords that you have in the actual video content, title, and description. To be specific, you want to make sure that you have the keywords *2014*, *Honda Odyssey*, *Toyota Sienna*, *Better*, and *New Jersey*, in the description. You cannot just throw keywords in the description and expect Google to like it. You must write compelling text copy that is unique, useful, and relevant.

Let's break this down. If you were a Honda salesperson, you would be very interested in getting people who are thinking about buying or leasing from your direct competitor (Toyota Sienna) to change their minds and buy or lease from you! So, you create a (positive) propaganda video, stating that the Honda Odyssey is better than the Toyota Sienna. In the description of that video you are going to write a compelling break down of all of the reasons (real reasons) why the Honda is truly better than the Toyota. There might be some things that the Toyota is better than the Honda in, but of course, you are not going to mention those things. The point is that utilizing the relevant keywords for keyword consistency, you are simply going to validate your video content and your video title:

The 2014 Honda Odyssey Is BETTER than the Toyota Sienna Marlton, New Jersey

Here is an example of a good description for that video:

http://www.hondamarlton.com - 856-418-4285

If you are considering a Honda Odyssey or a Toyota Sienna, call me. I would be happy to explain both vehicles so you can make an educated buying decision. As a matter of fact, I would be more than happy to show you a side-by-side comparison of both the Honda Odyssey and the Toyota Sienna.

In the interim, please review these major third-party websites that have reviewed both minivans and share their results. You will see clearly that the 2014 Honda Odyssey is clearly the best minivan.

Kelley Blue Book weighs in on the 2014 Honda Odyssey versus the Toyota Sienna.

http://tinyurl.com/7rze4cx (KelleyBlueBook.com)

For a detailed review on the 2014 Honda Odyssey, you should read why Edmunds.com thinks it's one of the best minivans on the market.

http://tinyurl.com/m26ok4s (Edmunds.com)

If you are in Marlton, New Jersey, or *anywhere* in the state of NJ, I can help you find the right vehicle for you.

http://tinyurl.com/lrkofuy (Google Maps)

I know you might be thinking that that is a lot of words for a description. The reality is that you can shorten it if you want. But for the purpose of this book, I want to show you a thorough example. YouTube allows for up to 800 words in the description, so the description is within YouTube's guidelines. The main strategy that I want you to take away from this example of a proper video description is as follows:

- You want to make sure that you create unique content. You do not want to cut and paste from another video campaign or from online or from anyone else. Google is a jealous oracle. Google wants only unique content.
- Make sure that you put your contact information on the very first line in the description.
- Make sure that you remember to use the "http://" before your URL.
- I would include a phone number in your contact information.
- Make sure you write the content in useful, relevant way. Make sure that you are writing it for people, not the search engine. Make the content interesting, like ad copy.
- Make sure that you have keyword consistency within your text content. If your video is about 2014 Honda Odysseys and Toyota Siennas and that is what your title is, then you are going to want to make sure that you have those actual keywords sprinkled throughout the description, not saturated in the text. Make sure that the keyword consistency is in relevant places. You are not randomly sprinkling keywords just to have them in there. In the example that I used, the keywords were used only where it made perfect sense for them to be.
- Include external links in your description, but not just any random links. You want to have links that go to authoritative websites that are relevant and consistent with what your video campaign is about. Let me elaborate on this important detail.
  - The first link I included in that description was for www.KelleyBlue Book.com. KBB is one of the most respected third-party websites in the entire automotive sales industry. It is a consumer-driven resource with credibility and respect—not to mention that it has tens of millions of unique visitors per month. So, embedding a link to a site of that caliber is good, but what is even better is that the link did not go just to the home page of KBB.com. Instead, it went to the actual page on KBB.com that compares the 2014 Honda Odyssey and the 2014 Toyota Sienna. So, think about that for a second: Google reads, sees, and hears your entire video campaign. Google is going to see/hear your actual video content and read your title, description, and the link you have embedded to KBB.com.

Google will give validity or credibility points for the fact that you are sending people to a *major*, credible website that is relevant to the topic that you are focusing on in your video. It will also recognize that KBB.com is an authority in the automotive and consumer resources industry. Google will also be able to read the destination (other end of the link) of the link. It will realize that this major, international authority of automotive reviews has web pages that are completely dedicated to 2014 Toyota Siennas and 2014 Honda Odysseys, and to comparing the two different minivans and identifying which one is better. So Google puts all of these pieces together.

- Actual video content
- Title
- Description
- Links

And then says (not literally), Wow! This video *must* be about "2014 Honda Odysseys and Toyota Siennas." Everything supports that it is what it says it is.

- I put multiple links in the description to make sure that I validated to Google that this video is exactly what I say it is. The second link went to edmunds.com, which is literally the number one consumer resource for automotive researching. This time, though, instead of sending the link to the page on edmunds.com that compares the 2014 Honda Odyssey and the Toyota Sienna, I created a link to edmunds.com that went to the web page that detailed only the 2014 Honda Odyssey, breaking down all of the features and benefits.
- The third link is a special strategy that I use. I created a link to Google Maps for the geo-targeted validation, which means that if we are targeting Marlton, New Jersey, we want our video to show up on the first page of Google when someone is typing Marlton and/or New Jersey (or NJ). By going to Google Maps and typing in the address to the dealership in Marlton, New Jersey, or by simply typing Marlton, New Jersey, you can create a geo-targeted location on Google Maps. As a matter of fact, it will include the latitude and longitude of your destination. You then can convert that actual Google Map–specific page to HTML code or to a link. This is similar to getting validation and consistency points by linking to KBB.com and Edmunds.com, but those

links were created to boost credibility and consistency that the video was in fact about 2014 Toyota Siennas and Honda Odysseys. By creating the link to Google Maps with the specific location mapped out for Marlton, New Jersey, you are telling Google that in fact this video is relevant and consistent and in some way is about Marlton, New Jersey. You are even linking to Google itself . . . Google Maps!

Secret Tip

You will see within my description that the links I embedded looked like this: http://tinyurl.com/lrkofuy. It seems like a normal link, but actually it is a resource called a *tiny URL*, from a website that shortens URLs so they can fit easier in places like a YouTube description or a Twitter tweet.

The actual length of that "http://tinyurl.com/lrkofuy" might shock you:

https://www.google.com/maps/dir/marlton+new+jersey/marlton,+nj/@39.8912197,-74.9561652,13z/data=!3m1!4b1!4m13!4m12!1m5!1m1!1s0x89c133b2ba79d77b:0x91dfe942d6db646!2m2!1d-74.9218324!2d39.8912248!1m5!1m1!1s0x89c133b2ba79d77b:0x91dfe942d6db646!2m2!1d-74.9218324!2d39.8912248?hl=en

That is the real link. And unless you have a resource that I am about to give you, that is what it would look like if you simply cut and pasted it on your website, blog, social media, or anywhere.

The site www.tinyurl.com is an amazing free resource that will shorten any URL. TinyUrl.com just turned that 276-character URL into a "tiny" 26-character URL. This is a great resource, so use it!

META-TAGS/KEYWORDS

The keyword/meta-tag section for your videos is exactly like traditional SEO. You want to make sure that you keep the continuity with your meta-tags/keywords, exactly how you have kept the continuity with your video content, title, and description. The keywords/meta-tags that you use for your videos need to be consistent with the keywords that you have used throughout the entire video SEO campaign. For example, if "The 2014 Honda Odyssey Is Better than the Toyota Sienna, New Jersey" is your video focus, your title as well as your description perpetuates this theme. And that is exactly what you need to do in the keywords/meta-tags section of your YouTube video.

I recommend that you utilize 8–10 meta-tags or keywords. Each meta-tag can be 120 characters. So, you can make keyword phrases, questions, or simple individual keywords.

Here is the list of recommended keywords for the Honda car salesman's video SEO campaign for "2014 Honda Odyssey Is Better than the Toyota Sienna, NJ":

1. 2014
2. Honda Odyssey
3. Toyota Sienna
4. Better
5. Review
6. Reviews
7. New Jersey
8. NJ
9. Minivan
10. New

Keep in mind what you are doing is just further validating to Google that your video is actually what you say it is about. The way you accomplish that is simply with the details. You need to make sure that you dot all of the I's and cross all of the T's.

ADVANCED SETTINGS

Category Section

This section is pretty simple and self-explanatory. There are only 15 different categories that YouTube allows you to pick from:

1. Autos & Vehicles
2. Comedy

3. Education
4. Entertainment
5. Film & Animation
6. Gaming
7. How-To & Style
8. Music
9. News & Politics
10. Nonprofits & Activism
11. People & Blogs
12. Pets & Animals
13. Science & Technology
14. Sports
15. Travel & Events

You want to make sure that you choose the category that is going to fit your video as well as what you want to be categorized in.

A quick tip about the category: You might want to use the keywords in the category section in your video's title, description, and keyword sections. For example, in our current scenario I would recommend that you choose the "Autos & Vehicle" category for the video on "2014 Honda Odyssey Is Better than Toyota Sienna, NJ." You could have auto, autos, vehicle, vehicles, or all of those words in the description and keywords section; this is optional, but it would make sense for the overall campaign.

VIDEO LOCATION

YouTube allows you to actually register the location of your video. All you have to do is type in the town, city, state, and country, click "search," and it will find it on the map using exact latitude and longitude. Once you click "save," you will have successfully plotted your video's location on the YouTube global map. This is awesome, because the vast majority of your videos (if not all) should be geo-targeted. This is another validation for YouTube that your video is what you say it is. Think about it: If your video is titled "2014 Honda Odyssey Is Better than Toyota Sienna, NJ," it would be a good idea to go into YouTube's Video Location and register Marlton, New Jersey, as the location of that video.

SUBTITLES AND CLOSED-CAPTIONING FOR YOUR VIDEO

Subtitles and closed-captioning features for your video are for the hearing impaired, just like the "alt tags" on a web page are for the visually impaired. And just like with alt tags, a transcription of your video and closed-captioned text can and will be recognized by Google and provide you with additional SEO opportunities.

The best way to create subtitles and closed-captioning for videos is using transcripts. Transcripts are easy and contain only the text of what is said in the video. The good news is that they do not need time codes.

One of the most important aspects of a transcript is the "automatic timing." YouTube's speech (audio) recognition software automatically matches your captions with what is verbally spoken in the video.

There are two ways that you can transcribe (create a transcript of) a video properly:

1. Directly typing text into YouTube

   In the YouTube Video Manager section where you are editing your video, look above the actual video and you will see "subtitles and CC"—click that. It will allow you to type directly into the transcript text box.

2. Uploading a transcript file

   Create a script of what was said in the video. In essence you are creating a "Word" document for the audio transcript of what is said in your video. Make sure that you create a plain text document. You might need to convert the format, depending on what type of software program you are using to type out the document.[12]

ANNOTATIONS

Annotations are a great way to increase engagement with your viewers and get them to increase time spent with your content. Annotations are clickable text overlays on your videos. You can get very creative with how you utilize them to maximize opportunities with your audience.

---

[12]*Source:* https://support.google.com/youtube/answer/2734799?hl=en.

Here are some awesome ways to use annotations to maximize your audience's experience while watching your videos:

- Direct viewers to additional (relevant) videos
  - Sequel or prequel videos
- Direct viewers to specific playlists
- Direct viewers to your social media platforms
  - Facebook
  - Twitter
  - Instagram
  - Google+
  - LinkedIn
  - Flickr
  - Pinterest
- Direct viewers to your main website
- Direct viewers to a shopping cart or ecommerce site
- Direct viewers to an event (workshop, concert, speech, etc.)
  - www.eventbrite.com
- Direct viewers to specific product or service pages within your main website based on content discussed in your video
- Create calls to actions(CTAs)
  - Subscribe to my channel
  - Comment on this video
  - "Like" this video
  - Share this video
    - Social media
    - Facebook
    - Twitter
    - LinkedIn
    - Google+
    - Pinterest
    - Embed this video
    - On a website
    - On a blog
    - Email this video[13]

---

[13] *Source:* www.youtube.com/yt/playbook/annotations.html.

There are multiple factors that contribute to your video SEO strategies' success or lack thereof. The first factor is the elements in the traditional SEO strategy:

- Video content
- Root file
- Title
- Description
  - Text content
  - Keyword density and consistency
  - Keyword relevancy
  - Links
- Meta-tags/keywords
- Category
- Location
- Subtitles, closed-captioning, and transcript
- Video thumbnail
  - Make sure that you choose a good-looking thumbnail for your video or upload a custom one.

Those things are only about 25 percent of the overall success of the video SEO campaign. There are three other important factors that YouTube looks at when ranking your videos:

1. Trust and authority
   - As mentioned earlier, it is imperative that you focus on building not only an individual video's rankings but also the entire channel's value
2. Proper Channel Set Up
   - Properly optimizing the channel
   - Using all of YouTube's resources for channel creation
   - Choosing a proper YouTube domain name
   - Choosing appropriate channel art
3. Engagement
   - Getting subscribers (lots of them)
   - Getting channel likes (lots of them)
   - Getting overall channel views (lots of them)
   - Getting overall channel shares (lots of them)
   - Getting overall channel comments (lots of them)

The value and equity that the channel generates will benefit the individual videos.

Back in the day I used to have numerous YouTube channels. As a matter of fact, I still have seven or eight YouTube channels that have thousands of videos. I have not updated these channels in years, but they exist. On the other hand, for the past couple of years I have focused solely on my main YouTube channel, www.youtube.com/SeanVBradleyTV, which as of August 2014 has the following:

- **1,045,592 views**
- **3,280 subscribers**
- **2,408 videos**

That is 100 percent organic. I have not sponsored any videos, boosted any videos, or paid to drive traffic to my site. Because I have a completely organically grown YouTube channel with so many videos, subscribers, views, and comments, YouTube acknowledges that I have a trusted and respected "authority" channel within my niche (industry), which means that YouTube will give brownie points to videos that I publish from this channel.

VIEWER ACTION AND REACTION

YouTube wants to provide people with what they want—the most incredible relevant, unique, and powerful video content. One way that YouTube decides which videos are awesome and worthy of high rankings is by how viewers engage and react to videos that are uploaded. For example, if a video is uploaded and viewers watch the video for only a few seconds and then abandon the video, that is a clear sign to YouTube that the video does not meet the YouTube standard of excellence. And if that scenario keeps playing itself out, viewer after viewer, YouTube will bury that video. The same goes if a video has an abundance of negative comments or thumbs down. That is why those features are there—for YouTube to quantify the value of the video content uploaded on its platform. On the flip side, if a video gets a lot of the following, it will develop YouTube equity.

- Positive comments
- Playlist adds
- Thumbs up
- Playlist adds
- Favorites
- Video responses

YouTube will consider these types of videos worthy of high rankings, as well as useful, relevant, and important.

SHARING AND RECOMMENDATIONS

When people share, post, link, embed, and/or recommend your video, this also adds to the SEO rankings. This is magnified when these people or websites have authority or established credibility with YouTube or Google.[14]

Here are a couple of examples of how seriously powerful video SEO can be.

If you Google "**2014 Honda Odyssey NJ**," out of 1,120,000 results you will find *two* videos on the first page of Google. Actually, they are in first-position and second-position, natural Google! Two different videos show up for a Honda car salesman that works in a dealership in Marlton, New Jersey. The campaign is so powerful that you don't even need to type in an exact town. These two videos show up prominently on the first page of Google for a search throughout the entire state of New Jersey! Just to be crystal clear, these results are typical of a multimillion-dollar car dealership; it is *not* normal for a frontline salesperson to have this type of online visibility or digital marketing resources. The best part is that these videos were created, uploaded to YouTube, and search engine–optimized from a cell phone and all for *free*! That's right—the average car dealership in the United States spends approximately $60,000 per month in advertising, and they don't see results like this, at this magnitude. Yet a frontline employee can have more powerful results than an entire dealership and for free!

Want further proof? Look at the entire page: Out of the 1.1 million results, the car salesman shows up twice with video organically. The salesperson works for "Burns Honda," and Burns Honda does *not* even show up once organically! That is *crazy*![15]

If that wasn't an amazing enough example of the true power of video SEO for your marketing initiative, try a different search. Google "**2014**

---

[14]*Source:* www.tagseoblog.com/video-seo-youtube-ranking-factors-infographic.

[15]*Source:* http://www.google.com/?gws_rd=ssl#q=2014+Honda+Odyssey+NJ.

Toyota Sienna NJ": This is the direct competitor of the Honda Odyssey. Look what shows up! (See Figure 5.6.)

Out of 453,000 results again, first- and second-position, natural Google is the Honda car salesman, with the same videos! What is truly remarkable is that this Honda salesperson sells *only* Hondas. And his videos show up more than *anything* else on a search for "2014 Toyota Sienna NJ." Furthermore, his are the *only* listings that are non-Toyotas on the page. He is the only Honda dealership that shows up.

This is a truly advanced strategy that I created for this salesperson. This is a strategy that Honda should and would pay a small fortune to accomplish for itself. This is also a strategy that every single Honda car dealership in the state of New Jersey should and would pay a lot of money to accomplish. Every Toyota dealership should have this level of SEO capability for their own franchise, in their own backyard. But as you see in this example, they don't. And remember that the Honda salesperson accomplished all of this video optimization and video domination for free on his iPhone.

SYNDICATION AND SUPPLEMENTAL UPLOADS

Now that you have your video SEO strategy in place, and you have created a checklist of "what to do," "when to do it," and, most importantly, "how to do it," you are empowered to create a great video SEO campaign. But how do you keep it working? How do you achieve longevity with Google?

Simple: by syndicating your video SEO campaigns. That means that you should have multiple accounts with different video search engines:

- Dailymotion
- Howcast
- Vimeo
- Flickr
- Pinterest
- Vine
- And many more . . .

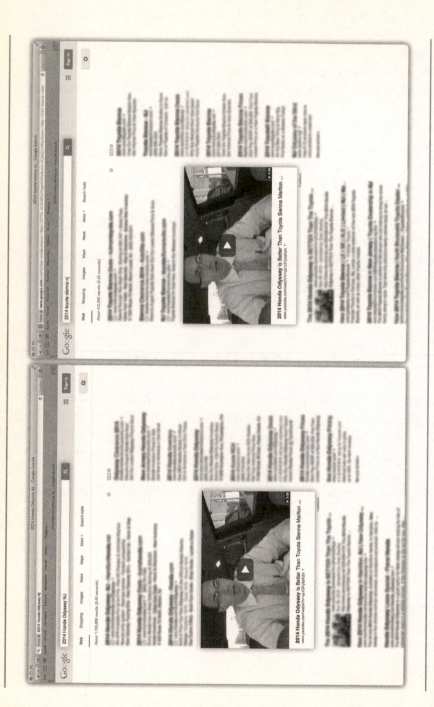

FIGURE 5.6 This VSEO example shows how prominently a YouTube video is displayed, regardless of the search term. When optimized properly, you can target key competitors and dominate the results page.

Source: www.google.com/webhp?tab=ww&authuser=0&ei=V275U-bCO4WlyATqpoDADw&ved=0CBsQ1S#authuser=0&q=2014+toyota+sienna+nj.

That's right—just as you should create a YouTube channel, you should also create additional channels on these other video search engine platforms (also considered social media platforms). You must take your time and properly set up each of these platforms the right way, so you can maximize the potential SEO opportunity that they will yield if you set them up with the right:

- URL
- Title
- Description
- Content
- Meta-tags/keywords
- Links
- Artwork

Once you have these additional video search engine platforms set up and optimized the correct way, then it is time to start uploading video content to these engines. Here are some powerful tips:

- Try to use *unique* footage if at all possible.
  - If you do not have unique footage, then make the footage unique by adding "bumpers," meaning different "intros" and or "outros."
  - You can use some of the video content as "b-roll" or running footage and edit new footage into it.
  - You can buy stock footage to edit into your video content to make it new and unique.
  - You can change the graphics and edits to make the video unique.
  - Make sure that you use different thumbnails.
- Make sure that you optimize the video(s) uniquely.
  - Title
  - Description
  - Content
  - Links
  - Keywords
  - Geo-targets
  - Transcripts

Another type of syndication is through social media. You can integrate most video search engines with social media. Specifically, you can connect your YouTube channel and other video search engines to your other accounts:

- Facebook
- Google+
- Blogger
- Reddit
- Tumblr
- Pinterest
- LinkedIn
- StumbleUpon
- Digg
- And more . . .

That means that if you took the time when you set up your channel to connect all of your social media to your video search engine(s), when you upload a video you could easily "push" it to all of those social media platforms without having to log in to those platforms directly. You can push right from the actual video on your video search engine.

This is important for several reasons. First, part of YouTube and Google's algorithm for ranking your video is the amount of views, likes, comments, and shares. So, syndicating or pushing the video to your network is like giving your video a shot of adrenaline. The people who see the video on your social networks can not only engage the video but also expose the video to their network, and so goes the "viral" aspect of possibilities. The second aspect is convenience. To be honest, it would be a pain in the neck to constantly log in to 10 different social media platforms just to deploy a new video. It is just so much easier to be able to do everything from one platform.

If you Google "**2014 ridgeline lease Tampa**," you will see a great example of the Googleopoly strategy in full effect.

Out of 686,000 results, the dealership Brandon Honda ranks four times organically and also shows up in first position in PPC. There are two videos on the first page of Google. One video is a YouTube video and the other video is a Dailymotion video. This is my point *exactly*! If you upload to only one video search engine, like YouTube, you limit your opportunities to rank on the first page of Google and win with

Googleopoly! Furthermore, there were five third-party lead source provider sites. Two of them, AutoTrader and TrueCar, are billion-dollar corporations. They make their money selling leads to the dealership at a much higher cost than acquisition. So, Brandon Honda's prominent position not only gives them major visibility in their primary market area but also neutralizes their competition. By competition I mean both other car dealerships and third-party lead source providers.

There were 21 total positions on page one of Google for this search, including organic and paid search engine results.[16] It is beyond awesome that this dealership shows up five different times out of the 21 on the first page of Google. This example personifies "winning the game of Googleopoly."

SUPPLEMENTAL UPLOAD TIP

You want to make sure that you develop a strategy to keep creating and deploying video-optimized content to your YouTube channel and all other video search engines. That is right; you want to keep uploading content. Video SEO is similar to conventional SEO. You do not want to let your content get stale—Google wants you to keep updating your website content, wants your website to have a blog (for fresh content), and wants you to constantly add unique and relevant content to it. Well, the same goes for videos, YouTube, and all other video search engines.

LOCALIZED VIDEO SEO

One last strategy for video SEO is creating "localized video SEO," meaning that instead of utilizing a video search engine to upload videos and optimize them, you can create your own video player or buy a video player plugin, design additional web pages, embed the video player on the new pages, and then, using traditional SEO, optimize the page with proper keywords, etc.

You might be surprised that you will also be able to achieve Google page one dominance this way.

---

[16] *Source:* www.google.com/#q=2014+ridgeline+lease+tampa.

BONUS SECTION: VIDEO SUGGESTIONS

Sometimes people get intimidated by making videos. Don't be! Don't be too critical of your videos. Obviously, try to make them as awesome as you can. But, unless you are trained professionally, don't expect your videos to come out like George Lucas or Steven Spielberg. Follow the rules of engagement I have set forth in this chapter, but the most important thing is to just start making videos. You will get better at making them with experience.

Another stress factor for people is deciding what kind of videos to create. You have a myriad of options to provide a tremendous amount of value with a diversified video content library.

Here are some videos that a car salesman could produce:

- Client reviews (testimonials)
- Product reviews
  - A walk-around for each vehicle in the lineup
    - Features/benefits
    - Professional reviews
- Comparison videos
  - Compare each of your vehicles against each of their competitors.
  - Examples
    - Honda Accord Is Better than Toyota Camry
    - Honda Accord Is Better than Nissan Altima
    - Honda Accord Is Better than Ford Fusion
    - Honda Accord Is Better than Chevrolet Malibu
    - Honda Accord Is Better than VW Jetta
  - Examples
    - Honda Civic Is Better than Toyota Corolla
    - Honda Civic Is Better than Nissan Sentra
    - Honda Civic Is Better than Ford Focus
    - Honda Civic Is Better than Chevrolet Cruze
    - Honda Civic Is Better than VW Beetle
- "How-to" videos
  - "How To" Avoid getting screwed when buying a car
  - "How To" buy a new car
  - "How To" buy a used car
  - "How To" lease a car
  - "How To" get a car when you have bad credit

- "How To" set up Bluetooth in your car
- "How To" use satellite radio in your car
- "How To" set your garage door opener in your car
- "How To" use OnStar
- "How To" get roadside assistance if you have a flat tire
- Value package proposition (why buy from us)
  - What is different and better about you than everyone else?
    - Free delivery to your home and office
    - Price protection guarantee
    - Owner rewards program
    - Three-day "love it or exchange it"
    - Free oil changes
    - Free car washes
    - Loaner cars
- Message from owner or general manager
  - Mission statement
  - Personal guarantee of 100 percent client satisfaction
- Department introduction videos
  - Sales department
  - Service department
  - Parts department
  - Finance department
  - Aftermarket/accessories department
  - Bad credit department
- Community involvement videos
  - Charities
  - Local government
  - Car shows
  - Special events
  - Holidays
- Aftermarket/tuner cars (like *The Fast and the Furious*)
  - Videos of hot cars

If you are not in the automotive sales industry, you might be asking what kind of videos you should create. You need to focus on your knowledge and expertise. Whatever industry you are in, whatever your subject matter expertise you have, all you need to do is map out an outline of potential videos like I did for the car salesman example.

Just remember that the vast majority of people go online to read, research, and surf—not to buy. Don't get me wrong; there is a lot of online buying going on, and I am going to focus on monetizing, but I just want to point out that the vast amount of people are doing other things besides buying things online. So, take advantage of that. Focus on what you or your product or service specializes in, and that will be the category you focus your video library on.

I am a great example of this working beyond expectations. I personally have over 6,000 videos published online. And, as mentioned, I have over 2,400 videos on one YouTube channel, www.youtube.com/seanvbradleytv, and have over 1,040,000 views. I have millions of views just from my YouTube videos (combined with my other YouTube channels). That is not even counting my other video search engines.

Here are some of the types of videos I have uploaded:

- Training videos
  - Automotive Internet sales
  - Automotive phone sales
  - Automotive business development
  - Digital marketing
    - Video SEO
    - Social media
    - Website design
    - SEO
    - And more . . .
  - Time management/organization
  - Leadership
  - Entrepreneurship
  - Making money
    - I have my own weekly Internet TV show, called *Make Money Mondays*.
  - Videos of my travels all over the world
    - All over the Unites States, including Hawaii and Puerto Rico
    - Russia
    - Italy
    - France
    - Mexico
    - Haiti

- Jamaica
- Bahamas
- My martial arts training videos
  - Brazilian jujitsu
  - Karate
  - MMA
  - Training
  - Capoeira
- Tutorials
- Webinars
- Entertainment industry
- Family videos
  - Kids
  - Wife

My life is like a reality TV show—I live my life very transparently online. I have a large following of fans and friends who eat up all of my content. Not all my content is for everyone. There are some people who watch my videos not because of my professional career but because they love the family and travel aspect of my life, while others are inspired by my success and business videos. My point is that there is content for everyone. Actually, there is more than enough content.

Video SEO Resources

There are technology resources that can assist you with streamlining your video SEO initiatives. One of these is software called *OneLoad*, formerly *TubeMogul*. OneLoad is to video as HootSuite is to social media. OneLoad allows you the opportunity to consolidate all of your video search engine accounts (one login and one password), so that you can log into one platform and upload one video, and it will syndicate across all of your video search engine platforms automatically. The only challenge is that you will still have to go in and do the individual SEO. Also, it will be the same video asset, with no modifications. So, you are deploying duplicate video content. This isn't totally useless because you can still have completely unique video optimization in all of the categories. However, I highly recommend that you utilize totally unique video assets across your different video search engine platforms. I mention OneLoad only to let you know that the technology exists and more importantly what the shortcomings are. I personally would never utilize this software.

There are other companies that have full-blown video SEO software that will do everything the right way:

- Produce and edit high-quality professional video assets
- Upload to numerous video search engines
- Cut, code, and optimize unique content

There are also companies that will manually do video SEO. They have years of experience with a trained staff of professionals.

The best part about video SEO is that it is organic and free! That's right—you can (and will) achieve Google page one dominance (organically). You can do everything yourself for absolutely no money out of pocket. Or you can outsource it for a fee. The choice is yours. Just like you can mow your lawn or you can hire a landscaping company.

ADDITIONAL RESOURCES

Learn more about how to properly optimize your online videos, including new techniques, guided tutorial videos about editing, and so much more, by visiting www.googleopolybook.com/video-seo-strategy.

CHAPTER **6**

Social Media versus Social Media Optimization

There is a difference between social media and social media optimization.

Social media is all about being social. That is the point and the reason it is called *social* media—constant updates on what you are doing, what you are thinking, where you are going, what you are eating, and who you are hanging out with. This would also include wishing people a happy birthday, happy anniversary, or happy holiday, as well as random thoughts, fears, excitements, frustrations, loves, hates, and everything in between.

Social media is also about sharing content that already exists. People are 1+ing, retweeting, liking, pinning, and commenting all over the Internet. Major sites like MTV.com, FoxNews, CartoonNetwork, BMW, and U.S. Airways all have content that is shared.

Social media optimization (SMO), on the other hand, is the strategy of creating compelling enough content that other people want to engage and share, by:

- Liking
- Recommending
- Commenting
- Creating video responses
- Retweeting
- Revining
- +1
- Repinning
- Sharing
- Embedding your link(s)
- Embedding your video
- Embedding your picture or infographic

- Linking
- Promoting
- Telling people about it

Social media content can rank on the first page of Google and achieve POD.

THE SOCIAL COMPONENT OF SOCIAL

Social media is the number one form of communication on the planet, and Facebook itself is one of the largest websites on the planet. Social media has changed the world literally on a communication level and even on a political level. Social media has been the catalyst in revolutions and even in perpetuating regime changes around the world. No one can deny the power of social media on a social level. Social media has also revolutionized the entire advertising and marketing industry.

The marketing potential of sites like Facebook, Twitter, LinkedIn, and Instagram (just to name a few) is tremendous. The ability to interact in real time with your current and past customers as well as prospects and fans is incredible. However, we're not going to talk about any of those things here. Right now, we're going to go into the effects that social media has on the search engines. Then why even mention it at all? Because I think it is important for you to know and respect the full power social media can have for your overall strategy. I could write an entire book (and might) on social media. This book is about winning the game of Googleopoly, and a large part of that strategy is going to be utilizing social media search (engine) optimization, also known as *SMO*.

For many, it's their secret weapon. Because so few people or businesses are using social media for its tremendous SEO benefits, those who are properly utilizing it are achieving incredible success.

It really comes down to four aspects, which we'll cover here.

SHARING MEANS ATTENTION

For years, the search engines were all trying to figure out how to apply social media to their ranking algorithms. Google purchased several social media sites that all failed (other than YouTube, of course) before finally deciding to build its own in the form of Google+. Microsoft went so far as to buy directly into Facebook itself and currently still owns a large portion of the largest social network in the country.

The search engines had the data. They could read the pages. They could judge the links coming in from other sites. They could tell how long people would spend on sites and whether they were finding what they were looking for based upon people bouncing back to the search to look at other results.

The one thing they couldn't understand was sentiment. They had no way of telling if people really liked what they found on the other side of the click. This is where social media comes in. Social media sites know what we like. They know our tendencies. They understand that if we share a piece of content, whether it's an article on a news site, a video, or a helpful page on a website, that we likely found value in that page.

The search engines coveted this information, and today they have a way to measure it. We'll discuss that component later because it's an extremely controversial topic, but there's one thing that is not in question: They like the attention that social sharing gives to web pages.

If content on your site is worthy of being shared on Facebook, tweeted on Twitter, or pinned on Pinterest, it likely has an opportunity to get other people to like it. The search engines take that portion of the data—attention—and measure it based upon other signals.

For example, if a video gets shared on Facebook by a lot of people, it's very likely that some of the people who see it on Facebook will like it as well. If they happen to own a website that is relevant to the topic of the video, they can embed that video on their website.

It goes further than that. Links play a major role in the way that search engines rank pages. By sharing on social media, you'll be able to get more people linking to your content because they're able to find it. The more that you expose your content on social media, the more likely it will be that someone will link to it. This is the way that Google's own employees place value publicly on social media sharing. They embrace this portion of it and do not try to hide it. The other aspect is something they do try to hide, but first let's discuss the people sharing the content.

Quality of Shares

In today's world, with so many social and search engine spammers, the search engines have tried to determine the best way to decide whether a share is valid. It does not cost much money to get 100 fake Twitter accounts to tweet a page, but the search engines realize that these shares are worthless. They have not and likely will never come out and admit this fact, but testing at every level by top SEOs indicates that this is the case. You can't fake out the search engines for long.

Beware of websites that offer to get fans, followers, +1s, and so on. These companies are a dime a dozen and for the uninformed might seem like a great idea. For a measly couple of hundred dollars you can buy fans. The reality is that they are not real. They could be coming from shell accounts that are just created for the sole purpose of selling their "likes," "friendship," "retweets," or "+1s," or they could be coming from known spam accounts and provide negative backlinking to your account, jeopardizing your initiative even before you had a chance to get it off the ground.

There is another reason to be very cautious about buying fake friends, followers, and fans. Most of these social media sites have their own algorithms, like Google and YouTube. Facebook has its own algorithm as well. And part of that algorithm is the reactions or responses when you post comments. For example, if you have only 200 friends on Facebook, you post a status update or a picture, and you get three or four comments, it is what it is. On the other hand, if you bought 1,000 fake friends or followers, you post that same status update or picture, and you receive only three or four comments, it is going to look very bad to Facebook because it's going to look like you have 1,200 friends and only three or four interacted with your content. It is going to give a signal to Facebook that the content is not interesting or your friends don't find it interesting. This can be completely false because you in fact do not have 1,200 friends—you have only 200. There are more detriments to buying fake friends and followers, but I think I made my point. Remember it takes a long time to be an overnight success.

If you are going to take advantage of social media as a way to improve your search exposure, you must embrace social media one way or another. Most become active on social media sites, sharing their own content and encouraging friends and family to do the same. This might seem like a cheap way of doing it, but local businesses can get a great benefit from this.

If you are a local business, you absolutely want to encourage people to "check in" on Facebook when they enter your establishment. Lots of businesses even provide incentives or coupons for people checking in.

I have seen numerous businesses—restaurants, diners, car dealerships, and more—use this to their advantage. More than half of Facebook users have at least 200 friends in their social network (the true average is 130 friends).[1] So, if a person checks in on Facebook that they are at Karina's Cafe, it will display on their time line, where some or all of their friends will see. A business couldn't ask for more! It is word-of-mouth advertising on steroids. In addition to having prospects and customers check in to an establishment, it is a great idea for *you* to check in to your establishment. Everyone on your timeline will see where you are. This will create top of mind awareness (TOMA). I highly suggest that if you are a business owner or a manager to ask all of your employees, general contract agents, vendors, partners, and friends—anyone and everyone—to check in. I mentioned Facebook regarding checking in, but the truth is there are several other major sites that also allow you to check in:

- Google+
- Yelp
- Swarm by FourSquare

To be clear, people will be able to see these check-ins forever after, not just when someone checks in at an establishment. So, obviously if someone checks in, it will show up in real time on their time line. But if someone was looking at a person's time line from three days ago to three years ago (whenever), they will still be able to see that check in at Karina's Cafe.

For larger companies, you cannot do it on your own. Either way, there are plenty of gurus and social media experts out there who can help you. Beware! Just as you now know that quality matters, you'll want to make sure that they know it as well. Check on the quality of the people sharing your posts. If the quality is low or if they appear to be spammers, let them go. They will do more harm than good.

Reread what I just wrote: quality over quantity. You want to make sure that the people who are retweeting your tweet, liking your Facebook status update, repinning your Pinterest post, etc. are quality

---

[1] *Source:* www.pewresearch.org/fact-tank/2014/02/03/6-new-facts-about-facebook/.

people. If they are an authority in your industry, that is, of course, better than some random person or, worse, a fake account liking or retweeting your post.

SOCIAL SIGNALS

Earlier, I discussed a controversial topic regarding social media and its effects on search engine rankings. That controversial topic can be summed up as *social signals*.

Microsoft acknowledges that Bing looks at Facebook, Twitter, and Pinterest. Google acknowledges only that it looks at Google+. They both look at these and many other social media sites, but they will likely never admit it. Why? Because they want to get organic data. They know that with social media, it can easily be manipulated.

If the search engines let the cat out of the bag that social signals had an impact on rankings, there would be businesses and marketing agencies around the world trying to figure out how to game the system. It already happened once. From 2006 to 2012, Google acknowledged that inbound links from other sites affected search rankings. As a result, search engine optimizers started figuring out ways to generate more and more inbound links. They would exchange links with each other. They would buy links. They would go "link farming," a practice notorious both for its effectiveness and its eventual cataclysmic decline.

On April 24, 2012, Google put an end to low-quality links with the release of the Penguin update. This had a major effect on the rankings, taking websites that once dominated on search and making them plummet down the rankings. Companies got mad. SEO firms shut down. It was an apocalyptic end to a very easy way to optimize.

Today, social signals fall under the same category, but the search engines will do whatever they can to hide this fact. They do not want to make the same mistake they made with links by letting the cat out of the bag. Instead, they will say that social signals don't exist until they're able to come up with a method of understanding how to read them properly.

Social signals are the actions themselves between a web page and social media sites. Anything that happens on social media sites that pertains to a web page is monitored and understood by the search engines. They know if a page has been shared. They know how many times it has been liked. They can see how many comments were attached to it, how many times it was retweeted, and even where it was shared. This is especially useful for local optimization; if your page is about Atlanta sushi bars and it's shared 10 times in Atlanta, those shares will have more of an impact on the rankings than if it were shared 100 times from various places around the world.

If it happens on social media sites, it is likely indexable by the search engines. This is where they get tricky. Google will say, "We can't index much of Facebook," which is true, but that's not what it is really seeing. It is looking at the page itself and social sharing buttons that are on a good chunk of pages on the Internet. This data gives Google an idea of the public sentiment toward a page. That's the data that it covets—Google wants to know what content we like.

As a basic strategy, try to make sure your content is "shareworthy." Use images often—social media is visual. Embed videos. Make sure your text content is long enough to be useful but not so long that nobody will read it all the way through. Lastly, make sure that if content should be shared, that the page has easy-to-use sharing buttons to encourage the social signals.

THE MOST IMPORTANT COMPONENT: PAGE ONE DOMINATION

The search engines are always changing. Today, social signals are important. Tomorrow, other forms of sentiment might be more important. One thing that will remain a constant for the near future is that social media sites can rank well on the search engines, giving you more pages that you can use to dominate the search engine results pages.

Every time you have one of your pages ranked for a search, it means another page (possibly a competitor) is ranked lower. You want your social profiles to rank for branded searches as well as unbranded searches.

The search engines already love to rank them, so this isn't hard. The biggest mistake that so many businesses make is that they try to do too many social sites. They hear that there are dozens, hundreds, even thousands of social media sites, and they figure that they should be on all of them, but that's not the case. In fact, by focusing on the right ones, you'll be able to maintain the highest chance of dominating on search.

The important networks today are as follows:

- Facebook
- Twitter
- YouTube
- Google+
- Pinterest
- LinkedIn
- Flickr

There are others that are rising, such as Instagram, Tumblr, and Scoop.it, but use these only if you have the available bandwidth. The only thing worse than missing out on a social network is to have one that's abandoned because you couldn't keep up with it.

It is important to note that not all social media sites are equal, and not all social media sites have the same SEO value. Just like in the game of Monopoly, not all of the properties have equal value. The same goes for social media and Googleopoly. As mentioned previously, there are so many choices to choose from. Here is the list (and order) that I suggest you follow as you implement your strategy.

I won't be able to go over all of these here, because the subject of social media could take up an entire book. If I don't elaborate on each of the different platforms, don't worry. The strategies and advice I detail in these platforms will be applicable for all of the social media platforms. There is no need to be redundant in this chapter.

- Google+
  - This is obvious, because Google owns Google+ and is going to use all the data that you generate from your Google+ Business or Personal account to determine your SEO relevancy on multiple levels. First, as mentioned with social signals, what happens on your Google+ page will influence Google's decision on where and how to rank your content. Also, Google Reviews is tied to your Google+ Local Business Page. Online reputation is one of the most import factors in people's choice of product, service, company, brand, etc.
  - Google gives prominent placement and visibility to Google Reviews (a future chapter will go into this).
- Facebook
  - Facebook is the largest social media site in the United States (and world for now). It has major credibility on the search engines,

so if you build a strong Facebook business page or personal page and develop it properly, you will be able to get your Facebook page to rank on the first page of Google.

- The social signals from people checking in at your local business are great SEO juice.
- Facebook is a great place to post:
  - Coupons for your business
  - Embedded videos
  - Client or fan reviews/testimonials
  - Pictures
  - Infographics
  - Tips
  - Advice
  - Subject matter expertise
- Flickr
  - Flickr is to images what YouTube is to video. Flickr is considered a social media platform, but it can also be considered an image (or picture) search engine.
  - Image optimization is almost as powerful as video SEO and it is as quick.
  - You can optimize individual images on the Flickr channel and potentially get those individual images to achieve Google page one domination.
  - The Flickr channel itself is also search engine optimizable for Googleopoly.
  - Flickr also allows for video upload as well as video SEO.
- Pinterest
  - Pinterest is another very popular image SEO platform with the same capabilities as Flickr.
  - Pinterest also allows for video upload as well as video SEO.
- LinkedIn
  - LinkedIn is a "professional" social community. But it has all of the functionality of a traditional social media platform, including social signals SEO value.
  - You can post articles and blog posts to LinkedIn that can and will get ranked if you optimize properly.
- SlideShare
  - SlideShare is to PowerPoint what YouTube is to video.

Having the pages and profiles is one thing, but now you have to get them ranked.

To accomplish this, you'll need to do two important things. First and foremost, make sure your company's social media pages and profiles are robust. It doesn't take much time to fill out your address, website, and other important parts on your social pages. Some websites are even attaching websites to social profiles. Google+ and Pinterest allow users to verify their ownership of the company website. This gives them higher relevance, and they will be more likely to rank on branded searches.

Once your pages are complete with all of the relevant information, it's time to get active. Post—often. You don't have to overpost, but be sure to post often enough to keep your page in the conversation. If you stop posting, your page has a greater chance of falling off the search results pages.

The second thing you can do to get your pages ranked is to link to them from your website and blog. This is easy—there are plenty of buttons available to create these links. If it's a direct link, you have a better chance of having it rank.

For certain businesses, it's harder to get these pages ranked. If you do these two things and your pages are still not showing up on page one, you can try to link to them from other websites as well. This should be rare. If you have an active page or profile and you link to it from your website, there's a great chance that it will rank for important keywords, such as your name.

By utilizing social media to take up real estate on the search engines, you're not just helping to push down competitors. It can be beneficial for pushing down other things, such as bad reviews, negative press, or third-party sites trying to make money off of your business name.

Social media is an important part of the search engine game. Regardless of whether you believe in social media as a valid marketing venue for your company, one thing is certain: it's definitely beneficial when it comes to controlling what people are seeing on the search engines.

Let's break down some of the main social media platforms for SEO.

GOOGLE+ LOCAL BUSINESS

Google+ is the most important social media platform. It is owned by Google and links to other important tools and platforms that you are going to need, like Gmail, Google Analytics, AdWords, Google Reviews (for your business), and YouTube! That is right—in order to use the powerful video SEO strategies on YouTube that you learned in the last chapter or the SMO strategies for Google+ in this chapter, you are going to need to have a Google account—a Gmail account. Once you create a Google account (Gmail), you will be able to access all of Google's tools, including Google+.

The next step after creating your Google account is to claim your business page. That means that you need to validate that *you* are the owner of that business and are allowed to be the manager of that business listing. You can authenticate by validating via a phone call from Google, or they can mail you a PIN, which you can activate on receipt (this is how I had to validate Dealer Synergy).

Here are some powerful tips to maximize Google+ for SEO.

Headlines

Google+ posts are like miniature blog posts. It is very important to utilize a proper header, both to gain attention of the searcher as well as differentiate yourself from the plethora of content on Google.

Google will use the first words of your post in two important ways:

1. Google will merge your headline with the title tag of the post.
2. The headline will be displayed in Google's search engine results page (SERP).

The more searchers notice your Google+ page, the more likely they are to react and engage with your content. Comment on it, +1, embed your video, share it, etc.

Text Content

Do not be lazy and just cut and paste links into your Google+ account. You want to make sure that you add text content, details, and descriptions ("meat on the bone") for the search engines to index, and that will enable searchers to better understand the value of your content, in order to engage with it as well as to share it.

Images

Almost all of the top posts on Google+ use images. So, it makes sense to include images with your posts. I highly recommend using unique images if possible. Take the time and pick the right image with the right quality. Sometimes, people get lazy and don't include an image, or it is poor-quality or the wrong version for the web.

Videos

Embedding videos will increase your engagement ratios. People prefer video content over all other content—but *not* just any video. It needs to be unique, relevant, compelling, fun, interesting, and/or useful.

#Hashtags

Google uses hashtags and semantic analysis to form relationships between topics. This helps organize and recommend content for searchers. It is very important for you to use hashtags in your posts. You can teach Google what is most relevant as well as what content is similar and consistent with your post by using these hashtags.

Targeted Sharing

Make sure that you share your posts with all of your circles and individuals.

Setting your post to "public" might seem like the best opportunity for visibility, but if you also add all of your circles to the public post, it will increase your exposure. You have to be careful, because if you do this too much, you might be considered too spammy. Tread carefully because this is a great resource. You do not want to overdo it.

Google+ Comments

Similar to Facebook's plugin for comments, you can embed Google+ comments on your blog. This is great because when someone leaves a comment on your post, they are given the option of sharing their comment with their Google+ circles. This will significantly increase engagement and therefore your SEO.

Interactive Posts/Calls to Action (CTAs)

With interactive Google+ posts, you are able to customize how your content is displayed and, more importantly, create specific calls to action for your unique product, service, or business.

Google has an awesome list of CTAs that you can embed in your post. You can get a full list from the resource Google Developers.[2]

Some CTAs include the following:

- Add me to your contact list.
- Add an item to a shopping cart.
- Add an event to my calendar.
- Apply for a job.
- Book tickets to a concert.
- Buy an item.
- Check in to a location.
- Compare different products.
- Watch a video.
- Contribute to a cause.
- Download a document.
- Listen to a song.
- Read an e-book.
- Reserve a table at a restaurant.
- Sign up for a newsletter.
- And many more . . . [3]

Google+ Local Business has some pretty powerful additional resources, the most important of which is Google Reviews. I explain online reputation, Google Reviews, and more in Chapter 8.

FACEBOOK

You need to use your Facebook for more than social interaction. Facebook is an SEO incubator for your business. When someone searches for you or your business, you want to make sure that your

---

[2] *Source:* https://developers.google.com/+/features/call-to-action-labels.
[3] *Source:* http://moz.com/blog/google-plus-tips-seo.

Facebook page shows up. For example, if you Googled Dealer Synergy, on the first page you will find www.facebook.com/DealerSynergy.

URL

Just like traditional SEO, it all begins with the URL. Make sure that you choose a specific, custom URL. I suggest that you use the name of your business. Or you might want to use a subject matter expertise, service, and/or a geo-target. For example, here are some Facebook URL ideas (these are hypothetical).

- www.facebook.com/customwheels
- www.facebook.com/KarateMarltonNJ
- www.facebook.com/NissanWoodbridgeNJ
- www.facebook.com/BrooklynPizza
- www.facebook.com/DentistChicago
- www.facebook.com/AtlantaMusicProducer

When someone Googles *anything* that you do or offer, you want *your* Facebook page to show up on the first page of Google. If your Facebook page is www.facebook.com/110004034rsdf, how are you going to show up if someone is Googling "Brooklyn Pizza"? You aren't, but if you owned www.facebook.com/BrooklynPizza, and someone Googled "Brooklyn Pizza," you might show up on the first page. But if you had a productive Facebook page that got a lot of engagement and the social signals were high, you most likely would rank on the first page of Google.

Category

Make sure that you choose the most relevant category for your business. You also have the opportunity for three subcategories. Choosing the proper category enables Google and the other search engines to properly rank you. But it is also important for Facebook, as well as the users on Facebook. There are numerous ways someone can search within Facebook and narrow down those searches. Take your time and make sure you are optimized for your profit centers and/or for your main focus.

About Section

The About section is like the meta-description of a traditional website. You want to make sure that you completely fill out this section. And you want to fill it out for SEO, which means that you want to make sure that it is detailed and focused on these points:

- Name of your company
- Phone number
- Email address
- What products and services you offer
- Your value package proposition (why buy from you)
- Credit, awards, citations
- "About your company"
- Your staff or team
- Geo-target your location of business or service or your primary market area (PMA)
- You want to make sure that you use proper keyword density and consistency.
  - Make sure that you use the name of your business sprinkled in the description.
  - Make sure that you use the keywords of your product, service, and or geo-targeted area sprinkled in the description.

Remember to write the About section like ad copy. Make it interesting for people, not spam content for the search engines.

It can get indexed, and that index will be crawled.

Posting Content

Posting content is one of the most important aspects of social media and specifically Facebook. You want to make sure that you post only quality content. Both Facebook and Google have algorithms in place that use social signals to track the value of content that you post. Social interaction and social engagement are an important factor for ranking you, your page, and its individual content on Google. You want to focus on producing only high-value content. That means creating and posting content that people are going to want to comment on, like, share, engage, embed, or repost.

At one point it was all about getting "likes," to the point where people started buying fake followers and fake friends to boost their "like" count. Likes do not matter anymore, or they don't matter nearly as much as they use to. Now it is all about engagement. As a matter of fact, there are companies that specialize in tracking social media engagement between most of the major platforms. One site/service that is popular is Klout (www.klout.com). Klout integrates with Facebook and other social platforms and details all engagement with your friends, fans, and followers. What matters more than how many friends, fans, or followers you have is what they do with you. Do they engage with you? Do they really care about what you say? Do you influence them? That is the most important—engagement and influence.

Understanding How to Work Facebook's Algorithm

Secret Tip

To go deeper, it's not just about quality content. There is so much content out there on the Internet that you need to step it up even further and go to remarkable content. A step further than that is remarkable content that is likable and shareable.

Here is the difference between quality and remarkable content:

Quality content: Unique content that is clean, grammatically correct, professional, and useful.

Remarkable content: Quality content that triggers a need or addresses an interest that is shared by many people. People are compelled to engage it. People can't help themselves but to comment on it, share it, like it, hate it, talk about it, etc.

Example: There are many political posts or #TrendingTopics on social media that receive a lot of attention. It doesn't necessarily mean all feedback will be good. It just means that there is content posted that incites people or is provocative or intriguing to the point that people are compelled to engage with it and/or share it.

Remember that you are looking for the trifecta regarding your content—it should be unique and remarkable and make people take some type of action.

Superduper Secret Tip

This is a *major* tip that will prove invaluable to your Facebook strategy:

You want to be vigilant with your Facebook notifications. You must monitor your "actions per hour." When you post an update, a picture, a video, or any other type of content, you want to make sure that you have at least one interaction per hour. If after two to three hours you do not have an interaction, then you need to delete that post and repost something else that will be remarkable and get people to engage.

There are a lot of people who spam Facebook and kill the Facebook algorithm. The truth is that you do not have to constantly be posting content on Facebook. What you want to do is work the algorithm and ride the algorithm all the way up the rankings for Facebook.

Let me digress for a moment to discuss the reality of the Facebook visibility situation. You might be shocked to know that it almost doesn't matter how many friends or likes you have. Let's say you have 1,000 friends on Facebook and you post a status update. I assure you that your 1,000 friends will not see your post. Only about 5–10 percent of your friends will see your post on their time line. That means only 50–100 people will see your post out of your 1,000 friends. This is because Facebook doesn't want people to get pissed off about being flooded with content that sucks or that they are not interested in. So, Facebook uses an algorithm to measure multiple things:

- Content you are posting
  - Are people liking it
  - Sharing it
  - Engaging it
  - Reading it
  - Watching it
  - Sharing it
  - Enjoying it

- Content your friends like
  - What content are they looking at
  - What are they searching for on Facebook
  - What are they liking
  - What are they sharing

Based on those variables, Facebook will match up relevant content and interest with people who will possibly be interested in those things.

Posting content that isn't remarkable will hurt your Facebook ranking. So, it really doesn't make sense to constantly post content that people don't like, don't comment on, and don't share. All you are doing is digging a deeper Facebook grave, because you are dead in the water.

Advice

This has nothing to do with SEO, but while on the topic of Facebook, I want to give you some powerful advice: You need to buy Facebook ads if you want to be successful on Facebook. You don't have to spend a ton of money either. For about $200–$300 per month, you can have a powerful Facebook ad campaign. And it won't matter how many friends or likes you have (you are going to need at least 100, but that is nothing). You will be able to reach thousands in your targeted audience easily. Facebook is a publicly traded corporation and a for-profit company. It wants to monetize. If you participate in Facebook ads, you will be able to target specific people:

- Male/female
- By age groups
- By interests
- Geographically

Or you can target your friend network, which includes your friends' friends—anyone who likes you or your post as well as their friend network. As long as you are willing to invest money, Facebook is willing to give you unlimited access to its members.

Another Tip

All comments need to have a reply. Make sure that you respond to each and every comment post. As a matter of fact, I would try to interact with everyone who engages you and/or your posts as much as possible. You could potentially turn a simple post that had four or five comments into a post that has hundreds by responding to all of the comments. You could even cut and paste links from other Facebook posts (or other social platforms) in the comment thread of a particular post if it is relevant. Remember the goal is interaction.

PINTEREST AND FLICKR

Flickr and Pinterest are image search engines as well as social media platforms. As mentioned earlier in this chapter, a lot of the top posts on Google+ as well as on most of the search engines are pictures and images. There are so many people searching for the following:

- Pictures
- Graphics
- Logos
- Stock photos
- Infographics
- And more . . .

You have the ability to organize all of these assets in one place as well as optimize them for individual and platform ranking on Google page one.

Flickr and Pinterest are to pictures/images what YouTube is to video. You can optimize both the platforms as well as the individual images within the platform. And the same strategies that you learned in Chapter 5 for video SEO are applicable here for image optimization.

Here are the areas you want to focus on when optimizing your Flickr and/or Pinterest platforms, as well as the images within those platforms:

- URL/domain name
  - Make sure that you create a URL that has a focus—the name of your brand, product, service and/or a geo-target.
  - For example:
    - www.flickr.com/dealersynergy
    - www.pinterest.com/seanvbradley
    - (*not* real) www.flickr.com/DetroitFlorist

- Title
  - It is important to make sure that you create the title by anticipating what someone will type into Google. When someone types something into Google, you want your Flickr and/or your Pinterest platform or the images on the platform to rank on the first page of Google.
- Description
  - This is similar to the description in a YouTube video or the meta-description on a traditional web page:
    - Make sure that you describe the image and details surrounding the picture.
    - Be sure to use keyword relevancy and keyword density in your description.
    - Make sure that you add a couple of links in the description to add more SEO value to the image.
    - Be careful *not* to embed links to a monetized site from Flickr, like your website or a shopping cart. This is strictly against Flickr's guidelines. It will *delete* your account—I found out the hard way. I optimized a recording artist's Flickr account that had over 1.5 million views, and the account got deleted with no warning whatsoever. This was my wife's account (Karina Bradley). It is clearly stated in Flickr's user policy that it forbids using the platform to try to monetize. However, using Flickr to win the game of Googleopoly is totally okay!
    - There are no such restrictions with Pinterest. As a matter of fact, Pinterest is a great resource for creating a backlink haven and SEO relevancy (with the right content to the right links). If you have backlinks in your description that go back to your main website or a product/service page and someone repins your pin, that will be good for SEO.
- Tags
  - Make sure that you follow the same rules and strategies when filling out the proper keywords/tags on both Flickr and Pinterest.
  - Make sure that you are not keyword stuffing. Focus on what that particular strategy is for that particular image.
  - Always begin with the end in mind. Ask yourself, "What do you think someone will type in Google that will lead them to this particular image and ultimately *me*?"

- Geo-target
  - Similar to YouTube's geo-targeting capabilities
    - Make sure that you attach a specified geo-targeted location to each and every image within the platform
    - Geo-target strategy is for:
      - Where you or your product or service is located
      - Where you want to "conquest" from

LINKEDIN

LinkedIn is the number one "professional" social network. Most people utilize LinkedIn to create business opportunities, find employment, or advertise a job opportunity. There are multiple opportunities within LinkedIn for content to be ranked favorably by Google:

- LinkedIn groups
- LinkedIn articles or blog posts
- LinkedIn careers

If you Google "career Philadelphia," out of 154 million results on the first page of natural Google is a LinkedIn job directory that was updated only four hours ago! (See Figure 6.1.)

1. Jobs in Philadelphia, PA | LinkedIn
2. www.linkedin.com › Jobs › Pennsylvania
3. Cached
4. LinkedIn
5. Loading . . .
6. Four hours ago - Apply to 10832 *jobs* in *Philadelphia*, PA, on LinkedIn. Sign up today, leverage your professional network, and get hired. New *Philadelphia*, PA . . .[4]

PRIVATE LABEL YOUR OWN SOCIAL NETWORK!

Now that you see the tremendous power social media has for your business, I am going to give you even more amazing information.

---

[4]*Source:* www.google.com/?gws_rd=ssl#q=career+philadelphia and www.linkedin.com/job/jobs-in-philadelphia-pa/.

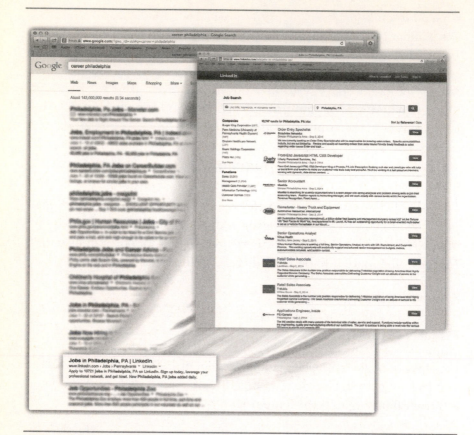

FIGURE 6.1   This is how a Google search of "career Philadelphia" returns a LinkedIn query for all jobs in the Philadelphia area.

You can create your very own "Facebook," "Google+," or "LinkedIn"! That's right—you can create your own social network. There are two easy resources that you could utilize:

Ning: www.ning.com

BuddyPress (WordPress plugin): www.buddypress.org

Facebook, Google+, and LinkedIn are worth billions of dollars, and you can create your very own full-blown social community or social network for virtually nothing or for less than $100 per month.

There are additional customizable social platforms besides Ning and BuddyPress, but they are the easiest and most cost-effective solutions on the market today.

There are numerous reasons why I would highly suggest that you create your very own social media network and add it to your overall marketing and advertising strategy. To have your very own social community platform where you can interact with your current clients, past clients, and all of your potential prospects is amazing. To have real-time interaction and the ability to identify clients' wants, wishes, and needs is priceless. However, as it relates to winning the game of Googleopoly, having your own social network is phenomenal for SEO. I have discussed how much SEO "juice" Facebook, Google+, Flickr, YouTube, Instagram, and the rest of those social platforms have. They have a tremendous number of people on those platforms who are constantly uploading content. So, imagine if you had your own platform!

One of the best things I ever did for my core business at Dealer Synergy, which provides training, consulting, and digital marketing for the automotive sales industry, was to create my very own social and professional network called www.AutomotiveInternetSales.com (AIS). (See Figure 6.2.) Here is the breakdown of AIS:

- Over 10,000 unique visitors per month
- Approximately 4,000 members
  - Members have to create a full-blown profile, like with Facebook, Google+, or LinkedIn
- Over 2,000 articles and blog posts
- Over 900 videos
- Over 2,000 images/pictures
- Over 150 public and private groups
- Dealer of the Month
- Vendor of the Month
- Free resources
- Make Money Mondays
- True Vendor (vendor rating system and directory)
- Blog
- Forum
- Events calendar
- And much more . . .

FIGURE 6.2 www.AutomotiveInternetSales.com is a full-blown social networking site run on the Ning platform. More than 4,000 members log in to read blog posts, catch up on forums, or view photos and videos, which are posted daily.

I created www.AutomotiveInternetSales.com on the Ning platform, and it costs me less than $100 per month. My vision was to create the most powerful social and professional community in the entire automotive sales industry. I wanted it to be like Facebook, LinkedIn, CNN, and Google+ combined, specifically for the automotive sales industry. And that is exactly what I did! We are ranked as one of the best automotive sales professional communities in the entire industry.

I seriously could write an entire book just on Ning and creating your own private professional community. But the bottom line is that AIS is phenomenal for SEO! If you Google "Automotive Internet Sales" out of 76 million results, in first-position, natural Google is www .AutomotiveInternetSales.com.

It is *very* important to remember that it is not merely enough to have your own private social platform like Ning or BuddyPress. Once you have established your social community, you want to make sure that you follow the rules of engagement for SEO. The most incredible aspect of your own social media platform is the fact that you and all of your members will be able to create unique and relevant content that can be optimized:

- Blog posts
- Pictures
- Videos

And all of the content that is created on *your* social platform can be syndicated to all of the traditional social networks, like Facebook, Google+, Pinterest, LinkedIn, and so on.

You want to make sure that you map out a strategy of which social media platforms you want to utilize. Once you have mapped out each of the platforms that you want to utilize in your overall Googleopoly strategy, then you should clearly map out what type of content you are going to have on each of the platforms, as well as what your SEO content focus will be. To be specific, you do not want to simply sign up with 5 or 10 social media platforms and try to just wing it. There is obviously a lot going on and a lot of opportunities to go in multiple directions. I feel that if you do not do a good job of mapping out your wants, wishes, expectations, and a detailed road map, your strategy might get compromised. You can't build a brand-new house from scratch without blueprints; the same goes for your SMO strategy.

Remember that social media is a moving target. It is evolving at quantum speeds, and there are always new, awesome social media platforms popping up. Part of the extra value of buying this book is that you have an incredible resource at www.GoogleopolyBook.com for *free*. I will be updating important details, facts, strategies, and new social platforms to keep you and your Googleopoly strategy on the cutting edge of technology.

ADDITIONAL RESOURCES

With an ever-changing list of popular social networking sites, as well as changing guidelines and etiquette, stay up-to-date on what works, what doesn't, and what's coming up next by visiting www.googleopolybook .com/social-media-optimization.

CHAPTER 7

Strategies for Mobile Dominance on Google and Web Success

Up to this point, everything I have talked about has primarily had to do with aligning your website strategies with the guidelines and criteria that Google has created in order to create a better and more organized web. Previous to the mobile boom that has taken place in more recent years, any discussion about achieving high Google ranking has been centered on desktop devices, such as home computers or laptops. But with one in every five people on the planet having an Internet-connected smartphone, Google has placed emphasis on making sure that the desktop version of your website translates to the mobile web.

When you align your web strategies with those recommended by Google, it's important to understand that doing so will render your site far greater rewards and preferential treatment, further empowering you to dominate online and achieve success.

Previous chapters mentioned that 95 percent of search traffic doesn't even search past the first 10 organic search results (i.e., the first page of Google). We also know that Google wants to direct you to sites that provide a great experience and relevant information based on your search query to stay aligned with its primary objective as a search engine. So this fact really simplifies Google's dilemma, because while Google is going to return 1,000 results for every search, only 10 or 20 will rank high enough to even get noticed by majority of web users.

31.3 PERCENT OF ALL WEB TRAFFIC COMES FROM MOBILE DEVICES!

This is significant because it represents a 34 percent year-over-year increase in mobile traffic from the fourth quarter of 2012.[1] On top of that, more than half of mobile traffic to websites comes from organic search, which is an impressive representation of user search behavior and the devices people are using to both search for and browse your website.

These high numbers also represent something greater than just the device people are using to find information. They also represent fundamental shifts in how information is searched for and found.

Now that you can see how popular mobile search is, let's take a look at Google's published philosophy and how it fits in with creating a solid mobile search optimization strategy.

1. Focus on the user and all else will follow.

"Since the beginning, we've focused on providing the best user experience possible. Whether we're designing a new Internet browser or a new tweak to the look of the homepage, we take great care to ensure that they will ultimately serve you, rather than our own internal goal or bottom line. Our homepage interface is clear and simple, and pages load instantly. Placement in search results is never sold to anyone, and advertising is not only clearly marked as such, it offers relevant content and is not distracting. And when we build new tools and applications, we believe they should work so well you don't have to consider how they might have been designed differently."[2]

The user is number one on the 10-item Google philosophy list!

Let's take a look at number 5.

5. You don't need to be at your desk to need an answer.

"The world is increasingly mobile: people want access to information wherever they are, whenever they need it. We're pioneering new technologies and offering new solutions for mobile services that help people all over the globe to do any number of tasks on their phone, from checking email and calendar events to watching videos, not to mention

---

[1]*Source:* www.internetretailer.com/2014/02/06/mobile-devices-account-nearly-third-web-traffic.

[2]www.google.com/about/company/philosophy/.

the several different ways to access Google search on a phone. In addition, we're hoping to fuel greater innovation for mobile users everywhere with Android, a free, open source mobile platform. Android brings the openness that shaped the Internet to the mobile world. Not only does Android benefit consumers, who have more choice and innovative new mobile experiences, but it opens up revenue opportunities for carriers, manufacturers and developers."[3]

As you can see, mobile is here and it's growing. As I mentioned earlier, one in five people on the planet have a mobile phone. Google cares about our experience and is always looking for ways for their products to be mutually beneficial for all users.

Since mobile usage has become much more abundant, there has been a debate about which mobile software technologies provide the best fit for achieving a solid mobile strategy. There are three different mobile website formats to consider, without even mentioning native iOS or Android apps. For the purpose of this book—winning the game of Googleopoly—let's take a closer look at the three prominent mobile website formats and how they can be used to help you dominate online.

Before taking a closer look, it's important to understand that no matter what you do, the first thing should be to identify your online objectives. Doing so will help you eliminate the formats that don't align with your objectives or goals and help the winning format rise to the surface.

Dedicated Mobile Websites

A **mobile website** offers a simplified small screen, visually optimized layout and browsing experience, which traditionally contains only the most important elements of your full desktop website. Even though smart phone browsers can display almost any modern website, the aim of a mobile website is to deliver a streamlined experience for the user. You've probably viewed a website on your phone before that is not mobile-friendly; they require you to pinch and zoom and scroll all over the place with your fingers to navigate through the site.

Mobile websites can be inexpensive to design and develop, and there are mobile design generators out there that will allow you to adjust various elements of the site's design, from color to button style, relatively

---

[3]www.google.com/about/company/philosophy/.

quickly. You will need to make sure that when a web user types in your domain from a mobile device that the mobile version of the website is detected and therefore shown instead of the full desktop site. The most typical way to do this is through a mobile detection script that you add to the header section of your website. Browsers report the device they are on to the server that serves your website; all you need to do is listen for it and respond with instructions about what "skin" to use to display your website.

Here's the code: https://code.google.com/p/php-mobile-detect/.

If you have the design chops, you can design the mobile skin yourself; otherwise, a professional designer will need to create it for you. The detect code can be a simple add for some, and maybe a little more complex for others; the design can be as simple or complex as you desire. If you go the detection route, you'll need to also consider tablets and small laptops in your design planning. You can detect each different device and display a different mobile skin for each one. This is important because a typical mobile site that works great on 320px phone is a terrible user experience on a 7″-plus tablet or laptop. You'll want to build out several designs for the myriad of different devices and decide which skin to use for each device that you detect. (See Figure 7.1.)

A disadvantage of mobile websites is quickly discovered when it comes to mobile SEO because they often exist on a mobile URL (e.g., m.yourdomain.com). The reason I see this as a potentially negative aspect of mobile websites is because you are starting from scratch and have to build up the authority, linking, and structure of a completely separate domain. Having said that, if you have a developer who is really familiar with mobile websites, they can use a unified URL structure (which we'll look at ahead), which means that instead of having to use a separate domain, the mobile version of the code can exist in the same file as the full website code and therefore use the same URL.

Because mobile usage is so high, and we're talking all about how to achieve Google page one dominance, it's best to weigh the benefits of delivering a streamlined user experience against the disadvantage of having to maintain a secondary domain on top of your existing full URL.

Adaptive Website Design

Without question, one of the biggest debates when it comes to mobile website design formats is between adaptive and responsive websites.

FIGURE 7.1   Kayak is an online travel site where you can book hotels, cars, and flights. The desktop version has a clean design and is easily navigated. The mobile version, which is very different from the desktop site, still maintains a similar style while oversimplifying the user interface.

Though each format aims to achieve the same objective, the approach for both of them is different.

The simplest way to define adaptive websites is that they use a library of static dimensional breakpoints to cover the most common screen sizes—namely, mobile (320 pixels wide), tablet (720 pixels wide), and desktop (960 pixels wide). Adaptive websites are similar to dedicated mobile websites in that they don't load automatically. They first detect the type of device that the website is being accessed on and then deliver the properly sized layout to view.

There are two main benefits for choosing an adaptive website for your mobile strategy. The first is that they are relatively inexpensive to develop because you are focused only on creating layouts for three different device dimensions instead of an optimized experience for all sizes. Second, if your existing desktop website contains a large library of images that won't scale well, taking the adaptive route may be the best approach.

Responsive Website Design

The rival of adaptive websites is different because instead of requiring multiple design files or a detection script, responsive websites can offer an optimal mobile website because they scale to any and all device screen sizes.

Something to consider is that a responsive website may be more work for a web developer to create upfront (and therefore be a little more costly), but they are typically well worth the investment since you won't need to make adjustments for different devices. Do the work once, and it's done. In order to combat expensive development costs, it's worthwhile to note that there are several web development companies who have created Wordpress, Drupal, or Joomla responsive website templates that cost under $100. What's valuable about that is that the expensive design and development work has already been done, and you won't have to worry about paying another developer to create a site for you from scratch.

Likely the top reason to consider using a responsive website as part of your mobile strategy is because, believe it or not, responsive is what Google not only loves but also highly recommends that you use. Remember my earlier point about aligning your mobile strategy with Google's vision?

There are good reasons why Google recommends responsive design as well. For example, because responsive design requires only one design, one URL, and one code, page, and content set, it is extremely easy for Google to crawl and read your website. To validate this further, here is what Google has to say about responsive design:

> Sites that use responsive web design, i.e. sites that serve all devices on the same set of URLs, with each URL serving the same HTML to all devices and using just CSS to change how the page is rendered on the device. **This is Google's recommended configuration.**[4]

When it comes to mobile SEO, responsive sites are also much easier to maintain. Unlike dedicated mobile websites that require a primary and secondary "m." version of the domain to maintain, responsive websites

[4]*Source:* https://developers.google.com/webmasters/smartphone-sites/details.

use only a single URL. That means that the SEO work that you've done to build up the domain authority and rank of your website isn't in vain. The authority and rank are unified between your desktop and mobile site because they are the exact same site!

The same SEO best practices that exist for the desktop version of your website also carry over to the mobile version. Depending on the mobile website format that you choose, aside from user experience and ease of access, your concern should be making sure that all of the pages, SEO meta-settings, and content that exist on your desktop site also simultaneously exist on your mobile website.

With wearables hitting the market now, like watches, glasses, and who knows what else, responsive design is looking more appealing and will definitely save you time and headaches down the road.

Do it for your users or do it for Google search placement, but no matter what, you need to have a mobile solution in place if you are going to succeed on the web.

"Should I use a different domain for my mobile website?"

Using .mobi is .ridiculous. Don't use a different domain. The reason you see so many websites using a different domain for the mobile site is simply this: It's easier for a website vendor that wants to sell you a mobile site to build it on a different domain. They can build the site without ever needing to access your website and host it on a .mobi version of your domain, which is always available, because they are stupid, and when it's done all they need to do is add the detection script.

Here is why it's a horrible idea:

It cuts your traffic in *half*!

Half of your traffic is coming from mobile devices, and half of mobile traffic is coming from search. Do you want Google to have to figure out which website to send the traffic to? The fact is .mobi is always a disaster for website traffic and will kill your traffic from mobile search.

Regardless of whether you use a responsive design strategy or a detection strategy, it is incredibly important that you use a unified URL structure on all versions of your site. With a unified URL structure you can send an email with a link to any page of your website, and the user will land on that page no matter what device they visit the site with.

For example, Frank can send an email to a customer after calling him about his selection of skateboard wheels with this link in it: http://FranksSkateBoards.com/trucks-and-wheels (not a real site).

If Frank has a unified URL structure, his customer can open that email, click the link, and see his selection of wheels, regardless of whether she is using her phone, tablet, laptop, or desktop computer.

If Frank signed up for a .mobi website and is running multiple domains, he has to send her this email:

> Hi Sheila,
>
> Please check out our wide selection of skateboard trucks and wheels. If you are using a mobile phone go to http://FranksSkate Boards.mobi/I-Hope-This-Works, if you are browsing on a desktop or laptop you can visit our main site, http://FranksSkate Boards.com/trucks-and-wheels, or if you are using a tablet or similar device, please find another device to view our great selection of skateboard wheels.
>
> Thanks,
>
> Frank

However, most businesses with a .mobi website don't email this way. They just send the link that they see on their computer, http://FranksSkateBoards.com/trucks-and-wheels, to the customer, who promptly clicks the link on their phone. They then get a "404 page not found" error and search elsewhere for their skateboard wheels.

Why would Google reward this? It doesn't.

Google and your customers will reward you for using a unified URL structure. This is impossible with a different domain because of the different domain extension:

http://FranksSkateBoards.mobi/skateboards

is not the same as

http://FranksSkateBoards.com/skateboards

even if it redirects. It's a bad idea—don't do it. Use a unified URL strategy.

PPC ADVERTISING ON MOBILE

Okay, so now you've got a great thumb-friendly mobile site that can rank organically and your customers love it. How about mobile paid search advertising? While paid search can be frustrating in general because so many people run ad blocking software and/or completely ignore the paid areas of search results pages, it actually works great on mobile! One of the main reasons is that it is so unavoidable.

When you perform a Google search on your desktop computer, you can see the organic results with your eyes. Most of us have trained our eyes to skip the paid ads or have completely blasted them out of existence entirely with free ad blocking extensions! It doesn't work that way on your phone. Ad blockers don't work on the phone, and you have to physically scroll past the ads with your finger to get to the organic results. Remember 51 percent of mobile traffic to your site comes through search and it is the same for your competitors. Wouldn't it be nice to force your competitors' customers to see ads for your website and business every time they search for them?

Mobile advertising is powerful stuff because, unlike traditional desktop search advertising, your prospects have to look at the ads to get to the information they are searching for. Of course, the ideal is that you are there on top when they get to the organic results, but let's face it—the most competitive and lucrative search terms are going to take a while before you start ranking number one organically. You can be running a mobile advertisement on that term you want so badly, and it will show up in front of searches in the next five minutes!

And mobile phone users can't help but look at them!

Google AdWords offers the ability to automatically adjust your bid amounts based on the user's device. If you are already running a Google AdWords campaign for your business and assuming you've already squared up your mobile website and fired the jerk who sold you a .mobi, try increasing your bids on mobile by 20 percent or more and watch what happens.

Just like the lottery, you've got to be in it to win it.

To summarize, be sure you have a great mobile strategy because:

- Your users care.
- It's almost one third of all web traffic and growing at a rapid pace.
- Google cares.
- It helps you rank organically.
- You can easily swamp your competitors with powerful ads that their customers can't ignore.
- More than half of mobile traffic comes from search.

Remember to maintain a unified URL structure regardless of how you choose to design the site so that Google and your users can find what they are looking for.

HOW MOBILE USERS SEARCH

After covering different mobile website format best practices, it's time to shift direction away from what you should be doing to how people are using their mobile devices to search. I should mention that even though I have already touched on some mobile SEO tips and tricks, going deeper into how people search will bring up some more SEO points.

A few years ago, when Apple introduced Siri, the operating system's virtual voice recognition assistant, the way users interacted with their phones changed forever. Shortly thereafter, Google launched its version of a virtual assistant with the release of its Google Now software. Each advancement in artificial intelligence technology also brought with it shifts in how mobile users use their device to find and access information.

Consider the primary difference in conducting a web search from a desktop device and from a mobile device. As an example, let's say that I'm in need of vehicle repairs and maintenance services. From a desktop, I might search for something like "cheap mechanics in San Diego, CA," and the search engine will go to work, finding me websites that are as relevant as possible to what I've typed in.

Since Google knows the physical location where I'm conducting that search, it will do its best to deliver me search results as close to my physical location as possible. Research suggests that mobile users are more concerned about the "here and now" than desktop searchers, so adding a layer of locality to your web strategy is going to deliver you far superior results.[5]

Now add the location-based data to a mobile device, and the difference in how the search is conducted. "Okay, Google, where is the best place to get the air conditioning in my car fixed for cheap and near to my location right now?" "Where" searches from a desktop computer are merely implied questions and much more consolidated (because, let's

---

[5]*Source:* http://mobithinking.com/best-practices/mobile-seo-best-practices.

face it—who wants to type all of that out?); mobile users are conducting voice searches, which automatically become much more conversational and better enable Google to understand the bigger picture of what you are trying to find.

This is where the Hummingbird search algorithm update can really come into play for your online strategy, because if you are focused on making sure the content on your website is incredible to begin with and your mobile website aligns with what your objectives are, you have a greater power to show up more prominently for relevant searches from your desired target audience when they are searching from their mobile.

Once a mobile user finds a link to content or information that is enticing, the next step is to be aware of how impatient mobile users are. As a best practice, make sure that your mobile website loads in one second or less, or you will risk losing the interest of a potential customer or brand ambassador. To assist with making your website as fast as possible, in August 2013, Google announced new speed guidelines for smartphone sites.

Google recommends that most important information on any page on your site should exist above the "fold"—in other words, above where the content gets cut off naturally by the bottom of your device's screen. It also mentions that the "above the fold" content should be fully loaded and displayed on the user's handset in less than one second! If you think that sounds incredibly fast, you'd be right, especially considering that the average phone load speed is around seven seconds for the majority of mobile sites currently.

Lastly, in speaking of mobile page load speeds, it's important to ask yourself how long you would expect someone to wait for your site to load. If you agree that one second is unrealistic, further ask yourself if the content on your website currently is worth waiting for. Doing so will help you identify whether your current website is offering the right level of value to begin with.

Mobile searchers are also highly social, so encouraging social sharing is an absolute must as part of your mobile strategy. At first glance, this may not appear to have any value for your Google mobile strategy, but consider that according to Facebook, 74 percent of its monthly global visits come from mobile devices. The objective with social sharing is to get more eyes on your content. Driving traffic to your site can translate to offsite SEO opportunities because the more eyes you get on your content, the more likely someone will be influenced to write and link to your website, thus enhancing the authority of your site and gaining it more favor in the eyes of Google.

Do not hesitate to make your mobile site as easy to share as possible. Aside from merely trying to please Google, the more eyes on your business or brand, the more opportunities you get to do business, just as discussed in Chapter 1.

As you can see, having a mobile strategy in place is absolutely vital to achieving success online with Google. Mobile usage is still on the rise (if you can believe it), and there is no indication that it is going to stop growing bigger and bigger year after year.

To briefly recap, your mobile strategy priorities (in no particular order) are as follows:

1. Identify your objectives.
2. Select a mobile website format that best meets your needs.
3. Make sure your desktop SEO work seamlessly carries over to mobile.
4. Remember how mobile users search.
5. Closely follow Google's mobile speed guidelines.
6. Make your mobile content as shareable as possible.

Following these six guidelines will help you leverage an online mobile marketing strategy that delivers results and places you in the good graces of Google.

ADDITIONAL RESOURCES

For additional resources on how you can best optimize your site and online assets for the most popular mobile devices, please visit www .googleopolybook.com/mobile-dominance-strategies.

CHAPTER 8

Online Reputation Optimization

There are multiple layers of online reputation or reputation management. There is the obvious "reputation" aspect of it. Perception is reality. What people see, they will believe. It is like back in the day—when something was on television, it had to be real. Today if it is on Google, it must be real. Or if "Google says . . . ," it must be real. As mentioned earlier in Chapter 2, Jim Lecinski from Google wrote the book *Winning the Zero Moment of Truth*, or ZMOT. What he said is that more than 80 percent of all transactions in the United States start on search engines. And the number one influence point is online reputation—the "zero moment of truth." When someone reads a Google review, a Yelp review, or a MerchantCircle review, it can and will cause them to react to the person, product, or service differently. An online review on Google will influence a person's buying decision. Google places a very high level of value on reviews, especially on reviews people leave on Google+ Local Business/Google Reviews.

There is another reason why reviews are so important to Google. Google wants to give people what they are looking for, when they are looking for it. Google wants to give the absolute best possible results—that means the best possible person, place, product, service, thing, and so on. Google knows that 95 percent of people do not go past the first page, so out of thousands, hundreds of thousands, or even millions of search results, Google has to provide the absolute best options for the searcher. If Google provided crappy results, bad companies, horrible restaurants, or dirty hotels, people would stop using Google to find things.

It is in Google's best interest to provide the absolute best possible solutions for searchers. So Google's algorithm has multiple signals that it looks for in order to rank favorably on page one.

A brand, person, or company's online reputation is one of the most important aspects of successfully creating a fan base or selling a product or service. Both understanding online reputation and creating an online reputation management strategy are crucial for not only your success but also your brand's longevity. I will not be going into detail about online reputation, other than with respect to its SEO value. However, I feel compelled to point out to you how serious this subject is and how important it is for you to make sure that you not only understand the concept but also create an online reputation management strategy for your brand. There will be more information on online reputation at www.GoogleopolyBook.com.

ONLINE REPUTATION OPTIMIZATION

Online reputation optimization (ORO) strategy is what it sounds like. It is the optimization of your online reputation. Specifically, it is having all of your online reviews and testimonials show up on the first page of Google, organically. To win the game of Googleopoly, you want to acquire as much Google real estate as you possibly can. I highly suggest that you create a thorough strategy to engage as many reputation sites and business directory sites as possible that allow people to rate/review you or your business.

There are multiple "hit points" if you can dominate Page One of Google with positive reviews. Obviously, you will have the Googleopoly strategy in full effect, but the additional value is that you will have the right real estate dominating Page One of Google. Not only are you going to be all over the first page of Google, but also you will be there with the most influential pieces of content possible—online reviews!

The following is a list of **mandatory** online reputation sites that you need to utilize in your strategy.

Google Reviews

This one is a no-brainer; you have to make sure that Google+ Local Business is totally set up, not just for the social media and SMO value but most importantly for the online Google Reviews. Google Reviews rank higher than all other reviews. In addition to Google Reviews ranking more powerfully than any other reviews, Google displays its reviews more prominently. This will include a whole section on the first page of

Google, with a star rating system, number of reviews, review score, and even a link to the Google+ Business page.

If you Google "Ford dealers Philadelphia," you will see six different dealerships' Google Reviews prominently on the first page of Google (see Figure 8.1).

FIGURE 8.1   Google compiles search results based on Google Reviews. They are organized by their relevance, ranking, and number of reviews. By also linking to Google Maps, the company's address and phone number appears, making it easy for users to get in touch with and visit the business.

Pacifico Ford has the most reviews and the highest rating: 134 reviews with a 4.7 (out of 5 stars) rating. Not only does Pacifico have supreme placement in the Google Reviews section, but also it has the best rating. A prospect is almost surely going to choose that dealership over the Dunphy dealership, which has one review and no rating. A prospect would surely choose Pacifico over a dealership that has no ratings and doesn't even show up on the list of possibilities.

Zagat Ratings

Let's dive into restaurants for a moment here and show you how much Google values reviews. In 2009 Google was in discussions to acquire Yelp for $500 million. That deal fell through, and in 2011 Google acquired Zagat for $151 million. It wasn't a half billion dollars, but $151 million is still a lot of money to pay for a company that reviews businesses. But Google had a vision and an understanding that people (searchers on Google) want to know what other people think about things. People want to avoid making bad decisions and wasting money on subpar restaurants (as well as companies, products, services, people, etc.).[1]

If you Google "seafood restaurants New York City," you will see a large black bar on the very top of Google that is above the PPC ads. In that bar are Zagat reviews for 22 restaurants that fit the search criteria.

In the black bar are graphics/pictures of food, restaurants, etc., which draw you in. Then, of course, there are the names of restaurants, the star ratings, the types of restaurants, and the number of reviews. There is everything you need right there on the first page of Google. You do not need to go anywhere else. If you click any of the options in the black bar, it will open a Knowledge Graph on the right-hand side.

Here is an example. If you clicked the "Blue Water Grill," you would see what is shown in Figure 8.2.

The Knowledge Graph is tied to the Zagat review/rating system and provides very important information:

- Address
- Phone number
- Pricing
- Hours of operation

[1] *Source*: www.forbes.com/sites/chrisbarth/2011/10/27/google-paid-151-million-to-get-zagat-ditch-yelp/.

- Reservations
- Menu
- Star rating system (reviews)
- "Also searching for." This is an important feature that gives searchers additional options and ideas they might not have known about.

FIGURE 8.2   The Blue Water Grill is a great example of how Yelp and Zagat have been integrated into Google search results. Photos, a map, phone number, website, and additional details, as well as multiple review sources, provide users a full range of content to help them make informed decisions.

Yelp

If you Googled "Chinese food San Francisco," in addition to the Zagat/Google black bar on the top of the first page, you would find numerous Yelp reviews and ratings (see Figure 8.3).

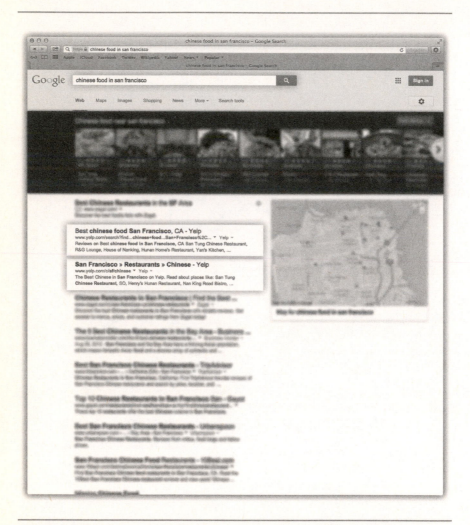

FIGURE 8.3   When you Google "chinese food in san francisco," you'll see that the first two organic results are from Yelp. When you combine the power of Google's algorithm and Yelp's partnership with Apple (and consequently Siri), it's more important than ever to have a profile on Yelp.

Yelp is a major online review site that ranks very high on Google. It is arguably the most powerful and most relevant review site. The only problem is that Google doesn't own it. So, it won't rank as well as Google Reviews or Zagat, but it still has major value and more specifically it has major SEO value.

Another major aspect of Yelp is that it is partnered with Apple and powers Apple's Siri search results and reviews. For example, if you are one of the 500 million people who purchased an iPhone and you tell Siri, "Ford dealership Philadelphia," "seafood restaurants New York City," or "Chinese food San Francisco," Siri will return with Yelp reviews, *not* Google reviews. So, Yelp is still a major force to be reckoned with. Make sure that in addition to creating a Google+ account so you can create a Google Review strategy or a Zagat account so you can create a Zagat strategy, you add Yelp to your arsenal for ORO resources.

Here are additional resources that you should also sign up your business for so you can start to harvest online reviews that will rank on page one of Google:

- MerchantCircle
- Yellow Pages
- White Pages
- Citysearch
- Foursquare

There are a myriad of important and useful websites, directories, and listing sites that you can utilize for your brand, company, product, or service. This can get confusing or cumbersome, so there are software solutions that you can utilize that will streamline and organize the process. One tool I suggest that you look into is Yext (www.yext.com). Yext will first scan to see how your brand/company is listed in all of the top directories and business listing sites.

Human Resources

Most people have no idea that there are human resources websites that have tremendous SEO value for online reviews. But these online reviews are not like traditional reviews. These are employment reviews! That's right—there are multiple websites that allow (actually encourage) employees to rate and rank where they work. This makes all the sense in the world. If you were looking for a job, you don't want to go work for a horrible company or a terrible boss. So, these websites are in existence to provide the job seekers some sort of transparency about what they might be getting themselves into.

Here are the two most powerful websites that specialize in this:

1. Indeed.com
2. Glassdoor.com

I encourage you to create accounts (profiles) on both of these websites and set up the profiles the proper way with relevant keywords for a viable SEO strategy. Once these profiles are created for your business (brand), I would encourage all of your employees to fill out positive reviews about your organization:

- Full-time
- Part-time
- Interns
- General contract agents (1099 employees)
- Frontline level
- Senior level

By creating human resource review site profiles, you are creating additional indexable content that can (and will) rank on the first page of Google.

Industry Review Sites

Let's use examples from the automotive sales industry:

- Edmunds.com
- KelleyBlueBook.com (KBB.com)

Another major opportunity is to connect with industry-specific review sites. These sites are powerful because they have a specific and relevant audience already built in. For example, in the automotive sales industry, the top two websites that consumers and shoppers visit are Kelley Blue Book and Edmunds.com. These sites generate millions and millions of unique visitors per month. They are primary information sites to assist the shopper/buyer in making an educated buying decision on their next automotive purchase. These sites already have powerful

SEO value. A car dealership or an automotive salesperson would be smart to direct their clients to both of these websites and fill out an online review on their dealership (or them as a salesperson). Or they can send an email campaign with a link to either KBB.com or Edmunds. The overall objective is to get online reviews at places that specialize in online reviews, especially industry-specific online review sites.

To give you a different example about how this works, let's use the hotel industry. Google "best hotels Beverly Hills," and you will see an almost complete first page of Google saturated with online reviews:

- Zagat reviews
- PPC reviews
- Hotel comparison (sponsored)
- TripAdvisor
- Expedia
- Hotels.com

You want to not only utilize review sites but also incorporate industry-specific review sites for even more relevancy.

Personal Review Site (Blog Site)

I am going to go into detail regarding blog sites/ancillary websites for SEO value in the next chapter, so I am not going to go into detail right here. However, I will say that it would be an *amazing* idea for you to create your own review site! You can create (for free) a review site using WordPress for your company or brand. It is simple—here is the roadmap:

- URL/Domain
  - I suggest something simple, like www.ABCCompanyReviews.com (the name of your brand or company and then "Reviews.com").
- I suggest a blog format because it will be very easy to update all of the reviews that you receive on a daily or weekly basis.
- Make sure that you upload text reviews.
  - You can get quotes directly from clients or fans.
  - You can extract quotes from video testimonials from your clients and make text quotes.
  - Scan letters, cards, or thank you messages into digital format.

- Pictures: Get pictures of your clients. Get pictures of *you* and your clients, your clients at your events, and your clients with your products.
- Videos: Video testimonials are one of the most powerful pieces of review content that you can acquire.
- Syndicate content: Get all the reviews that you receive from all other sites:
  - Google Reviews
  - Zagat
  - Yelp
  - Yellow Pages
  - MerchantCircle
  - Foursquare
  - TripAdvisor
  - Hotels.com
  - Edmunds.com
  - GlassDoor
  - Indeed.com
  - And so on . . .

You can cut and paste them into your blog site.

INTERACTION WITH REVIEWS

Getting more reviews and having these sites rank for your name is just the start. The real juice begins when people read them. We already know how prominently the star ratings show up on Google, but that's just an overview. Depending on your type of business and the type of customers you attract, there's a good chance that you can make a huge impact on potential customers.

Every review should receive a personalized reply, preferably from the owner or general manager of the company. Let me repeat that for emphasis: *every* review should receive a personal reply from the owner or general manager. It doesn't matter if you're getting reviews every day. Time must be set aside for immediate responses so that no review sits there for longer than one business day before becoming a conversation rather than a monologue.

This works for two reasons. First, it's respectful to your customers. This should be obvious. If someone takes the time to say something about your company, good or bad, they deserve to receive a reply. The other reason is that Google loves these types of interactions. If you ask them, they'll deny it. If you ask SEO experts who have been doing this for a while, they will verify that interactions help your review pages get ranked higher in the searches.

There are exceptions. Sites like Ripoff Report and other "parasite sites" rely on business names to drive traffic to their sites. In essence, they hold you hostage by posting these negative reviews and hoping that they rank for your name so you have to address them.

Don't.

Your natural instinct will be to defend yourself, but if you validate these sites, it will only get worse. Focus on the strong sites—BBB, Yelp, Google, etc.—and let the parasites sink.

Turning Bad into Good

Most businesses are scared to death of negative reviews and rightfully so. A few bad reviews can get people to stop doing business with you if they believe that they're going to be working with an unreputable company.

What's worse is that people love to look for dirt on companies that they're considering working with. You could have dozens of good reviews, but people visiting these sites will skip most of those and look for the one-star reviews.

It's not all bad. You can turn it around and make it work to your advantage. How you respond to complaints can position your company in a positive light. Nobody expects a business to be perfect. We can't make everyone happy 100 percent of the time. Negative experiences happen to every business, and your response is extremely important.

Secret Tip

You have to be careful with your wording, not just because of the repercussions, which we'll discuss ahead, but because of how Google reads the statement.

Negative phrases, such as "I am sorry," "bad experience," or "big mistake," get read by Google and can influence whether it "recommends" your company in the form of organic listings. To be specific, you might think that you are saying something

(continued)

(*Continued*)

nice, like "I am sorry you had a horrible experience at our restaurant. Let me make it up to you." Google is going to understand that there were numerous negative keywords and phrases from *both* the person leaving the review and the business itself. The more negative keywords and phrases, the more Google will place that business in the "bad" category. When I teach businesses this reality, they seem shocked that Google has the ability to understand the meaning and inferred meaning from the type of language used in the reviews, both from the user and the supplier standpoints. So, be *very* careful what you say and how you respond to reviews. Google is listening. . . .

First and foremost, avoid acknowledging wrongdoing. Don't say things like "We're sorry you had a bad experience" or anything that puts your business in a purely apologetic light. A better way to put it is to empathize and try to open communication rather than simply trying to make it right.

This is hard for a lot of businesses. In the real world, we tend to want to say we're sorry and to offer some sort of compensation. This is a mistake in a public forum like online review sites because it encourages people to leave more bad reviews, thinking that they're going to get something for free if they complain about it.

Here's an example of how to respond empathetically to a bad review online:

Mrs. Customer:

Thank you for your feedback. We strive as a company to be perfect in all of our interactions, but there are always instances when perceptions are not aligned. We would love to discuss this further with you directly. Could we discuss this in person or on the phone as I want to give this personal attention?

Sean V. Bradley
CEO
555.555.1234

(Continued)

An interaction like that following a bad review tells Google that you want to make it right without acknowledging that you did anything wrong, while still telling anyone reading reviews that you care and you want to make it right. It's challenging because you have to play to two different audiences, but a properly worded response can go a long way to helping you on both ends of the spectrum.

Sharing Makes It Even More Visible

Utilizing social media channels also has a double benefit for your business. When you have great reviews that you want to share, be sure to put them everywhere you can:

- Your website
- Blog
- Facebook
- Twitter
- Google+
- YouTube

That last one should have caught your attention. How do you share a Yelp review on YouTube? For some businesses such as mine, we meet face-to-face with customers and we're able to get actual video interviews with them. That doesn't work for most businesses, but that's okay. You can still take advantage of reviews.

It doesn't take extreme video editing skills to grab screenshots of your best reviews and put them into a nice visual media file that can be uploaded to YouTube. Add some music, tag it properly as discussed in the previous chapter on video SEO, and voilà! You have a video review.

These can be very powerful for one major reason. When people do a search for your business reviews, there's a great chance that your properly optimized video will rank on the first page.

I have already identified how powerful videos and video SEO are. So, I highly suggest that you create a video review or video testimonial strategy for yourself and/or your business.

Here are some best practice tips for creating the best video reviews:

- Make sure that you diversify the types of reviews that you create. For example, if you were a car dealership or an automotive salesperson, you would want to get video reviews from your happy clients. But diversify your testimonials by:
  - Expectations
    - Price shoppers
    - Convenience shoppers
    - Specific vehicle shoppers
    - People who hate car salesmen
    - Credit-challenged people
    - People interested in selling their trade
  - Geographics: Review from people in a certain area
    - People who live in the primary market area of the dealership (people who live close to the dealership)
    - People who live in areas outside of the dealership's primary market area (these areas are "conquest" territories)
  - Demographics
    - Minority communities
    - If there is a Hispanic community, get reviews from Hispanic clients
    - If there is a Jewish community, get reviews from Jewish clients
    - If there is an African American community, get reviews from African American clients
  - Law enforcement and military
    - Clients in uniform
    - Senior citizens
    - First-time buyers
    - Families
    - Credit-challenged

As you can see now, creating reviews is more comprehensive than just sticking your camera phone in someone's face and asking for a "quick review." You need to create a strategy. I know that I used an example for the automotive sales industry. But the concept is simple and can be applied to all industries. Basically, you want to diversify your video reviews. You want to think of your audience—all of them. What is it that they want, need, or expect? What is important to them? Once you understand what these things are, then get video testimonials/reviews from all of your current and past clients and make sure to diversify your library of video reviews. So, when people are searching for you or your company, product, or service, they will collide with all of these video testimonials.

As I mentioned earlier, I have over 600 different video reviews/testimonials. All you have to do is type in "Dealer Synergy reviews" or "Sean V. Bradley reviews" in YouTube, and they will all show up. They are all diversified reviews. I have segmented them for:

- Me (Sean V. Bradley) personally
- Dealer Synergy Reviews (my training and consulting company)
- Internet Sales 20 group (my three-day workshop)
- Different audiences:
  - Dealer principals (multimillionaire owners of car dealerships)
  - General managers
  - Sales managers
  - Internet directors
  - BDC directors
  - Appointment setters/Internet sales coordinators
  - Car salesmen
  - OEM reps (automotive manufacturers)
  - State dealer associations
  - FranklinCovey students
  - Raving fans that say that I have changed their lives
  - Other industry experts who give powerful reviews
  - I even have my direct competitors provide video reviews on how awesome my workshops are

In addition to video reviews on YouTube and other video search engines, there are other sites that you need to syndicate your online reviews to, including your own site. The sharing and linking will help your strong reviews rank well on the search engines. Share them on Facebook, Twitter, and Google+. Syndicate them to your blog and website. There are widgets and plugins available that will pull these reviews onto your website and blog and then link back to your reviews themselves. When you acknowledge the reviews and review sites with your own properties, Google is more likely to give them credibility as a result.

Remember, there is no trick to beat Google. You can't fake or scam Google (not for long). Google feels so strongly about online reviews that it published a book called *Winning the Zero Moment of Truth*, which states that reviews are a huge influence factor and contribute to the prospect's Zero Moment of Truth. Google also went on a mission to acquire the most powerful review companies in existence and almost bought Yelp for a half of a billion dollars but at the last minute dropped that acquisition attempt and instead purchased Zagat for $151 million. Google gives preeminent position on the first page of Google for Google Reviews and Zagat Reviews. Google also integrates the Knowledge Graph with its online review platform(s).

Use this information to create an ORO strategy. Use online reviews to achieve Google first page domination.

ADDITIONAL RESOURCES

Online reviews are so influential that every business and brand must be constantly monitoring their reputation. Find more resources to keep you current on your online reputation management and optimization strategies by visiting www.googleopolybook.com/online-reputation-strategies.

CHAPTER 9

Secondary Websites for Search Dominance

So far, we've covered how you can make your primary website rank better. We've shown you how social media pages and profiles can affect both your primary website rankings and how they rank themselves on searches. We've discussed review sites that also rank for your business by name and how to take advantage of them, but there's one final piece to the puzzle that's necessary to fill all of the holes.

You want to completely dominate the first page of Google, particularly when people search for your business by name. Google limits the number of times that a website can appear for individual searches, so there are other spots that need to be covered. This is where secondary websites come into play.

Secondary websites come in a variety of types. In an ideal situation where you're able to dedicate a good amount of time to the game of Googleopoly, you'll have many of these secondary sites out there taking up space on searches and generating more business.

Here are some of the different types of secondary websites:

- Blogs
- Microsites
- Customer appreciation sites
- Focus sites

Let's take them in this order and describe what benefits they bring, how they are created, how they are maintained, and what they can do to further your business.

BLOGS

The weblog started growing in popularity around the turn of the century. Websites have been easily available for people for over two decades, but they were clunky and often required technical expertise to build and maintain them. The rise of the early blogging platforms made it possible for everyday people without technical training to put up a personal site on which they could express their thoughts and share with others.

They were journals online. Literally, they were weblogs of our lives. The term was eventually shortened to *blogs*, and they have grown in popularity over the years. Today, there are around a quarter of a **billion** blogs floating around on the Internet, though most are completely abandoned by their original builder.

Blogging for your business is a way to give a personality to the company. They can be used to establish expertise. They can even be used to promote things happening from day to day at your business, like sales, employees of the month, and customer testimonials.

Types of Blog URLs

There are three types of blog domains that can be used:

1. www.companyname.com/blog
2. blog.companyname.com
3. www.companynameblog.com

There are advantages to all three options. The first option puts the blog in a folder on your website. This allows you to continuously add content to your primary website the way that Google wants you to do. Most SEO professionals and even Google recommends this way, but shortly we'll explain why it's not the way that I recommend.

The second option creates a subdomain for the blog. This used to be the best way to do it and is the way that Google has always run its own internal blogs, but things have changed. They were once considered to be completely separate websites from the primary domain. Today, Google is shifting toward viewing them as branches of the primary in most cases. It uses exceptions for the sites where this is impossible, but for your business, this is the least appealing approach.

The last one is the one that I recommend. It puts your blog on a completely separate domain. It does not even have to be hosted in the same place. In essence, it can stand alone.

The negative of this style is that your primary website does not gain the SEO value of having content constantly added to it. For most businesses, that is an important thing. I know that you're not going to be like most businesses, so consider that last option as an advanced business owner's method for really dominating on search.

By keeping it on its own domain, you will be able to drive links to your primary website that has some benefit for its rankings. This is minor but it has an effect. Be warned, though. Each additional link to the primary domain reduces the effectiveness of the inbound links themselves. In other words, if you're continuously linking to your own website from your blog, eventually Google will stop giving you any value from those links.

The biggest reason that you want to do it this way is because you'll be able to cover more real estate. As already mentioned throughout, it's important to cover as much search real estate as possible. This is the only way to successfully do it. Your blog on its own domain will be able to rank for your name as well as other searches in ways that the other two styles cannot.

ProTip

Many companies like to use the free subdomain blog services offered by companies like Wordpress, Tumblr, and Blogger. But hosting costs $10 per month, so there's no reason to use this method at all. It is less effective, and the money saved by doing it this way is minimal.

Blogging Software

Keep it simple. There are literally dozens of different blogging platforms available to use. Most of them are designed to highlight a special feature or to integrate with other software. In most cases, you should look at the various innovative programs available, but in the case of blogging, the major players have everything you need. No need to find the secret platforms. There's nothing worse than putting effort into something that may be obsolete in the future.

Despite a sea of blogging platforms, there are only four that are worth considering:

1. Blogger
2. Tumblr
3. Ning
4. WordPress

They have their benefits and weaknesses, and unlike most other things in this book, we're not going to give a solid recommendation. If you're using any of these, you'll be fine. Let's look at them individually.

Blogger

One might believe that since this is owned by Google, it's the one that is most favored by Google. That's not the case. In fact, one can argue that it's the second-most favored by Google on the list.

Blogger is a middle-ground type of software. It's more robust than some and simpler than others. It doesn't have the features or plugins that Wordpress has, and it isn't as easy as Tumblr. For this reason, it's a good platform for people who want a little of everything rather than a focus on the extremes.

Tumblr

This is the easiest platform to use for blogging. One can have solid posts up in literally seconds. If you see a video you like on YouTube and you want to share it with your readers, simply copy the URL and write a title and description. It resizes it appropriately and shares it on your blog.

Tumblr also has the biggest internal community. It is really a social media site that has decent blogging capabilities rather than being a blog that has social capabilities, but as a tool for business, the blogging aspect is more important.

Unfortunately, it is also the least robust of the group. You are constrained by the themes. Thankfully, there are plenty to choose from, but customizing a Tumblr blog to fit your needs can be more challenging than any of the other platforms.

It is also the least trusted by Google, meaning that you may have to work a little harder to get it appropriately ranked for your keywords.

Ning

This is the oddball of the group because it's not really a blogging site. It has blog features, and that's good enough for our purposes.

Ning is the easiest way to do collaborative blogging. In other words, you can have people within the community or industry participate in adding content to the blog. This can be very beneficial if you're planning on making your blog stand out and get serious traffic. It's worthless if you're not going to get a ton of people to the blog.

WordPress

Any of the previous three platforms will work for you nicely. I give a slight nod to WordPress as the best of the four.

It is the most robust. Many build complete websites on the WordPress platform. It also has the most options. There are tens of thousands of plugins, themes, and customizations that can be done to WordPress.

Most importantly, it's the most search-friendly from both an inbound perspective as well as an outbound perspective. The blogs rank better than any of the other platforms, and the juice that you send to your primary site has the most impact when coming from a WordPress blog.

The drawback is its strength. With any robust platform comes the need to understand it. With Tumblr, you can be up and running in moments. With WordPress, there's definitely a learning curve to getting it working properly. Maintaining it can be a challenge as well. It does not have the set-it-and-forget-it abilities of the other platforms.

If you want the best, you have to be willing to put in the effort. It's for this reason that I recommend any of the four. It all depends on how much you can do with your blogs. It's better to have a basic Tumblr blog that runs fine than to have a WordPress blog that you don't post to often because it's difficult.

What to Blog About

Believe it or not, everyone's a blogger waiting to happen. One does not have to be a Pulitzer Prize–winning journalist to post to a blog. You just need some ideas, a basic understanding of the English language (after all, you have spell check), and a schedule to sit down and blog for 30 minutes or more per week.

What you blog about depends entirely on your industry. If you own a restaurant, for example, it's easy to post image collages of various dishes, video blog posts of the chefs preparing a particular meal, or insights about the local community.

Here are some categories that most businesses could blog about:

- Industry innovations
- Industry news
- Special products or services
- Community events
- Local charities
- Local schools
- Individual customers
- Employee spotlights
- Interesting facts about your company and its history
- Interesting facts about your industry and its history
- Tips to help people use your products or services
- Reasons why people should use your products or services
- Anything that *you* like

This last one is the debatable one. There was an automotive industry blog where the company owner posted his wife's Thanksgiving turkey recipe. Some questioned what it was doing on an automotive blog, but it turned out to be extremely popular and shared well by the local community.

Some like to stay focused. Others like to branch out. The bottom line is that your blog should match what you know about and what you can write about. You're the expert. If you run a dry cleaning service, you know more about dry cleaning than any of your customers. Share your knowledge in your blog.

MICROSITES

There was a time not too long ago when microsites were all the rage for SEO. There were companies that specialized in creating hundreds, thousands, even tens of thousands of microsites that could be used for generating inbound links that helped the primary website rank for certain searches.

This was cut off completely. The Penguin update of 2012 eliminated these automated, low-quality links to the point that having them could actually do damage to your rankings. These networks were, for the most part, taken down. Several prominent SEO firms closed as a result.

A genuine, high-value microsite is one that works very similarly to your primary website. It can be an extension of your website, or it can be a stand-alone variation that covers a particular set of topics.

Unlike a blog, the content on a microsite is almost entirely set to drive business. That gives it the advantage of bringing more direct value to your business, but it also makes the site harder to get ranked for keywords.

A strong microsite is one that combines a little bit of everything. It has some pages of content that are similar to a blog that bring value to the visitor, but these pages should be timeless. In other words, since you're not posting content to it on a regular basis, the content should be able to stand on its own regardless of when it is seen. You wouldn't want to cover a particular event on a microsite, for example.

People often confuse microsites with landing pages or focus sites. A microsite can have landing pages, but a stand-alone landing page or squeeze page is effective only in certain situations and does not offer any value from a search perspective. When added to a microsite, this kind of page can act as a way to generate leads, while the rest of the site brings SEO value to your primary domain and also has the ability to rank in searches on its own.

When building a microsite, think of it as a smaller variation of your own website. Cut out the less important components. You shouldn't have an About Us page on a microsite, for example.

An example of a microsite would be a car dealer's inventory placed separately from the website itself. On the primary website, a dealership will have sections for service, parts, finance, specials, and the works. With a microsite, the home page would talk about the various models available in the brand. Then there would be the full inventory feed that creates pages on the site and takes them down when a vehicle is sold.

Microsites do not replace any aspect of the primary website. You should not direct people from your primary website to the microsite. The opposite can be done; there's nothing wrong with having a service or parts button that takes people to the appropriate pages on the primary website.

A properly positioned microsite will rank for the company by name and will also rank for the specific needs. In the previous example, you would put it on a domain like www.bradleyhondainventory.com.

It should rank for *Bradley Honda* as well as other terms, like *Honda Accord New Jersey*.

The disadvantage of microsites is that they require a good amount of effort to build. The advantage is that they do not require much effort to maintain. Build it. Add content every month or two. Let the search advantages permeate!

CUSTOMER APPRECIATION SITES

Appreciating customers is easy. As business owners, you know that your customers provide your paychecks and keep the business up and running. Most people appreciate their customers, but are they doing anything to show them this fact online?

A customer appreciation site fills this need. It's not for everyone. A roofing contractor, for example, doesn't have a whole lot to say about their customers other than to thank them. They don't have "regulars" because it's normally a one-time gig. They don't have fans because it's difficult to stand out for doing a great job. If the roof is done right, the customers are satisfied but they're not going to say, "Wow, he fixed our roof better than any roofer we've used in the past!"

For most other types of businesses, customer appreciation sites work nicely. They comprise two components: the customers' stories and offers from your business.

Many businesses have loyalty programs that come in the form of loyalty cards or online check-ins. These are ideal for helping to select the right people to put on a site. Coffee shops often have "buy nine, get the tenth free" punch cards. This is a great way to build a customer appreciation site!

When someone fills out their punch cards, the barista simply has to ask if they can be put up on the customer appreciation page. All they need is to have their picture taken with their favorite drink, a first name, and the way they order their drink. This becomes a post on the customer appreciation page and can generate fun, utilizing the principles of gam-ification. I won't go into too much detail—gamification could take up a couple of chapters and has nothing to do with search—but I suggest looking it up for your business.

What's the point of all of this? Yes, it's fun and gives your customers something that they can use to promote your business to their friends, but it goes further. First of all, it makes for great content that can be shared on your social media sites. Second, it gives you another site where you can have a constant flow of content similar to your blog. Third, it adds unique images to your web presence that can individually rank in Google image search.

The most important reason, however, goes back to what I discussed about reputation management. These types of sites can take up real estate for the all-important searches for your business by name, but they can rank for other important searches as well:

- "Company name" reviews
- "Company name" complaints
- "Company name" feedback

When people do those searches, they're deciding whether to do business with you. By positioning customer appreciation sites well on those searches, you'll be able to stand out from the competition. Remember, if they're researching you, they're probably researching your competitors as well. If they don't have a customer appreciation site (and they probably don't), then you'll stand out as truly appreciative of your customers.

FOCUS SITES

I saved this one for last because they're the most important secondary sites that you can have. For the majority of businesses, if you can put time and effort into only one type of secondary site, this is it.

A focus site is exactly what it says—it's a website that is focused on one particular topic. We've built thousands of focus sites over the years that have helped automotive clients dominate countless searches.

Here are some examples of focus sites that work in the automotive industry:

- Model-specific focus sites
- Auto service focus sites
- Used car specials focus sites
- Event focus sites
- Geo-targeted focus sites

With each of these, you want to remember to stay completely focused. It should go without saying, but it's easy to try to include too much. The goal of a focus site is to rank for very particular keywords. By adding too much that is off topic, you can prevent it from doing its job.

Why They Work

There are two primary goals for these sites: take up space on Google and generate business. Very few people search for "best lasagna in Newport Beach," but if you have an Italian restaurant in or near Newport Beach, you'll want to be ranked at the top for this term. There are national sites that usually rank for these types of terms, sites like Yelp and TripAdvisor. Your primary website has very little chance of ranking for this term and there's not enough traffic for it to put in the SEO effort to make it happen, but a quick focus site can do the trick!

If you put in the effort to build and maintain focus sites regularly, you'll start to see your name popping up everywhere in searches. Regardless of whether your business relies on leads, direct sales, or simply the branding and exposure required to drive people to your store, focus sites are an excellent way to get the search terms that your primary website can't easily get.

They're not limited to filling the gaps, though. Just because your primary website is ranked, don't think that you shouldn't build focus sites for those keywords. Remember, if you're ranked number one with your primary website and number two with your focus site, then everyone else on the front page has been pushed down and one competitor who was at the bottom of the front page is now on page two, better known as "the barren search wasteland."

How to Build Focus Sites

Let's say you're building a focus site about the 2015 Honda Accord. You would want it on a specific domain, like 2015hondaaccordnewjersey.com. Then you would want the title to be very specific: "2015 Honda Accord for sale in New Jersey."

The content on the site should be completely unique and relevant to both Honda Accords and New Jersey itself. It doesn't have to be "SEO-speak." Write the content naturally, and make sure that you're not copying and pasting the content from other websites across the Internet.

There are plenty of platforms available. If you're using WordPress for your blog and you're comfortable using it to build other websites, there are great themes already prebuilt that you can plug in immediately.

If you're using a web developer, he or she can build you a template that is similar to your primary website. All you need to do is replace the old content with fresh, focused content, and you can start busting out new focus sites every month.

One Warning

There is a thin line between marketing with focus sites and spamming with them. Just because you can build a ton of them, don't think that you need to flood the market. It's better to have one or two strong focus sites that actually rank and drive business than to have dozens or hundreds of them that do nothing.

It's okay to link back to your primary website on your focus sites, but do not put those links in the footer or sidebar. All links to your website should be contextual. They must be within the body of the content on the pages rather than stuffed at the bottom or on the side. Google views repetitive links from across a domain as spam.

USING SECONDARY SITES PROPERLY

I have clearly laid out how each of the four major types of secondary sites should be used. If you have the bandwidth to make them awesome, then do it. If you do not, be selective. It's much better to skip a type of secondary site in order to make the others strong rather than to stretch yourself too thin and miss out on the benefits from any of them.

Focus on quality above all else. This is a bulk play to some extent, but that bulk must be tempered with quality. Just because you build them doesn't mean the people will come to them. Put in the effort if you can or save them for later if you can't.

You should be using the techniques laid out in this book to promote these secondary sites as well. Apply strong onsite SEO principles to them. Generate links to them. Share them on social media. Just like with your primary sites, these secondary sites need SEO juice to work properly.

Lastly, do not let the secondary sites take away from your efforts on your primary site. These are luxuries. If your primary site is not in perfect working order and ranking well on searches, you shouldn't put your effort into these secondary sites. Save them for later when you've already dominated everything you can with your primary website.

ADDITIONAL RESOURCES

Learn more about advanced SEO tools such as secondary sites, blogs, microsites, and focus sites by visiting www.googleopolybook.com/secondary-site-strategies.

CHAPTER 10

Putting It All Together

I know your mind must be swooning after reading this book. There is a lot to it. There is a lot of information, but I did my best to not make this book too intense. I wanted to make sure that you had the secret formula of how to win the game of Googleopoly. I have been immersed in advanced digital marketing for 15+ years, and there is very little structured education and certification for the subject of Google, SEO, social media, online reputation, and all of the other parts of Googleopoly. Even on a collegiate level, there is no real curriculum; the schools that offer classes or degrees fall short because when someone graduates, almost all of their training is irrelevant or obsolete (things change so fast). Furthermore, each of the individual categories that I covered in this book has scarce training opportunity in the real world. But to break down all of the pieces of Googleopoly the way I have done in this book and present them as one synergistic strategy has rarely been done, and it is virtually impossible to find similar training and implementation strategies anywhere.

Here is a recap of everything covered in this book:

- **Visibility is the key.** It doesn't matter who you are or what you are—a person, company, product, service, or a brand—you will need visibility to grow your fan base, build your brand, and sell yourself or your product or service.
- There are so many opportunities for visibility, but there are also so many distractions. The best and most cost-effective way to achieve visibility is the **Internet**.
- There are many ways to engage in Internet marketing and advertising, but there is nothing more powerful than **Google**.
- You need to understand exactly what Google wants and understand the complete landscape of **page one of Google**.
- Chapter 3 introduced the **Googleopoly strategy**. Basically, the reality is that only 5 percent of people go past the first page of Google.

So, you want to show up as many times as possible on the first page of Google. The way you do that is to use a multiplicity of resources to dominate Google's search algorithm.

- **The elements of Googleopoly are:**
  - (Onsite SEO) Websites and rules of traditional SEO
  - Full breakdown of what Google's algorithm is looking for:
    - URL/domains
    - Title tags
    - Header tags (H1, H2, H3, etc.)
    - Meta-description (description)
    - Alt tags
    - Content
    - Links
    - Strategy/focus
  - Video and video SEO
    - Technology/resources
    - YouTube and video search engines
    - Optimizing videos for Google page one domination
    - Syndication
    - Supplemental uploads
  - Social media and social media optimization
    - Social media versus social media optimization
    - Social signals
    - Social networks
      - Facebook
      - Google+
      - LinkedIn
      - Flickr
      - Pinterest
      - Private label social networks
      - NING
      - BuddyPress
  - Mobile and mobile optimization
    - How important mobile is to Google and the future of SEO
    - Different types of mobile solutions
    - Mobile SEO

- Online reputation and reputation optimization
  - How very important reputation and reviews are to Google
  - Google ZMOT
  - Online reputation/review sites
    - Google Reviews
    - Zagat
    - Yelp
    - MerchantCircle
    - Glassdoor
    - Indeed
- Online reputation optimization
- How to optimize reviews for Googleopoly strategy
- Secondary websites
- Why the need . . .
- How to optimize secondary sites properly
- What is the strategy of secondary websites (to secure Google real estate)
  - Blogs
  - Focus sites
  - Customer appreciation sites
  - Microsites, etc.

After you complete this book, you need to start from the very beginning of and use it like a checklist with your brand or your business.

If you utilized one or two sections in this book for your own business or brand, you would be extremely successful and you would have a competitive edge against your competition. However, if you follow each and every section of this book, you will win the game of Googleopoly and you will *crush your competition*!

ADDITIONAL RESOURCES

For a quick overview and outline of all the content and information covered in the previous nine chapters, please visit www.googleopolybook .com/googleopoly-strategy-outline.

CHAPTER 11

Looking into the Future of Google and Search

Writing a book about a multibillion-dollar company that affects over 1 billion people on this planet can be intimidating, especially when the book is about a strategy that can show you how to dominate Google for your brand, company, product, or service. And to make it more interesting, Google changes its algorithm 500–600 times per year!

Because I wanted this book to be the most powerful book that has ever been written on the subject of digital marketing, search engines, and, specifically, Google, I decided to reach out to some of my colleagues, who are some of the best and brightest search engine experts and digital marketing gurus in the United States. As a matter of fact, my network's clientele generates billions of dollars in revenue annually. I also wanted to make sure that I had the most objective strategies and best practices, as well as all the secret tips I could get my hands on so I could give them all to you!

I had the honor of speaking to, interviewing, and brainstorming with the following people:

- Rand Fishkin, Cofounder of MOZ, best-selling author for SEO
- JD Rucker, President of Dealer Authority
- Michael Cirillo, CEO of FlexDealer
- Christian Jorn, President of Remora
- Tim Martell, President of Wikimotive
- Eric Miltsch, President of Command Z, automotive consulting

I asked my network of experts the same question for the last chapter of this book, the bonus chapter:

Where do you see Google going in the future as it relates to SEO?

SEO is rapidly becoming more of a significant strategic element of the marketing and communication efforts of today's business. SEO is no longer the lone responsibility of an overly aggressive web marketer simply looking to rank a website for basic keyword terms. SEO is visibility in today's world. It does not matter what industry you are in. It doesn't matter if you are a person, a company, an artist, a brand. Everyone needs to be visible in today's overly content- and stimulus-saturated world.

Integrated search efforts now involve multiple disciplines, strategies, and departments; public relations (PR), product marketing, copy writing, and even web development are contributing to successful search marketing initiatives.

We're experiencing a massive shift within Google as it moves from being a web of links toward being a web of linking people. The newest portion of content on the Internet is user-generated (social), and this helps create new opportunities for trusted, helpful content. Google is working tirelessly to add the information contained within this layer to the search engine results by connecting and ranking our social connections as well. This will help usher in a new age of implicit trust between strangers as they search for what's most important to them online.

Another item contributing to this change in behavior is the mobile device segment. Mobile devices have expanded the buying spectrum by introducing new scenarios, such as subconscious shopping behaviors further out in the buying phase, while also introducing new heights of instant gratification closer to the final decision-making stage. Google also knows that it must provide the most accurate and helpful local search results as well.

Local directory optimization is among the most neglected elements of a marketing plan, and it's quickly becoming one of the most effective ways to connect users and convert them into customers. Content that addresses both technical and social needs among local citations will have an immediate positive impact. Consistent business names, addresses, and phone numbers are vital. Other key elements, such as business categories, new images of the business, and positive reviews, not only help create customer actions but also are specific items Google looks for to create local search authority.

The final piece of this shift is the manner in which Google can understand the connection between words and actually understand the context of a page within a website. Google's ability to understand the meaning of words is helping build the Semantic Web. This will create an Internet that provides even more specific results when a user is seeking answers and information. It's this change that will push a new wave of marketing integration as companies see the opportunities to develop internal media departments who exist for the sole purpose of developing incredibly rich content.

Google's largest search engine update, called Hummingbird, is just the tip of the iceberg for its ability to help understand the context of pages and match those results to our specific intent. This will shape conversation search and create even better user experiences versus Google serving us plain vanilla marketing content. The content provided will be truly beneficial as the personalization will speak to us clearer than ever and eliminate ineffective and irrelevant content.

Add layers of social content being injected into the Internet every day, and you have another major contribution factor with the introduction of content that is conversational, influential, and trusted.

So, what does this all mean for the future of SEO?

As long as there are search engines, there will be a need to categorize, rank, and serve up content within the search results to users. The methods by which this is done need to change to provide a better, trusted user experience for Google's user base, while taking into consideration our changing device behaviors and including **more personal connections within the search results**.

The first expert I spoke with, **Eric Miltsch**, says he sees many other changes contributing to the evolving search ecosystem. His comments are as follows:

> Natural language search behaviors will continue to increase and improve, creating the need for more expert, authoritative, and trustworthy content that will answer specific questions users have. Google's ability to understand the content via machine readable data and Semantic Web technologies will shape this movement.

> Personalized search results will also continue to grow as Google connects social content to provide greater results by understanding context better. This will also help marketing messages speak directly to user intent even faster. Specific needs and desires will be spoken to directly, speeding up the decision-making process,

while also reducing the number of final sources needed to make a buying decision.

Topic modeling will replace the focus on keyword phrases and individual rankings as Google aims to provide more specific answers to our search queries.

The best SEO efforts going forward will also include more proactive web development and technical abilities referring specifically to mobile speed performance and more efficient site structure. Improving the user experience will include more than just content improvements; providing technology enhancements per Google's recommendations will also reward your search efforts.

Here's what **JD Rucker** had to say:

We've had a decade of search being pretty much more of the same. There have been great innovations, and the engines have developed methods of detecting the majority of spam, which is good. Now, Google is going to focus on reinventing search for the next decade.

They have a good chunk of the data they need. Now, they simply need to teach computers to truly understand humans. Their investment into quantum computing is the solution. Imagine personalized search that knows you better than you know yourself, literally. Google will have the ability to make recommendations to people based upon trends it has collected about individuals as well as outside forces. For example, if you tend to like restaurants that others have indicated put too much salt in their dishes, Google will know that you like salty foods without having to tell it that. You won't have to ask your mobile device to "Take me to McDonald's" or "Take me to an Italian restaurant." Instead, you'll be able to say, "Take me to a restaurant I'll enjoy."

It goes much deeper than that, but within a decade we will see search turning into much more of a direct knowledge, a recommendation engine, rather than a place to do search. It's very exciting to watch it unfold.

I asked internationally recognized SEO expert **Rand Fishkin**, "What is the most important opportunity (or thing) that a person or company can focus on to be successful with SEO, specifically how to dominate Google?" In addition to everything that was outlined in this book (all the unique Googleopoly strategies), Rand mentioned the following:

> People have their own expertise and knowledge and should focus on that. Google wants unique, relevant content and it wants a lot of it. So, people should focus on what they know the most about or what they specialize in and create diversified content on all of the mediums (Googleopoly strategies) accordingly.

Tim Martell of Wikimotive goes a step further and says that the content can't just be unique or relevant. It also must be *remarkable*! This means that the content you create must be so remarkable it causes someone to take action or experience emotion. This is what Google is looking for, says Tim.

Rand Fishkin and Michael Cirillo both predict that Google is going to enhance its Knowledge Graph search functionality. Specifically, Google is going to try to provide the most important and most searched information via the Knowledge Graph—it will provide not only information but also real-time resources and functionality. This is going to neutralize the need for the searcher to click through to a website. This will make it much easier to get information based on the context of your search.

To be specific, they predict that the Knowledge Graph will:

- Be broader
- Provide competing pricing
- Provide different restaurant options
- Provide different hotel options
- Provide "what other people searched for"
- Provide different automotive car models
- Provide the ability to search for a restaurant and book a reservation
- Provide the ability to check movie listing times and buy tickets

Here's what **Christian Jorn** had to say about the future of organic search.

Over the last five years we have seen Google completely change its business model from an impartial traffic director into a total destination website. I expect this trend will continue. Google is not a charity and stockholders demand growth. The only workable way that Google can keep up with these demands is by morphing into a new scrape and displace ideology. When Google went public in 2004, Larry Page said he wanted to get search engine users "out of Google and to the right place as fast as possible."

Now the only "right place" is a Google property. It will continue to gobble up entire industries, just like it did to the online travel and booking industries and the airlines. Google sees an opportunity to "be the value add" and turn everyone else into a commodity. It is these large industries that were its biggest advertisers and are in large part the reason for the wild success of Google. Scrape and displace is working well for Google now; the only question is will it work long term? I think no.

As for myself, I believe that Google will continue to evolve and will provide faster, more accurate search results. I believe that Google will utilize everything at its fingertips like social media, localization, personalization, ratings, and reviews to "think about" what would be the absolute *best* search return for an individual, instead of in general. For example, I believe Google will be able to recognize (and keep track) of an individual person's likes and dislikes, as well as identify what an individual's friends like or dislike. It will be able to see the types of things a person searches for , and the types of places a person checks into on Facebook or Foursquare. I also predict that Google will evolve its Knowledge Graph and make it more robust and real-time interactive.

So Google will combine the deeper details—more specific and more relevant search returns for an individual—with the more robust return via a Knowledge Graph. And that is just the beginning!

ADDITIONAL RESOURCES

Much has been covered in this book, but so much more information awaits you online. To learn about where Google will be moving in the future and how you can prepare a strong Googleopoly strategy for years to come, visit www.googleopolybook.com/the-future-of-google.

Index